D1334412

CHILDREN IN FOSTER HOMES

Theodore J. Stein
Eileen D. Gambrill
Kermit T. Wiltse

Introduction by
Neil Gilbert and Harry Specht

**Praeger Special Studies
Series in Social Welfare**

series editors

**Neil Gilbert
Harry Specht**

CHILDREN IN FOSTER HOMES

Achieving Continuity of Care

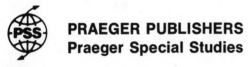

PRAEGER PUBLISHERS
Praeger Special Studies

New York   •   London   •   Sydney   •   Toronto

Library of Congress Cataloging in Publication Data

Stein, Theodore J
  Children in foster homes.

  Includes bibliographical references and index.
  1. Foster home care—California—Case studies.
2. Social work with children—California. I. Gambrill,
Eileen D., 1934–   joint author. II. Wiltse,
Kermit T., joint author. III. Title.

HV883.C2S73   362.7'33'09794   78-16927
ISBN 0-03-046421-8

PRAEGER PUBLISHERS
PRAEGER SPECIAL STUDIES
383 Madison Avenue, New York, N.Y. 10017, U.S.A.

Published in the United States of America in 1978
by Praeger Publishers,
A Division of Holt, Rinehart and Winston, CBS, Inc.

89   038   987654321

ACKNOWLEDGMENTS

The list of individuals who made the project possible is so extensive as to preclude acknowledging the contribution of each person by name. We would like to begin by thanking all of the "behind-the-scenes" individuals, particularly the administrators at both Children's Home Society and the Alameda County Department of Social Services, without whom there would never have been a project, and the tireless clerical staff at each agency. The day-to-day reality of the project was the work of 31 caseworkers at both Children's Home Society and Alameda County and of 7 supervisors at the latter. Their willingness to work with new methods of case management and to put up with all of the exigencies that are the essence of a research project is a statement of their concern for their clients and of their dedication to their profession.

CONTENTS

ACKNOWLEDGEMENTS   V
LIST OF TABLES   VIII
LIST OF FIGURES   X
INTRODUCTION   XII
by Neil Gilbert and Harry Specht

PART I

1.	FAMILY AUTONOMY VS. STATE INTERVENTION IN THE REARING OF CHILDREN	3
	Introduction	3
	Overview	6
	Notes	6
2.	DECISION MAKING IN FOSTER CARE	8
	Review of Current Research	8
	Exit from Foster Care	24
	Notes	34
3.	DESCRIPTION OF THE ALAMEDA PROJECT	43
	Population	43
	The Setting	44
	Selection of Cases	44
	Caseload Size	46
	Staff Workers	46
	Description of Cases	47
	Procedure for Dividing Cases Between Two Workers	50
	Data Collection Forms	52
	Notes	54
4.	RESULTS	55
	Case Outcomes	55
	The Process of Service Delivery	65
	A Search for Predictor Variables	79
	Limitations of the Study	93
	One-Year Follow-up	93
	Notes	100
5.	IMPLICATIONS OF THE STUDY	102
	Implications for Child Welfare Workers	102
	Implications for Supervisors	117

	Implications for Administration	122
	Data Collection	128
	Implications for Social Work Education	135
	Notes	139
6.	BARRIERS TO THE USE OF SYSTEMATIC CASE MANAGEMENT PROCEDURES	147
	Fiscal Constraints	148
	Agency Constraints	150
	Guidelines for Introducing New Programs	156
	Notes	158

PART II

7.	ASSESSMENT AND CONTRACTING	163
	Step 1: Identifying Parental Objectives for a Child's Future	163
	Step 2: Constructing a Problem Profile	164
	Step 2A: Beginning Problem Definition and Situational Examples	167
	Step 3: Problem Selection	173
	Step 4: Initial Specification of Objectives, Including Identification of Subgoals and Client's Assets	175
	Step 5: Formulation of a Treatment Contract	181
	Step 6: Gathering Baseline Data on Identified Problems	187
	Step 7: Specifying Additional Objectives	187
	Step 8: Amending Contracts	191
	Notes	192
8.	INTERVENTION	194
	Case 1: The Jones Family	194
	Case 2: Cynthia and Mrs. K.	206
	Case 3: The W. Family	223
	Notes	240

APPENDIXES		
A.	Project Forms	243
B.	California Civil Code Section 232	268
AUTHOR INDEX		271
SUBJECT INDEX		273
ABOUT THE AUTHORS		281

LIST OF TABLES

3.1   Experimental and Control Cases Volunteered for the Project and Those from Intake   45

3.2   Number of Experimental and Control Unit Children Entering Project, by Year   46

3.3   Conditions of Entry into Placement of Project Children   47

3.4   Number and Percentages of Children in Each Group, by Reason(s) for Placement   48

3.5   Ages of Experimental and Control Unit Children   49

3.6   Sex of Experimental and Control Unit Children   50

3.7   Racial or Ethnic Background of Children   50

3.8   Family Composition   51

4.1   Case Outcomes: Planned, Unplanned, No Decision   56

4.2   Restorations, by Year of Occurrence   57

4.3   Reasons for Miscellaneous Closings   58

4.4   Status of Adoption and Guardianship Cases   59

4.5   Children Categorized by Civil Code Section(s) Under Which Case Was Prepared for Court and Voluntary Relinquishments   62

4.6   Final Case Outcomes   63

4.7   Planned Outcomes: Year 2   64

4.8   Percentage of Contacts, by Case Outcome   66

4.9   Percentage of Interviews with Natural Parents, by Primary Type of Verbal Behavior Used in Interview   67

4.10   Percentage of Interviews with Natural Parents Devoted to Various Purposes   68

4.11   Percentage of Families with One–Six Problems Identified   70

4.12   Percent of Families with Each of 11 Identified Problems   71

4.13   Frequency and Percentage of Caseworker Contact with Collateral Resources   72

4.14   Contacts Between Project and County Workers for Four Time Periods   73

4.15   Purposes of Contacts Between Workers and Time Devoted to Each   75

4.16   Percentage of Time Spent in Personal and Phone Contacts over Six Time Categories   76

4.17	Number of Children, by Outcome Category, in Each Group	80
4.18	Percentage of Children in Three Outcome Categories, by Six Demographic Variables	81
4.19	Percentage of Experimental Group Children in Relative and Nonrelative Placements, by Outcome	82
4.20	Reason for Placement, by Case Outcome	82
4.21	Length of Time in Care, by Age and Outcome	84
4.22	Case Outcomes, by Time in Care	86
4.23	Correlations Between Length of Time in Care and Outcomes	87
4.24	Relationship Between Case Outcome and Time in Care	88
4.25	Number of Families, by Number of Identified Problems and Outcome	89
4.26	Identified Problem Areas: Resolved or Unresolved at the End of Year 2	90
4.27	Relationship Between Contracts and Outcome in Foster Care	91
4.28	Contract Status and Case Outcome: Verbal Contract Omitted	92
4.29	Decision Status of Children Headed out of Placement, One Year Later	96
4.30	Decision Status of Children Categorized as Long-Term Placements, One Year Later	97
5.1	Comparison of Major Types of Caseworker Verbal Behavior	110
6.1	Oregon Project Results, by Permanent Plan	149
8.1	Baseline Data Describing Verbal Interaction Between Mike Jones and His Father	200
8.2	Post-Negotiation Training Observational Data	208
8.3	Summary Baseline Data: K. Family	212
8.4	Coding of Tape-Recorded Material: K. Family	223
8.5	Verbal Interaction Between Mrs. K. and Cynthia Before and After Intervention	224
8.6	Drinking Behavior: Mr. W. over Seven-Day Period	229
8.7	W. Children's Compliance Behavior over Seven Days	229

LIST OF FIGURES

7.1   Beginning Problem Profile   166

7.2   Problem Profile with Examples and Identified Situations   170

7.3   Completed Problem Profile   171

7.4   Completed Problem Profile   172

7.5   Sample Contract Between Two Clients   183

7.6   Restoration Agreement   186

7.7   Contract Attachments: Plans for Goal Attainment   188

7.8   Sample Contract Between Client and Worker Regarding Trial Visit   190

7.9   Amendment to Contract: Additional Two-Week Visiting Schedule   192

8.1   Problems in Verbal Communication   195

8.2   Check Lists for Daily and Weekly Chores, and Dialogue Regarding Them   198

8.3   Contract Between Clients Regarding Daily and Weekly Chores   199

8.4   Contract Between Worker and Clients to Dismiss Court Dependency   202

8.5   Plan for Goal 1: Increasing Father's Approval Response and Son's Attending Behavior   203

8.6   Verbal Approval and Attending Behavior Check List   204

8.7   Plan for Goal 2: Negotiation Training   206

8.8   Percentage of Chores Completed: 14 Weeks   207

8.9   No Dialogue Relative to Chores: 2 Weeks   207

8.10   Verbal Interaction Between Father and Son Before and After Intervention   209

8.11   Form for Coding Observations   211

8.12   Contract Between Worker and Clients: K. Family   213

8.13   Plan No. 1: Increasing Verbal Repertoire and Nonverbal Behaviors of Mother and Daughter   217

8.14   Plan No. 2: Decision Making for Cynthia K.'s Future Living Arrangements   219

8.15   Extended Visiting Schedule and Worker Observations: K. Family   221

8.16   Contract for Restoration and Dependency Dismissal: K. Family   222

8.17	Problem Profile: W. Family	226
8.18	Recording Form for Baseline Information on Drinking Behavior and Children's Compliance Behavior: W. Family	228
8.19	Contract with W. Family	231
8.20	Plan for Chore Completion: W. Family	232
8.21	Plan to Reduce Mr. W.'s Alcohol Consumption	233
8.22	Plan to Increase Mrs. W.'s Free Time	234
8.23	Plan for Increased Visiting: Steven W.	235
8.24	Average Number of Alcoholic Beverages Drinks per Day by Mr. W.	237
8.25	Hours of Free Time per Day for Mrs. W.	237

INTRODUCTION
Neil Gilbert and Harry Specht

The purpose of this series of publications on social welfare is to provide social welfare scholars, policy makers, and planners with a timely source of high-quality research on the social services. The series focuses on analytic and evaluative studies of social service program planning and implementation.

The academic and professional audience for literature on social welfare and the social services is growing rapidly, as reflected by the fact that several journals in this field have been initiated in the last few years. The explosive growth and transformation of social services that has occurred in the United States since the mid-1960s has created an increased demand for current information on the social services. In the relatively brief period between 1962 and 1975, for example, federal social service grants under the Social Security Act alone increased from $194 million to $2.5 billion; the middle class has become eligible for many social services previously reserved for the poor; and social service programs have broadened considerably to include such diverse provisions as "meals on wheels," day care, and transportation, as well as traditional clinical counseling services and services for children.

It is a recurrent complaint of social welfare planners that they lack "hard" data about the outcomes of social service interventions. Program descriptions abound, and there is a surfeit of material that deals with the values and objectives of social welfare programs. But systematically gathered evidence about the outcomes of, and relative costs and benefits of, social service programs is harder to come by. This series is intended as a contribution to the effort to build a scientifically based knowledge about social welfare.

The authors of this volume have studied the continuity of care of children in out-of-home placement. They compare the effectiveness of a systematic case-management procedure using behavioral intervention methods with more traditional methods of resolving identified problems. Their objective is to develop a decision-making framework that can be used by practicing child welfare workers in a variety of settings. They describe how their findings can be used by child care workers, supervisors, administrators, and social work educators. In addition, they analyze the barriers to the introduction of systematic case management procedures that are found in child welfare agencies.

The authors provide a detailed description of the process used to help the experimental group, and three case examples are given so that readers can see the application of the methods in specific instances.

Annually, close to one-half million children in the United States are in foster care. As the authors note, more than half of these children will spend all of their minor years in out-of-home placements. Child care professionals can learn a good deal from the work of Stein, Gambrill, and Wiltse that will enable them to enhance their contribution to the social welfare of these children.

PART I

1

FAMILY AUTONOMY VS.
STATE INTERVENTION
IN THE REARING OF CHILDREN

INTRODUCTION

Throughout American history there has been an interplay between parental rights to rear their children without outside interference and the right of an external agent to intervene. Family autonomy was favored from colonial times until the mid-nineteenth century, when the state's role in defining social expectations for the rearing of children and in providing substitute care for children who were said to be receiving inadequate parenting began to broaden. Today the state articulates its interest in child rearing primarily through child labor laws, comprehensive and compulsory educational programs, and (to a lesser extent) through programs such as Head Start and state-supported day care.[1]

Society's right to intervene directly between parent and child is supported throughout neglect and dependency statutes that establish the jurisdiction of the juvenile court over these matters. Public education and public day care programs affect nearly all children at some time in their lives. Our concern in this book is with a small portion of all these children, the estimated 420,000 for whom the state has assumed the role of substitute parent through the provision of foster care services.[2] Since the late 1950s the system that serves these children and their families has been subject to scrutiny and criticism. These studies are reviewed in this book, revealing a complex and often contradictory picture. This is the case for a variety of reasons that we shall consider in Chapter 2. One concern we view as fundamental to understanding a number of the difficulties that will be described is the objective of state intervention. The concern can be clarified by considering the standard for juvenile court intervention. There are good reasons for using this reference point even though, on a national basis, only half of the children in care are there under court directive.[3]

Statutory law reflects prevailing cultural norms and mores, and so provides a ready basis for understanding the attitudes and beliefs of a community regarding child rearing.[4] Laws establish the conditions under which the community has "decided" that it can intervene in family life.[5] In addition, ever since the Children's Charter was presented at the White House Conference in 1930, there has been a growing sentiment for the development of a "Children's Bill of Rights."[6] Should this come to pass, it is the court that will be looked to for enforcement of such rights. It is likely that the role of the courts will expand partly as a result of economic factors, since the federal government reimburses the states for a considerable percentage of the costs of maintaining a child in care if the child is eligible for AFDC and is a dependent of the court. (The amount of federal contribution varies, state by state, and is contingent upon the per capita income in the state. California, which is considered a "rich" state in per capita income receives a maximum reimbursement of 50 percent for maintenance costs. Massachusetts, by contrast, receives 75 percent reimbursement.[7]) Also, there is a thrust to look to the courts to resolve the problems of children who are "drifting" in foster home care, particularly those initially placed on a voluntary basis.[8]

Since the late 1800s, when the first juvenile court was established, judicial decisions about the welfare of children have been based on the concept of acting in the child's best interest.[9] The concept embodies the humanitarian concerns of society for its children, and as a philosophical position it ranks with such other American values as an individual's right to self-determination. Philosophical positions, however, rarely make good guides for action and, in fact, may create a great many difficulties when we lose sight of them as ideals and begin to act as though they represented goals within our grasp. A primary source of difficulty lies in the "distance" between what we are able to accomplish, given man's state of knowledge at any point in time, and what an ideal directs us to accomplish.

Objectives that are attainable can be viewed as lying within the domain of science; the distance between these goals and those represented by ideals lies in the realm of values. They are subject to discussion and debate, but not to resolution in the present. We would now like to consider briefly the extent to which the "best interest of the child" standard serves to support or preclude a scientific stance toward casework service delivery. Our concern lies in what Thomas Szasz calls the "scientific vs. moral" aspects of any issue that is socially defined as a problem.[10] For our purposes the problem may be any one that might serve as a basis for state intervention in family life. We will consider the example of parental heroin use, casting this first into a scientific, and then into a moral, framework.

Let us assume that a parent uses heroin, spends many of his or her waking hours in pursuit of the drug, and neglects to feed the child adequately. This can be viewed as a scientific concern if we define the problem as "inadequate nutrition," and identify the current physical consequence for the child. We can then hypothesize the probable long-range consequence if this state of affairs continues. For example, depending upon the degree of malnourishment, a child may die. We can hypothesize that the child's current physical condition will improve if he or she receives foods that are high in nutritional value. These foods can be provided, and the effects upon the child's health objectively assessed. Thus, if the problem is inadequate nutrition, we can identify what the parent will have to do differently if he or she wants the child back. Heroin use becomes a moral issue when we define it as a problem but cannot say why it is a problem. As Troy Duster points out, "Once there is firm, adequate knowledge about the physical effects [of drug use] for example that it destroys body tissue, then the social response should be directed toward the destruction of body tissue" (and not toward the use of the drug).[11] We would argue that unless we can identify what is happening to a child because of a parent's use of a drug, removing the child cannot be said to be in the child's best interest.

A society can elect to legislate against certain behaviors that it defines as "bad," and legislation invariably reflects social morality. In fact, historically, neglect laws have been concerned primarily with moral conduct; and even today "More states have statutes regulating moral neglect than physical neglect."[12] State power has been used to reinforce public morality rather than to protect children from neglect.[13] However, insofar as we do not concern ourselves with whether the issue lends itself to a moral vs. a scientific view, a child can be removed from its parents any time the beliefs and values of the "dominant sector of society" are violated.[14] Children have been removed because the court disapproved of the parents' life style or child rearing practices. Removal has occurred, for example, because the parents were not married, because the mother frequented taverns or had male visitors overnight, because the parents adhered to extreme religious beliefs or lived in a communal setting, because the parent was a lesbian or male homosexual, because the parents' home was filthy, or because the woman was the mother of an illegitimate child.[15] In none of these cases was there evidence of harm to the children.[16] In such instances, socially unacceptable behavior of the parents is condemned on the pretext of acting in the child's best interest.[17]

When a moralistic approach takes precedence over a scientific approach, discretionary decision making based upon personal value judgments and opinions is encouraged. Such a nonscientific decision-making base undermines the whole purpose of state intervention to protect children, thereby making it difficult to establish accountability for services provided. Accountability for services provided is a major problem confronting social work as a profession.

We will now turn to a more detailed examination of the decision-making process in the foster care system—a process that can guarantee equal services to all children only insofar as decisions are made on a scientific, as opposed to a moralistic, basis.

OVERVIEW

This book is divided into two parts. In Part I, a review of the foster care literature is presented in chapter 2. Our concern is with the current state of knowledge in a number of different areas that constitute foster care services. We shall, for example, consider the decision-making process, case planning, service delivery, the role of collateral resources, and the diverse responsibilities of the public welfare agencies that administer foster care programs. In each of these areas, we shall view problems that have been identified and recommendations that have been made for change. In addition, data will be reported on the numbers of children that leave foster home placement and the various "routes," such as restoration, adoption, and guardianship, through which they leave. Reports from experimental studies that have tried to increase the numbers of children who move out of foster care also will be presented. Chapter 3 describes project methodology and presents demographic information on the children and their families. Results are reported in chapter 4. The section begins with an overview of case outcomes and presents data describing the process of service delivery. It concludes with a focus on the predictive value of a number of variables in relation to case outcomes. Implications of the study are addressed in chapter 5, specifically, the value of this work to child welfare workers and supervisors, administrators of child welfare agencies, and social work educators. The focus in chapter 6 is on impediments to implementation of the findings of this study. Attention is directed to agency- and court-imposed barriers as well as to those resulting from values and attitudes held by child welfare workers.

Part II contains two chapters. The first chapter describes in detail each of the steps in assessment and contracting with clients. The second focuses on intervention. Three cases drawn from the project are described in depth. These illustrate the assessment and intervention methods employed by project staff in decision making and case planning.

NOTES

1. Michael Wald, "State Intervention on Behalf of Neglected Children: A Search for Realistic Standards," *Stanford Law Review* 27 (April 1975):985–1040.
2. National Association of Attorneys General, *Legal Issues in Foster Care* (Raleigh, N.C.: Committee on the Office of Attorney General, 1976), p. 1.
3. Robert H. Mnookin, "Foster Care—in Whose Best Interest," *Harvard Educational Review* 43 (1974):158–97.
4. For discussion of this issue, see Hillary Rodham, "Children Under the Law," *Harvard Educational Review* 43 (1974):1–28; Phillip Selznick, "Sociology of Law" (Berkeley: Center for the Study of Law and Society, University of California). (Mimeographed.)
5. Rodham, op. cit., p. 4.

6. Beatrice Gross and Ronald Gross, eds., *The Children's Rights Movement* (New York: Anchor Press/Doubleday, 1977), pt. 3.

7. See Jessica S. Pers, *Government as Parent: Administering Foster Care in California* (Berkeley: Institute of Governmental Studies, University of California, 1976), p. 79; Allan R. Gruber, *Foster Home Care in Massachusetts* (Boston: Governor's Commission on Adoption and Foster Care, 1973), p. 12.

8. Discussions of increased court involvement in voluntary placements are found in Trudy B. Festinger, "The New York Court Review of Children in Foster Care," *Child Welfare* 54 (April 1975):211–45; State of Calfornia, Department of Health, *Family Protection Act of 1976* (Sacramento: the Department, 1977), "Children's Social Services, Adoptions and Foster Care," U.S. Congress, House, *Foster Care and Adoption Reform Act of 1977*, 95th Cong., 1st sess. (Washington, D.C.: U.S. Government Printing Office, 1977).

9. Sanford N. Katz, "Child Neglect Laws in America," *Family Law Quarterly* 9 (Spring 1975):3–5.

10. Thomas Szasz, *Ceremonial Chemistry* (New York: Anchor, 1974), p. 4.

11. Troy Duster, *The Legislation of Morality* (New York: Free Press, 1970), p. 236.

12. Wald, op. cit., p. 1033.

13. Mnookin, op. cit., p. 190.

14. Rodham, op. cit., p. 50.

15. Mnookin, op. cit., p. 185; Wald, op. cit., p. 1023.

16. Wald, op. cit., p. 1033.

17. Detailed discussions of this issue are found in Mnookin, op. cit.; Wald, op. cit.

2

DECISION MAKING
IN FOSTER CARE

REVIEW OF CURRENT RESEARCH

There are approximately 420,000 children in foster care in the United States.[1] Data gathered since the early 1960s from various parts of the country suggest that more than 50 percent of these children will spend their lives in out-of-home placement and that their being in long-term care is not the result of purposeful decision making.[2] In fact, the opposite is said to be the case: that they have been allowed to "drift into the limbo" of long-term care as a result of nonplanning.[3] Our objective here is to clarify why this situation exists, and to consider recommendations that have been made to resolve this problem. We shall begin by considering studies that have tried to describe the process by which caseworkers make decisions. Following this, we will examine what is known about case planning and service delivery, and will consider the role of the welfare bureaucracies that administer foster care programs.

Factors Related to Placement

Since the late 1950s, the suggestion has been made that research in child welfare should focus on the decision-making process, so that the variables that enter into any given decision can be delineated and a decision-making framework to guide child welfare workers can be developed. In 1959, Martin Wolins suggested that the criteria used to determine whether placement is appropriate be studied in addition to the outcomes of various placement decisions.[4] David Fanshel stated, in 1962, that child welfare services are characterized by a "number of well-defined decision making tasks, for example, the decision to separate children from their parents and decision in the selection of foster and adoptive parents."[5] He believed that these "choice points" would readily lend themselves to the development of research, and recommended that they be used to study the decision-making process.[6] Six years later, at a conference focusing on the use of manpower in social work, it was suggested that tasks for workers be defined relative to the major decisions made in foster care services.[7] The conferees noted, however, that in order to do this, one would have to know the basic decisions to be made in foster care and the professional skill required to make and to validate these decisions.[8] In 1970, Edmund Mech reviewed the literature on decision making in foster care, noted the absence of a framework, and recommended that one be developed.[9] These suggestions are repeated in subsequent literature.[10]

Let us now look at what is known about decision making in foster care. Bernice Boehm studied protective service caseloads in order to identify criteria used by workers in making decisions to place a child out of the home or to provide at-home services.[11] In 1962 she asked workers to analyze their cases and to indicate their criteria for reaching either decision. She reported that workers had a "tendency to use a model family as a frame of reference, and to evaluate problem behavior by the extent of deviation from ideal parenting."[12] She concluded, however, that all families "deviated markedly" from the model, whether or not their children were placed, and suggested that the problem at hand was to distinguish between placement and nonplacement families.

In the next stage of her research, Boehm asked workers to submit lists of "behavioral items" that they used to evaluate family adequacy. She factor-analyzed 140 items that yielded 12 "discrete behavioral dimensions," four of which dealt with maternal behavior and four with paternal behavior. Two focused on the child, and one each on "household management" and "family insight." The items covered a range of issues including the cleanliness of the home, parental use of alcohol, family insight, and emotional disturbance.

One hundred placement and an equal number of nonplacement families were rated by the workers on each item in each dimension. Using a five-point scale, workers were asked to indicate whether the item was "most like or most unlike the family."[13] Low scores were said to indicate greater degrees of family inadequacy. The most significant difference between placement and nonplacement cases was that the former had lower scores on every dimension of maternal behavior than did the latter. The only other significant difference between groups was that placement families scored lower on items of household management and family insight. Of the items dealing with the father, only his "interest in and affection toward the child" was related. None of the dimensions dealing with the child's behavior showed any relationship to the decision.[14] Boehm concluded that "the decision for placement is based largely on an evaluation of maternal care."[15] Alfred

Kadushin reported a study by Eugene Shinn that also pointed to "maternal pathology" as the most frequently cited reason for placing a child.[16]

Michael Phillips, Ann Shyne, Edmund Sherman, and Barbara Haring studied intake decisions for 309 children in three agencies located in two East Coast states.[17] Workers completed an intake and decision schedule containing information on the "social and behavioral characteristics" of parents and children, as well as the worker's decision for service.[18] Phillips et al. analyzed variables singly and in clusters to identify family characteristics most likely to result in a decision to place a child. No single item or combination of factors pointed strongly to a placement decision.[19] Of interest in relation to the findings of Boehm and Shinn, they noted that in two-parent families, "traits of the father were the single most important cluster of variables" in the decision to place, and that neither the "mother's functioning nor her relationship to the child were important considerations in reaching a decision."[20]

Scott Briar studied the basis for making foster home vs. institutional placement decisions.[21] He prepared two versions of a single case, in one of which a child was described as "seriously disturbed," and in the other as "mildly disturbed." Forty-three workers participated, 22 of whom received the first version of the case and 21 the second. Briar reports that there was a relationship between degree of disturbance and type of placement recommended, but that the direction of the relationship was variable and unpredictable.[22]

Mech reported a study that sought to delineate factors entering into the decision to maintain a child in care or return the child to its parents. Differential factors related to either decision could not be identified.[23]

Additional areas studied include inter-judge reliability in decisions made and the amount of information used by workers to reach a decision. Phillips et al. compared decisions reached by social workers with those of three independent judges, each of whom had more than five years' experience in decision making in child welfare.[24] The judges agreed with each other and with the workers on less than half of the cases; and when they did agree, they did not identify the same factors.[25]

Wolins, studying the process by which foster parents are selected, found that the reliability of decisions across judges was a function of the amount of information available upon which to base a decision.[26] Using seven actual case records, "worker-judges" were given either the entire record, randomly selected portions of the material, or information considered crucial to decision making. Agreement among judges was poor when they were given the full case record (chi-square of .47). When they received only information considered most important to a decision, reliability increased to .81. And when 80 percent of the material was randomly discarded, agreement was "nearly as good or better than with the entire case record."[27]

Theodore Stein analyzed 68 intake and service worker interviews tape-recorded by ten workers in a public child welfare setting.[28] Between 59 percent and 78 percent of the information gathered during intake interview was not related to the objective of reaching a placement decision, and between 22 percent and 90 percent of the information in service interviews did not relate to the interview goals set by the workers.[29] Naomi Golan found that workers gather excessive amounts of information in community mental health centers.[30] She reported a "lack of uniformity in the data gathered" by the 12 workers studied. There was either much information that appeared superfluous or omissions in data that appeared to be vital to decision making. She concluded that it "appears inescapable" that workers could carry out more economical and productive first interviews and arrive at more helpful decisions if they knew on what to focus and which areas would yield the most significant data.[31] Gathering unused information had also been found in the selection of adoptive applicants. In 1959, Donald Brieland tape-recorded interviews with 5 couples who were adoptive applicants, and played these tapes for 184 workers in 13 states.[32] During and after each interview, the workers were asked to judge the suitability of the couples as adoptive applicants. He reported that decisions were based on the information contained in the first half of the interview, and that the information in the second half bore no relationship to the decisions made. He concluded that workers become "locked into" a decision during the first half, and that the remaining data did not contribute to the final outcome in any way.

Role of Community Resources

Ann Shyne suggested that the availability of community resources influences workers' decisions.[33] She conducted a study of the decision-making behavior of social workers in 69 agencies located across the country for the Child Welfare League of America. She asked workers to state their "ideal" decision for 1260 cases and compared these ideal decisions with actual outcomes. Approximately two-thirds of the "ideal" decisions were "carried out or being arranged" at the time of her report.[34] The congruence between ideal and actual decisions varied from city to city, and was influenced by the availability of resources. For example, in Denver and Fort Worth, ideal decisions were carried out in fewer than 50 percent of the cases, while in Madison they were realized in almost every instance. Even though workers were asked to state their ideal decisions based upon the child's need, without regard to resource availability, there was a tendency to see needs in terms of available resources.[35]

Shirley Jenkins and Mignon Sauber had trained social workers and social scientists interview 425 families of children in care.[36] Their major focus was to identify changes that had occurred in the family during a 12-

month period prior to placement. Data on a number of dimensions, such as economic, social, and physical and mental health issues, were gathered during in-person interviews. Of concern to us here was the report by interviewers that 17 percent of the placements could have been avoided if homemakers, day care, or income supplementation had been available.[37] In contrast, Phillips et al. state that resources were unavailable for only 3 percent of the cases they studied.[38] Briar noted that "placement recommendations made by the workers were directly related to the placement practices in their employing agencies."[39] In discussing Briar's outcomes, Martin Wolins and Irving Piliavin hypothesize that one possible reason for his results may lie in deficits in resource availability.[40] Other investigators also have suggested that the availability of supportive services affects the range of alternative decisions.[41]

While it is possible that deficits in community resources may result in needless placement of some children, it also is possible that the recommendations made by other services—protective services, for example—may influence the child welfare worker's decision making. Donald Brieland et al. stated that "important decisions about children are made by others in the community before the social agency is even aware of the case."[42] The issue here is that a majority of families who come to the attention of foster care departments are already known to the community social service agencies.[43] Hence, they may come to the foster care department "labeled" as problematic or troublesome in some manner, and this may "set" the decision-making response of the child welfare worker. The concern here is an empirical one that has not been explored in its own right.

An additional concern in regard to community resources is the observation that workers fail to utilize those that are available prior to reaching decisions. For example, Alan Gruber reports:

> According to parents there was almost no consideration of options which may have intervened in the necessity of the child going into foster home care. Day care was talked about in less than 2% of the cases and other child care arrangements in 2.5%. Twenty-eight percent of the parents felt that day care alone would have been enough to make a substantial difference in the decision to place a child.[44]

It also has been noted that workers are "over reliant" on resources such as mental health professionals when they do exist, and fail to have mental health agencies share responsibility for making decisions.[45]

Case Planning and Service Delivery

Case planning and service delivery are seminal concepts in foster care.[46] It is expected either that those problems that necessitated out-of-home placements will be resolved through the provision of services to biological parents or that there will be planning for more permanent arrangements, specifically, adoption or guardianship.[47] (The expectation that services will be provided is embodied in the 1962 amendments to the Social Security Act reinforced by the federal government's assumption of 75 percent of the salaries of service workers.[48]) Despite this position, the available evidence suggests that plans are not made, nor are services provided, in a great majority of cases. In 1959 Henry Maas reported: "Agency relationships with most fathers and mothers of the children in care are such that, if parental conditions are to be modified the process will have to be one of self-healing without any assistance of casework services."[49] That this has changed little, if at all, is indicated by the studies below.

A. C. Emlen reports that 50 percent of the children's cases he studied in 15 counties in the state of Oregon had no case plans.[50] Between 62 percent and 77 percent of the children studied by Edmund Sherman, Renee Neuman, and Ann Shyne had no plans made for their futures.[51] From the results of his Massachusetts investigation, Gruber noted that "despite the temporary purpose of foster home care, 83% of the children had never been returned to their parents even for a trial visit."[52] Judicial review of 248 children in voluntary placement for between two and three years in New York City resulted in court orders for continued care for 40.3 percent, with court instructions to "explore the family's ability to resume care for the child, or to consider adoption or to *recommend some permanent plan* [emphasis added]."[53] In 1975, David Fanshel and John Grundy, reporting on all of the children in care in New York City, cited a figure of 30 percent as having no plans; and for children under two years of age, this increased to 60 percent.[54] Thirteen percent of the children studied by Kermit Wiltse and Eileen Gambrill had no case plans.[55] Remaining in foster care "indefinitely" is the "typical plan" for a child in placement in the state of Nebraska.[56] These figures might be higher still if one added all of the children designated as "long-term care" for whom this outcome is a result of "drift" or nonplanning.

Turning to service delivery, the evidence is unequivocal: of the natural parent, child, and foster parent triad, natural parents receive the least attention from social workers. In 1959, Henry Maas and Richard Engler reported that 70 percent of the fathers and mothers they studied either had "no relationship with the agencies responsible for the care of their children or their relationship was erratic or untrusting."[57] In 1961, Helen Jeter conducted a national study of the problems of children and their families.[58] Her data showed that no casework services were offered to the biological parents of 35 percent of the children in care.[59] In the results of his Massachusetts study, Gruber reports that 31 percent of the parents never see a social worker.[60] He also reports that through failure to receive services, 28.8 percent of the families reported that the situations necessitating out-of-home placement had not changed, and that for an additional 14.4 percent the family situation had "deteriorated." [61] The extent to which casework attention is on the child and foster parents rather than the biological parents is noted by Brieland et al. [62] They state that despite the goal of many agencies to restore children to their natural parents, the focus of concern at the conference was on the child in the foster home. [63] Investigators continue to document the absence of services to natural parents. [64]

Impediments to Effective Service Delivery

Why are there no case plans for such large percentages of children? Why do deficits in service delivery to natural parents exist? In the following pages we shall review various facets of child welfare services that have been said to explain these problems.

Casework Skills

It has been suggested that one of the reasons workers do not maintain contact with biological parents is that they lack assessment and treatment skills. [65] Skill deficits have been said to "perpetuate extended foster care." [66] The need to develop approaches to working with "troubled parents" is stressed in the literature, as is the necessity to provide in-service training to casework staff. [67]

Deborah Shapiro reported that experienced child welfare workers were more likely than were inexperienced workers to discharge children from foster placement during the first year in care. [68] Emlen did not find any consistency between a worker's length of experience and case planning. [69] He reported that "experience emerged as a force on the side of either drift or decisiveness." [70] Edmund Sherman et al. found that neither professional education nor a worker's experience was significantly related to outcome. [71]

Although the issue of the relationship between worker experience and case outcome is not settled, there are certain tasks that might facilitate movement of children but have little to do with experience. For example, there is evidence that the frequency with which parents visit their children is related to the probability of restoration. [72] At a minimum, workers can, and should, facilitate such visits. Paul McAdams has gone so far as to suggest that "Except in certain cases, workers would do well to push parents to visit their children early and regularly after placement." [73] There is evidence, however, that does this not occur, and that workers may in fact hinder visiting. Gruber reported that of the parents he interviewed, "60% stated that they did not see their children often enough and that 37.5% of these parents were prohibited from doing so by the social worker. An additional 20% said that contact with their children was discouraged by the foster parent."[74] Shirley Jenkins and Elaine Norman report a similar finding for 11 percent of the mothers they interviewed. In addition, 20 percent of the mothers "blamed the foster care establishment for setting inconvenient visiting times"; and "the same percentage accused agencies of trying to keep mothers away."[75] Fanshel attempted to identify variables that might be predictive of parental visiting, and found that only a "modest amount of variance could be accounted for by the variables he reviewed."[76] He suggested that the "extent to which agencies encourage visiting demands attention."[77] Jenkins and Norman found that "complaints of lack of encouragement of visiting" were numerous.[78]

An additional task in which workers can engage is maintaining contact with parents. Shapiro found that the only variable associated with improvement was "intensity of contact."[79] Stability of the worker, caseload size, and worker experience* were not significantly related to improvement in the family situation. A significant relationship between frequency of contact and the attainment of objectives also was reported by Sherman et al.[80]

Caseload Size and Service Delivery

Excessive caseload size has been said to militate against the provision of services to parents.[81] Shapiro suggests, however, that this is not the case. She reports a "bimodal relationship between caseload size and outcome," noting that workers with the lowest and highest caseloads discharged the greatest proportion of children.[82] To explain this finding, she hypothesized that workers with the highest caseloads may feel under heavier pressure to make decisions than other workers do. Hence, they may force, rather than delay, decision making. She concluded that caseload size may mean a different approach to case management, not necessarily diminished efficiency.[83]

Differential caseload management was noted by Jessica Pers, who found that workers "bank" cases that are "responding well to foster placement in order to free up valuable time."[84] Similarly, Gruber reported that cases were categorized as "active, inactive, and uncovered." Since some percentage of all caseloads probably are "inactive" for a variety of reasons, banking, insofar as this is a result of purposeful planning, would seem an appropriate approach to case management.[85] Edward Heck and Alan Gruber have developed a formula (Worker Effort Expenditure) for assigning cases that is based on activity rather than on quantity.[86] The value in recognizing activity as a crucial dimension in case assignment is noted elsewhere in the literature.[87]

---

*It was noted earlier that worker experience was related to moving children out of care. The distinction here is that worker experience was not related to "family improvement."

Collateral Resources

It has also been suggested that one of the reasons caseworkers do not engage in long-range planning for children in out-of-home care is that necessary services are not available through the public system.[88] In a similar vein, Norman Herstein asserts that the "power" a caseworker has to influence what happens to children in care is affected by "severe limitations in resources."[89] The position that deficits in the availability of resources restrict planning after a child is in care is similar to the assertion that resource deficits affect decision making at intake. We find arguments in the literature that the range of services should be increased.[90] Implicit in such recommendations is the assumption that the availability of services will result in differential outcomes for children in care, an assumption not supported by empirical evidence.

If community funds are expended to develop a range of supportive programs, there are two questions that should be answered. The first stems from the concern raised by Gambrill and Wiltse that workers exhibit a "mystical reliance" on the healing powers of mental health professionals.[91] Such a reliance can be seen in the juvenile court orders that parents participate in therapy*, and is at the base of recommendations that increasing the range of resources will make a difference in outcomes. However, the efficacy of treatment methods employed by these services has not been established; and even if empirically verified treatment methods are identified and employed, beneficial effects for clients are unlikely without the "integration of all the services given."[92] Coordination of services often does not occur, as illustrated below by Gambrill and Wiltse:

> The mental health worker (read community resource) decides what to work on in what period of time, and any reports that may be given to the social workers are usually in vague language, such as "Mrs. T. is making progress." Rarely does the mental health worker focus on the natural mother's parenting abilities or upon the areas that seem even slightly related to them. In fact, when asked how parenting abilities may be changing, the mental health worker may say that he is not working on that area at all, and furthermore, that the social worker should not place any pressure on the mother. This divergence of interests between the child welfare worker and the mental health professional was so frequently noted as to be of major concern. Hence, the mental health professional becomes the advocate of the mother, with little concern for the child. If the child welfare worker did not maintain her advocacy role for the child, then indeed the child had no advocate.[93]

---

* In California, when a child is removed under an abuse petition, therapy for the parent is a requirement before the child can be restored.

The need to develop and test different approaches to coordinating service and delivery and information exchange is recognized as one of the most pressing issues in child welfare today.[94]

Public Agency Responsibility

Ninety percent of the children in foster home placement are under the auspices of county-administered public welfare agencies.[95] Although the federal and state governments play a complex role in funding and specifying minimal services that should be available, primary decision-making responsibility in the state of California rests at the county level.[96] Describing county autonomy, Pers states:

> The counties set the payment rates for foster parents and institutions, determine how responsibility should be shared between the probation and social welfare departments and provide day-to-day casework services for children in care. The county probation and social welfare bureaucracy oversees the process by which children actually enter the foster care system, whether the juvenile court decides that they are "dependents" in need of care or their parents voluntarily decide to place them out-of-home.[97]

The role and responsibility of public agencies within the foster care system have been discussed in a number of studies. Major factors identified are discussed below.

Agency Policy and Objectives

Workers "rarely find written job descriptions or organized operations manuals to help them learn their jobs."[98] Formal training classes are not provided, nor are procedures offered to inform the new worker how he or she is to go about the job.[99] Gruber, in discussing cases in Massachusetts designated as "covered, uncovered, or inactive," noted a lack of criteria for deciding in which category to place any given case.[100] The "vagueness of agency philosophies, goals, and policies" contributes to what M. W. Bryce and R. C. Ehlebt call the "lack of clarity" on the worker's part as to who is responsible for service decisions, and encourages the "entrepreneurial discretion" that workers exercise in making decisions.[101]

Monitoring and Tracking

Clearly articulated agency objectives plus procedural guidelines and formal training will be of little value in lieu of a process to assure that objectives are pursued. Numerous recommendations to establish county and statewide monitoring systems to track each child entering foster home placement have been made.[102] The development of such systems has increased in recent years.[103]

A number of serious difficulties arise through inadequate case monitoring. For example, Gruber stated that the reasons given by caseworkers for the large number of children in Massachusetts said to be unadoptable were faulty. He noted that the lack of explicit policies and of mechanisms for assuring compliance with these policies deprived some children of adoptive homes. An additional problem in case management that could be overcome, in part, with a tracking system is reflected in the fact that in 72.5 percent of the cases workers did not know whether treatment programs recommended for the children had been carried out.[104]

In a similar vein, Emlen and Fanshel and Grundy suggested that routine screening procedures must be followed to insure that plans are made for children in placement.[105] In reference to the high percentage of foster children in New York City for whom no case plans had been made, Fanshel and Grundy pointed to inadequate case management and poor monitoring procedures at the public agency level as one explanation for this situation.[106] The absence of tracking procedures is particularly acute for children who are placed voluntarily, and therefore are not subject to review procedures that apply to children who are dependents of the court. Legislation in California has sought to remedy this situation by instituting a periodic court review of the status of such children.[107] Many investigators concerned with the drift of children into unplanned long-term care stress the need for regularly scheduled review of all children in placement.[108] However, even with a review mechanism, tracking may still be a necessity. New York City, for example, instituted a court review process for voluntarily placed children in 1971.[109] Four years after it was implemented, this review had been applied to fewer than 20 percent of the children under public agency auspices.[110] When such a procedure exists and is used, its potential for facilitating permanent planning can be seen in Trudy Festinger's report that the number of children designated as either in long-term care or as "unclear" decreased from 70.9 percent to 28.6 percent as a result of judicial review.[111] Similarly, John Steketee reports that in the first year of a mandated court review procedure in Rhode Island, the number of petitions to adopt children increased 100 percent; there was also an increase of 50 percent in petitions to terminate parental rights.[112]

Case record keeping that is neither standardized nor focused on measuring specific changes related to a child's future hinders careful monitoring of each child's progress. Record keeping is sometimes so bad that case records do not permit continuity of treatment across workers, and evaluation of effectiveness is precluded.[113] Gambrill and Wiltse report that there is a "large discretionary range as to what and when worker's activities are reported."[114] The need for standardized record keeping is made more urgent by the high turnover of child welfare staff, which has been said to contribute to the problems of foster care service delivery.[115] Problems created by staff turnover have not been fully explored; in fact, Sherman et al. indicate that staff turnover is not related to case outcome.[116] It would be reasonable to expect consistent record keeping to contribute a great deal to the solution of problems identified in future research.

Incentive Systems to Encourage Decision Making

In 1971, in order to increase the number of children returned to their parents or adopted, New York City instituted a system of incentive payments to private agencies.[117] For each child returned home after being in foster care for more than one year, the agency received $400, which was to be used to help prepare the family for the child's return. The agencies were paid $1,000 for each "hard-to-place" child adopted if the number of adoptions in any year exceeded the average for the previous three years. In 1973 the California State Department of Health recommended that a system of incentive payments be instituted.[118] The thrust of their recommendation was twofold; first, any savings that "accrue by diverting children from placement by maintaining them at home" should be made available by the state to the counties, in order to enhance preventive services.[119] The department further suggested the use of incentives for the adoption of the "hard-to-place" foster child.[120]

Delman Pascoe, in his review of seven foster care studies in the state of California, reports that the majority of his consultants did not support this recommendation. They felt that "Incentive payments are not necessary. The goal of returning children to their homes or providing permanent placement will be met by better organization, reduced caseloads, etc."[121]

However, the belief that "better organization and reduced caseloads" will result in changes in the status of children in foster home care is not grounded on empirical evidence. Several studies suggest that the belief that caseload size per se precludes effective service delivery is perhaps more myth than fact.[122] Even if such a relationship were to be found, current fiscal constraints preclude the expansion of social service programs.[123] Hence, adding new staff to reduce caseload size is not likely in the immediate future.

There is a growing recognition of the importance of incentive to increase the productivity of child welfare workers.[124] A number of nonmonetary incentives are currently being used for governmental employees in several states.[125] Measures employed by agency administrators to increase the productivity of child welfare workers include the following: clearly articulated agency objectives to reduce job ambiguity, particularly for new workers who are unfamiliar with agency goals; ongoing in-service training programs; clerical support to reduce the amount of time workers spend completing forms; feedback from administration about the purposes and outcomes of information that workers are asked to supply; involving staff in decision making that affects their day-to-day work; and support from legal staff to facilitate moving children through court termination proceedings and to subsequent adoption or legal guardianship.

The responsibility of public welfare agencies to create the conditions that would result in consistent case planning and service delivery is summed up by Edward Weaver: "Long-term foster care and continuity of planning and service-delivery cannot be achieved without a commitment from the administration. For effective action on cases to take place, policies should be directed to early diagnosis, planning and decision." [126]

Discussion

Implicit in each of the decision-making studies reviewed is the assumption that "something" guides workers in the decision-making proces. This is reflected in calls for a decision-making framework [127] that will identify criteria consistently used by workers in making decisions. This assumption is implicit in the expectation that experienced professional social workers, acting independently as judges, will agree in their decisions. Edward Foy has suggested the presence of a "collective practice wisdom," and Bernice Boehm speaks of an "accumulated practice knowledge" as the guide that workers employ in selecting among alternatives. [128] The studies reviewed suggest a failure to identify collective principles. As Phillips et al. have stated, there are "undoubtedly many instances in which practical experience leads to sound judgments about the needs of children, however, practice principles have not been articulated in sufficiently specific terms to meet the needs of the practitioner." [129]

Various alternative suggestions have been made regarding the bases of decisions. Among these are "idiosyncratic assumptions by the workers," "individual value systems," "personal discretion," and personal "attitudes and beliefs and expectations." [130] If individual values and personal discretion direct decision making, a still unanswered question is why choices are invariably in the direction of not making plans for children and not providing services to biological parents. Whether the issue is to remove or to return a child to its parent's home, the "best interest" standard calls for making predictions about the consequences to the child both now and in the future. Such predictions are difficult, and require a great deal of information when the concern is with behavior in the present. Those related to long-term concerns are even more so.

This problem is exacerbated by a focus on psychological issues. These usually are expressed in terms of a child's "need" for "normal experiences that produce feelings of being loved, wanted, secure and worthy," or for "continuity in relationship," or in terms of "rights" such as the "right to be wanted" or the "right to parental love." [131] Among the many problems in focusing upon psychological need is a lack of shared definitions of concepts such as "continuity, or the right to be wanted or loved." [132] We cannot satisfactorily identify the conditions that will produce these ends, nor can we determine, except in extreme cases, when they are not being met. Arlene Skolnick, in summing up the results of a 30-year longitudinal study at the University of California at Berkeley, and Sheldon White et al., in an extensive review of the psychological literature on child development, note the inability of theory to predict accurately what an adult will "look like" based on knowledge of childhood conditions. [133] Nevertheless, we act, and must act, as though such predictions were possible by making a chain of decisions that begins with the initial determination that a case should be referred to the court, the judicial decision to assume jurisdiction over a child, and a disposition that determines a child's future living arrangements.

We cannot provide answers to questions such as "Will a parent who abused a child ever do so again?" or "Will a parent who used drugs or alcohol ever resume their use?" Rather than certainty in our ability to make such predictions, we must face the fact every decision made for a child involves some degree of risk taking by the social worker or judicial decision maker. We expect that it is this inability to make long-range predictions that encourages social workers to delay decision making. However, unrecognized risks are accumulated by delay. Social workers do not seem to recognize the consequences that accrue from a failure to engage in case planning. They seem to seek resolution to this dilemma by accepting the rule "When in doubt, do not act." Perhaps they occasionally are rewarded for waiting by fortuitously acquiring further information that helps them make a decision. All too often, however, additional information does not emerge, because systematic steps are not taken to insure its collection.

An added concern is the tendency of social workers to diagnose pathology where none exists. [134] Given the two choices of diagnosing a parent as "healty" and returning a child, or diagnosing a parent as "sick" and maintaining a child in care, the chances of making an observable error are less with the latter choice. Several conditions in a public welfare context facilitate the likelihood that clients will be viewed in pejorative terms. The families of a majority of children who come into foster care are already known to social service agencies prior to placement. [135] When cases are referred from an outside agency, such as protective services or the police, or when the child has been declared a dependent of the court prior to the case reaching a child care worker, some degree of "stigma" is already attached to the parent(s).

One source of stigma that creates "blemishes of character" results from the assignment of labels. [136] A wide range of labels is seen in the foster care literature. Parents are generally described as neglectful, abusive, mentally ill, deviant, antisocial, or dysfunctional. The fact that a majority of children in care come from poor and minority families, while social workers from these groups are underrepresented in welfare departments, also encourages the application of deviant labels.[137] Middle-class therapists have a diagnostic bias with respect to lower-class patients. For example, given similar patterns of drinking behavior, the diagnosis of chronic alcoholism is significantly more likely to be assigned to lower-class than to middle-class problem drinkers.[138] Boehm, interested in the possibility of such a bias, compared 187 welfare clients with the population of their larger community on a number of socioeconomic indexes.[139] Commenting on what was described as the "marked contrast between [caseworker and client] groups," the "legitimate question was raised of possible bias on the part of predominately middle class group toward those of lower status."[140] Phillips et al. found that although only 6 percent of the parents reported emotional problems as the reason for requesting services, workers perceived such difficulties for 21 percent of the parents.[141] Jenkins and Norman, interested in the stigma resulting from the application of labels, recommend a "no-fault" foster care system that would eliminate the prevailing system of assigning blame to parents.[142]

Labeling may generate secondary deviance effects, thus encouraging inappropriate behaviors.[143] As Thomas Scheff put it, "When labelling first occurs, it merely gives a name to rule breaking. . . . When (and if) the rule breaking *becomes an issue*, and is not ignored or rationalized away, labelling may create a social type. . . ."[144] It is not unreasonable to suggest that when a child enters foster home care, an "issue" may be created. The "social type" or stereotyping frequently leads to "selective perception," in which an individual is seen in terms of the categorical definitions of the label.[145] Once this occurs, the likelihood of reactions based on inaccurate assessment is considerable. There is a search for information to support the label, which furthers the "pathologizing" of the client. Such information, when placed in case records, encourages the later reader of these records to perceive the client through the same filters. As Ervin Goffman points out when discussing case records, they typically

> . . . do not provide a rough average or sampling of past conduct. One of its purposes is to show the ways in which the patient is 'sick' and the reasons why it was right to commit him and right currently to keep him committed; this is done by extracting from his whole life course a list of those incidents that have or might have had 'symptomatic significance.'[146]

The picture presented above is hypothetical and incomplete. It is hypothetical because the role of risk taking in case planning and service delivery decisions, and the related factors, have not been investigated; nor has the labeling process and its possible effects been studied in a child welfare setting.

Summary

Prior to Maas and Engler's major investigation, children in foster home care had not been studied and described in any systematic fashion.[147] Their work provided seminal data about children in care. Two of their most germane findings—that once a child is in care for more than 18 months, the probabilities of its ever being restored to the natural parents are greatly reduced, and that casework services to natural parents are the exception rather than the rule—generated a great deal of concern and a number of empirical studies. Almost two generations have passed since their work was reported. Summing up the results of subsequent studies, it is to state that their major conclusions have been confirmed nationally, and that little seems to have changed.

Each time their conclusions are supported by subsequent studies, recommendations similar in content are reiterated. Earlier we cited the regularity with which is it suggested that the criteria used by caseworkers in decision making be studied and a framework to guide workers be developed. In addition, there are repeated recommendations for early and continuous case planning, for the offering of intensive services to biological parents, and for development of a broad range of ancillary community resources.[148] There is little empirical evidence to suggest that these recommendations have been carried out in a systematic fashion.

Deficits in casework skills and excessive caseload size have been offered as explanations for the absence of case plans and the failure to provide services to natural parents. Studies of the effectiveness of current casework treatment methods offer scant room for optimism. We have seen, however, that workers do not engage in helpful activities that have little to do with problem-solving skills, such as increasing parental visiting and maintaining contact with parents.

We also have considered a number of conditions prevailing in a public welfare setting that encourage viewing clients and their problems very negatively, and we suggest that this negativism hinders risk taking that is an inevitable part of any decision that will result in permanent planning for a child's future.

The child welfare worker is viewed as one segment of a complex system that includes the community, the public welfare bureaucracy, and the juvenile court. The worker's position in this system creates dilemmas. He or she is admonished to act in the best interests of the child while lacking the knowledge base to do so. Decisions are required that demand greater knowledge than is actually available. He or she is told to provide services to biological parents and to engage in long-range planning, yet supportive mechanisms, such as clear agency objectives and procedures, in-service training, legal consultation, and supporting incentives are not supplied; nor is his or her work carefully monitored and feedback offered. One way to resolve such dilemmas is not to act; the evidence suggests that this is precisely what occurs in a very high percentage of cases.

Below we shall consider each of several ways in which a child may leave foster home care and the problems associated with decision making at these various exit points.

EXIT FROM FOSTER CARE

Children who leave foster home placement do so in various ways. They may return to their biological parents or to relatives, or be placed in an adoptive home or with adults who become their legal guardians. Some leave only when they reach majority, others when they marry; and still others may be incarcerated in adult detention centers. When a child departs from foster care as a result of purposeful planning, the alternatives of choice usually cited in the literature are; first, restoration to natural parents, and, next, legal adoption.[149] While less frequently considered, the third preferred alternative is to obtain a legal guardian for the child.[150]

Restoration

A primary objective of foster care services is to restore a child to his or her biological parents.[151] This expectation is explicit in the service provisions of the 1962 Social Security Act amendments and in the state of California's Annual Service Plan for the 1975-76 fiscal year.[152] The infrequency with which this occurs will not come as a surprise, given our previous discussion regarding deficits in case planning and services to biological parents. In 1973, Jeter found that only 12 percent of 49,838 children in public welfare agencies were expected to be restored to their natural parents.[153] Henry Maas and Richard Engler predicted in 1959 that not more than 25 percent of the children they studied were likely to be returned to their parents' home.[154] Ten years later, when Maas followed up these children, only 38 percent had been returned.[155] Fanshel cites a figure of 60.7 percent as discharged to natural parents or relatives, or adopted at the end of five years in care.[156] Twenty-eight percent of these discharges occurred when the child had been in care for less than one year. Over the next four years, the percentage of discharge decreased to between 14 percent and 18 percent per year.[157] In 1973, Wiltse and Gambrill reviewed the case plans for 772 children in foster care in one county in California.[158] Of these children, 111 (15 percent) were headed for restoration to their parents. One year later 62 of these children (56 percent) had been restored and an additional 12 (11 percent) were still headed for restoration.[159] Fanshel and Grundy found that of 26,989 children in care in New York City, restoration was planned for 5,304

(19.7 percent).[160] In 1975 restoration was the plan for 257 children out of 2,657 (9.7 percent) in foster care in the state of Nebraska.[161] Emlen reports that 27 percent of the children in placement in 17 counties in Oregon had "restoration to their parents" as a case plan.[162] In the state of California 28,345 children were in foster care under both public and private agency auspices as of September 30, 1974.[163] In the three months between that date and the end of 1974, 3 percent had been returned to their biological parents. In a report from the state of Michigan, only 15 percent of 515 children entering care in the 1974–75 fiscal year were returned home within 12 months. After 15 months in care, only an additional 2 percent were returned home.[164]

Several experimental and quasi-experimental studies have been conducted in an attempt to increase the numbers of children returned to their parents.[165] Dividing case management responsibilities between two workers has been tried, with one worker responsible for services to biological parents and the other serving the child in the foster home. One of three studies in which this approach was used has yet to be fully evaluated; and another, while describing the method as "successful," does not provide comparative data against which this model can be evaluated.[166] In the last of these investigations, Sherman et al. conducted a one-year study in which 413 children were assigned to monitoring, control, or special worker groups.[167] Their study included all of the children in foster care in one public agency who were 13 years of age or younger, had at least one parent present in the community, and had been in care three years or less. In addition, cases entering the agency during the first eight months of the project were accepted if they met these criteria.

In the monitoring group, the only change in procedure was that workers submitted forms on each child every three months, so that movement during the study period could be tracked. No procedural changes occurred in the control group. Two of the agency's units were designated as special worker groups. Cases were divided between an agency worker, who was responsible for services to the child and foster parents, and two baccalaureate-level social workers with experience in foster care, one assigned to each group. The special workers were responsible for "intensive services" to the biological parent(s). Using the criteria noted above, agency workers in the experimental units were asked to refer cases from their active caseloads that "showed potential" for restoration but in which restoration was unlikely without additional assistance to the parents.[168] Intensive services were not defined. Process information was reported by workers on a monthly basis, and included the frequency and type of contact (such as in-person vs. telephone); the person with whom contact was made; service, such as financial and medical assistance, provided; topics discussed during the interview; and, using Hollis' typology of casework techniques, the predominant method employed. (Hollis' typology includes categories for describing the casework interview, such as the person who is communicating, the subject matter of communication, and the casework method employed—directive, structuring, exploratory techniques.)[169] A total of 75 out of 413 children (18 percent) were returned to their parents by the end of the study. Of these, 32 (28 percent) were in the control group, 27 (18 percent) in the monitoring segment, and 16 (13 percent) in the special worker group.[170]

Preventing children from drifting into long-term care and reuniting those in long-term care with their families were the two objectives of a one-year experimental study in New York City and two adjacent counties.[171] Cases judged by workers as most likely to benefit from intensive services within the time limits of the project were randomly assigned to experimental and control groups. Workers provided or arranged for a variety of services. Included were financial and housing assistance, counseling, vocational training, day care, and homemaker services.[172] Of 306 children in foster care when the project began, 47 percent of the experimental unit children, compared with 38 percent of those in the control group, had been returned to their own homes.[173]

Charles Atherton conducted a study in Illinois in which the supervisor of one foster care unit engaged staff in case reviews to consider the alternatives of restoration, adoption, and planned long-term care. The number of children returned home in a six-month period increased from 14 to 30.[174]

The studies reviewed above indicate that the percentage of children restored to their natural parents is small, ranging from a low of 3 percent to a high of 60 percent.[175] Data are provided in three of the four investigations in which the objective was to increase the numbers of children restored. One of these had no control group; hence the intensive supervision provided to workers cannot be considered causal to the increase reported.[176] Intensive services provided by experimental group workers in the study by Mary Jones, Renee Neuman, and Ann Shyne resulted in a greater percentage of restorations for experimental group than control group children. However, the difference was not significant.[177] The results of the Sherman et al. study are disappointing, showing a greater precentage of restorations occurring for control than for experimental cases.[178] The design of this latter study more closely resembled that of the Alameda Project than did any investigation reported in the literature, and will be evaluated in detail in chapter 4, which reports our results.

Adoption

When a child cannot be restored to its natural parents, adoption is the alternative of choice for establishing a permanent relationship between the child and the caretaking parents. The number of children adopted, like the number restored, is quite low. In 1963, Jeter reported that only 10 percent of the children in public agencies were receiving adoption services, and workers expected this outcome for only 13 percent.[179] (According to Jeter, "Adoption services may include any of the following: pre-adoptive study of the child, planning placement for adoption, pre-adoption supervision in an adoptive home and investigation at the request of the court of an adoption placement made independently of a social agency."[180]) In his ten-year follow-up Maas found that 21 percent of the children had been adopted. More than half of these children (12 percent) had been adopted within the first three years of placement.[181] Wiltse and Gambrill report that 48 of the 772 children in their study (6 percent) were designated as heading for adoption.[182] Less than 1 percent of the children leaving foster home care in California in the quarter between October 1 and December 31, 1974, were adopted.[183] At the end of a five-year longitudinal study in New York, only 4.6 percent of the children were placed in adoptive homes.[184] Adoption is the plan for 403 youngsters out of 2,657 (15.2 percent) in a study reported from the state of Nebraska.[185] Atherton reported that the number of children adopted increased almost five times—from 8 to 38—as a result of closer supervision and planning.[186] Sherman et al. reported a study conducted in one of the agencies that participated in Maas and Engler's 1959 investigation, in which aggressive court action was taken to free children who had been abandoned or whose parents could not be rehabilitated. In addition, services were provided to foster parents interested in adopting, and contact with natural parents was increased, so that a child could either be returned home or placed for adoption. In the second year after the study, the adoption rate more than doubled.[187]

In the study by Sherman et al., only 1 child was adopted, although this outcome had been planned for 26 children.[188] Irving Fellner and Charles Solomon report a 22 percent increase in adoptions after special group counseling in which parents were encouraged to work toward a plan for their children.[189] Festinger noted that adoption action was significantly greater (76.1 percent vs. 58.7 percent) for cases reviewed by the New York City court than for those not reviewed.[190] A 100 percent increase in adoption petitions was reported by Steketee following mandated court review of all children in care in Rhode Island.[191]

Time and a Child's Adoptability

The length of time a child has been in care affects the probability of adoption as well as of restoration. Fanshel, Maas, and Stein and Gambrill found that the majority of children who were adopted left care in less than three years.[192] It has therefore been stressed that adoption be considered in the early stages of a child's placement career.[193] It also has been proposed that monitoring systems be employed to track the movement of children so that appropriate and timely planning assures that children designated as "headed for adoption" are moved in that direction.[194] The importance of monitoring systems has been highlighted by several investigators. Gruber found that in 40 percent of the cases where workers believed that adoption was possible, the Massachusetts Division of Family Services had not taken action. Furthermore, in cases where petitions were filed, "one-half have been in court for one year or more with no action." [195] Seventy cases reviewed by the New York Court between mid-1972 and December 1973, were ordered freed for adoption. Festinger reports that as of May 1974, no action had been taken by the agencies on 40 of these 70 cases.[196]

Almost half of the children in care in New York City entered placement when they were three years of age or younger.[197] Fanshel and Grundy suggest that failure to return these children to their parents or to place them for adoption results in long-term care status. They found that for children under two years of age, adoption was planned for 18 percent while there were no plans for 60 percent. Although workers indicated that adoption was planned for a total of 5,628 children of all ages (20.9 percent), 47.5 percent of these children had yet to be freed. They noted that this figure represents many more children than are annually adopted in New York, and stressed the need for a monitoring system to insure that adoption actually occurs.[198]

In 1960 the State Charities Aid Association of New York reviewed the cases of 100 children in care at that time. The potential adoptability of these children was judged at three points in time: entry into care, two years after entry, and the time of the study. On the basis of reviews of case records, the Association staff felt that 45 percent of these children had been adoptable at some point in the past; but as of 1958, only 13 percent had been adopted.[199] A report issued by the California Legislative Audit Committee indicated that "4,950 children, representing 26.6% of the children in care, were unlikely to be returned to their parents and are, or were in the recent past, potentially adoptive." The report concluded that "Had effective adoptive services been made available during their 2nd year in placement, they would no longer be receiving foster care payments." [200]

Deficits in parental visiting are frequently discussed in connection with the need for monitoring systems. Gruber states with reference to his study of foster care in Massachusetts:

> 11% of the biological parents or guardians have not seen their child in foster home care for at least 6 months and, yet, the social workers have still designated the child as unadoptable because of parental interest. An additional 10% of the children so designated have only been seen once in a six month period and perhaps of greater concern is the fact that the child has been designated as unadoptable in 14% of the cases when the social worker does not even know the frequency of contact.[201]

Other investigators have reported that workers are optimistic that children will return home long after parents have ceased to demonstrate an interest in their child(ren).[202] Twenty-five percent of the children in Festinger's study had no contact with their parents since they were placed, and an additional 25 percent had not seen parents in six months or more.[203] A study of children in foster care in California in 1972 found that 32.6 percent were not visited at all by their parents, and the visiting record was unknown in 6.9 percent of the cases.[204]

Older Children

A child's age is said to be a deterrent to adoption.[205] According to Alfred Kadushin, a child of five is old by adoption standards.[206] While certain considerations, such as the child's interest in being adopted, the child's relationship to biological parents, and an adoptive couple's interest in having an infant, may be issues of concern in the adoption of older children, recent data suggest that there is "a trend toward increased adoptions of the older child."[207] There also is evidence that these children can be successfully placed.[208] Kadushin followed up a group of children one year after their adoptive placement. He was concerned with adoption failure, which was defined as the return of the child to the agency. Viewing failure relative to the child's age at the time of adoption, a bimodal relationship was found. The highest percentage of failures occurred for children who were placed between the ages of two and six years (56 percent). Failure rates for children who were placed when they were under two or over six were 14 percent and 30 percent, respectively. Fifty percent of the children who failed were successfully replaced.[209]

In New York City, adoption was listed as a discharge objective for 60 percent of the children between 6 and 9 years of age who had been in care between 10 to 21 years of age, who had been in care all of their lives, as suitable for adoption.[210]

Subsidized Adoption

Financial issues have been cited as barriers to adoption, and subsidies to adoptive parents have been suggested in the child welfare literature.[211] In 1972 the President's Commission on Population Growth recommended such programs, and by 1974 subsidy programs had been established in 39 states and the District of Columbia.[212] Eligibility for subsidy varies from state to state. Following recommendation of the President's Commission some states grant subsidies only on behalf of children adjudged hard-to-place; and available data suggest that programs often are limited in this way.[213]

California, while not restricting subsidies to hard-to-place children, encourages their use primarily for such children. Means tests are required in most states, and some require yearly renegotiation of the subsidy.[214] California limits the program to five years following the adoption.

The Child Welfare League of America, in conjunction with the Children's Bureau, has drafted a Model Subsidized Adoption Act.[215] Its intent is to permit public financial subsidy to facilitate the adoption of children. The Model Act, however, has yet to be adopted by any of the states.

Fanshel and Grundy suggest that the availability of subsidies may help to explain why such a high percentage of older foster children in New York City were reported by their workers to be adoptable.[217] Gruber noted that workers cited financial difficulties as obstacles to the adoption of a group of 127 children in placement. Seventy-seven percent of these workers stated that the children would be adopted if a subsidy program existed. He reported that Massachusetts had had such a program since 1972; however, at the time of his study in 1973, it had been used for only three children.[218] Emlen reports that while subsidies are available in the state of Oregon, they are a limited resource. He believes that financial barriers to permanent planning were rated "at least moderate for 25% of children in foster care" in Oregon.[219]

Termination of Parental Rights

Unless parents voluntarily relinquish a child, action must be taken to terminate their rights in order to free a child for adoption. Such action can occur in most states if the child has been abandoned or through petition to the court to sever parental ties following failed attempts to rehabilitate the natural parents.[220] The procedures and standards by which parental ties can be terminated vary considerably from state to state.[221] While abandonment is the most common basis for allowing adoption without parental consent, there is a legislative and judicial movement to permit children to be freed for adoption when their parents manifest disinterest or inattention, regardless of subjective intent to abandon the child.[222]

An attempt to standardize termination procedures is found in the Model Act to Free Children for Permanent Placement. The act, a project of the Children's Bureau, has been "submitted to H.E.W./O.C.D. . . . for review and dissemination."[223] Concern that adoption regulations be standardized nationally is explicit in pending federal legislation.[224] There are no national data on the numbers of children freed through court-ordered termination.

Several issues that hinder decision making at earlier stages of case planning are relevant to termination of parental rights. A decision to terminate means risk taking, and the social worker feels the weight of making long-range predictions. We have suggested that a decision to restore a child gives rise to questions such as "Will the parent ever abuse a child again?" or "Will the parent resume the use of drugs or alcohol?" At the point of decision making for termination, a series of "what if" questions often plagues the social worker. What if the parent recovers his or her mental health? What if a good adoptive home cannot be found?[225] The language of statutory law and of professional guidelines reinforces a concern with such predictions. Except for abandonment petitions, where the basis for termination is no contact between parent and child for a set time period (six months in California, a year in Massachusetts[226]) statutes of some states speak of terminating when it is in the child's best interest, or if the court finds beyond *a reasonable doubt* that return to parents would be detrimental.[227] The Child Welfare League of America recommends such action when "It has been established that parents will be unable or unwilling in the forseeable future to play a constructive role in a child's placement or plan his eventual return home."[228] The Children's Bureau suggests that agencies move toward termination when mental illness is likely to continue for a "prolonged indeterminate period."[229] We can only reiterate that such predictions are based on fragmentary knowledge. Fear of making a wrong decision often results in a failure to take any action.[230]

Additional issues are highlighted by a report from the state of Oregon.[231] Seeking to describe the barriers to freeing children for permanent placement, investigators surveyed 279 foster care workers in 29 counties. A 28-item questionnaire was administered to identify workers' attitudes toward court-ordered termination of parental rights. The major attitudinal factors to emerge as impediments to such action were the workers' perception of the court as a barrier and negative attitudes toward termination procedures.[232] A second phase of this project is focused on demonstrating ways of making more permanent plans for children, including developing procedures for more effective use of termination. The authors report that as cases were brought to the court, personnel began to see that these barriers were not so great as had been supposed.[233] This finding points to public agency responsibility to provide training and legal assistance if this case planning option is to be employed.[234] Their conclusions also reaffirm the need for agency policy. Clearly stated objectives and guidelines, not worker attitudes, should be major determinants in permanent planning for children.

One final issue returns our attention to case record keeping. Legal proceedings for termination action demand more stringent standards than do those used for initial removal.[235] Given the consequences of a decision to terminate parental ties, it seems reasonable to suggest that the specificity of data gathered by workers would strongly influence the court's willingness to terminate. We shall return to this last issue in the discussion of the project results.

The percentage of children adopted is smaller than the percentage restored; figures range from less than 1 percent to a maximum of 22 percent.[236] The importance of monitoring to assure consideration of adoption is highlighted by several issues raised in the literature. First, for a majority of children adopted, this outcome occurs within three years of their entry into care.[237] However, investigations have shown a failure to explore this alternative in the early stages of a child's placement or to consider moving to free the child for adoption when parents do not visit.[238] Studies have revealed a lack of definitive action for large numbers of children who are adoptable, and delay after adoption petitions have been filed or after children have been freed by the courts.[239] Although data on their long-range impact are still limited, adoption subsidies are increasingly being utilized to move hard-to-place and older children into adoptive homes.[240] The combination of inexplicit statutes and vague or misleading professional guidelines continues to direct social worker effort to making long-range predictions rather than to the use of explicit planning options. Social worker attitudes toward legal procedures and perceptions of the court as a hostile arena are added impediments to pursuing termination. Only as the public agency sets clear guidelines and provides training and legal consultation for casework staff will these impediments diminish.

Guardianship

Legal guardianship is of two types, of the person or of the estate. We are concerned only with guardianship of the person, in foster care meaning a foster parent or other adult who is given a legal status with reference to the custody of the child.[241] Legal guardianship is an alternative to adoption, establishing a permanent relationship without the supervision of a public or private social agency.

In instances where a child has been in a continuous placement with a foster parent, in an environment assessed as one in which the child should remain, but the foster parent feels unable to become an adoptive parent, guardianship is an alternative. Legally there are two seminal distinctions between a guardianship and an adoptive arrangement. First, a guardian is not responsible for financial support, nor are there rights of inheritance between child and legal guardian. Legal guardianship does, however, permit foster parents much more decision-making responsibility than they can exercise in the foster parent role. For example, they can decide where the child lives, they can control and discipline the child, and they have the power to consent to the child's medical care.[242] "Although many states call for judicial regulation and control of personal guardians, following the initial appointment, there is, typically, no court supervision, unless someone complains."[243]

Several writers have emphasized the value of guardianship as a way to provide both foster parent and child with a sense of permanence and a psychological bond that is not possible in a foster care arrangement.[244,] Whether this bond is in fact established has not been proved. In 1972 a report by the California State Social Welfare Board encouraged the use of guardianship because of the stability it can add to a foster child's life, and recommended the provision of legal services to foster parents wishing to pursue appointment as guardians.[245] A 1973 report by the State of California Department of Health set forth a contradictory position: "A review of the benefits and deficits of guardianship for children suggests that the assignment of guardianship rights to foster parents should be discouraged. Generally, the benefits devolve more upon the foster parents than upon the child."[246] It is not clear either from this report or from the available literature precisely what are the benefits and deficits to which they refer.

The 1972 recommendation regarding the provision of legal services to foster parents was not supported in a 1974 review of foster care studies conducted in California.[247] A reason given for not encouraging the use of legal guardianship in foster care was the lack of research evidence of its value to children. Two of the consultants gave the following reasons for their basis for rejecting this proposal:

> My experience with foster parents as guardians has been 100% negative. In almost every instance the foster parent has asked to be relieved of guardianship when the child becomes a teenager.

> Guardianship generally provides little protection for children and may prevent a responsible placement agency from acting in the child's best interest.[248]

Despite the above position, the value of guardianship for stabilizing a child's living arrangements is recognized in legislation enacted in California in 1976. The legislation directs the court to "order the appropriate [child welfare] department to facilitate guardianship proceedings . . . if the court finds that a specified minor is not adoptable."[249]

It is difficult not to be pessimistic about the current state of child welfare services. We find calls for more services, smaller caseloads, and more experienced workers, even though there is little evidence that these measures hold the answers. Additional services, whether given by public agency child welfare staffs or by other community agencies, cannot be expected to yield different outcomes for children in care if we lack empirical support for the effectiveness of methods used. Caseload size is not a meaningful yardstick. Caseload management, rather than caseload size per se, seems to make a difference. There is a surge of interest in improved and expanded monitoring systems, in the belief they will make a difference. Improved monitoring may lead to better case management procedures, provided supervisors use the information that is fed back to them to track cases within their units. A more optimistic view is possible if we glean from the literature those suggestions for change that are supported by empirical evidence and follow this with a systematic effort to implement these new directions in foster care practice and measure the results. This is precisely what the Alameda Project described in chapter 3 set out to do. The results are reported in chapter 4. The case management procedures that proved successful are described in detail in Part II.

NOTES

1. National Association of Attorneys General, *Legal Issues in Foster Care* (Raleigh, N.C.: Committee on the Office of Attorney General, 1976), p. 1.

2. A. C. Emlen and staff,*"Freeing Children for Permanent Placement"* (Portland, Ore.: Regional Research Institute for Human Services, 1975); Alan R. Gruber, *Foster Home Care in Massachusetts* (Boston: Governor's Commission on Adoption and Foster Care, 1973), p. 72; Helen R. Jeter, *Children, Problems and Services in Child Welfare Programs* (Washington, D.C.: Children's Bureau, 1963), p. 87; Henry Maas and Richard Engler, *Children in Need of Parents* (New York: Columbia University Press, 1959), p. 356.

3. David Fanshel, "The Exit of Children from Foster Care: An Interim Research Report," *Child Welfare* 50 (February 1971):65–81; Jeter, op. cit.; Maas and Engler, op. cit.

4. Martin Wolins, *A Proposed Research Program for the Child Welfare League of America* (New York: Child Welfare League of America, 1959), pp. 13–14.

5. David Fanshel, "Research in Child Welfare: A Critical Analysis," *Child Welfare* 41 (1962):484–507.

6. Ibid., p. 485.

7. Donald Brieland, Kenneth Watson, Philip Hovda, David Fanshel, and John J. Carey, *Differential Use of Manpower: A Team Model for Foster Care* (New York: Child Welfare League of America, 1968), p. 8.

8. Ibid., p. 10.

9. Edmund V. Mech, "Decision Analysis in Foster Care Practice," in Helen D. Stone, ed., *Foster Care in Question* (New York: Child Welfare League of America, 1970), pp. 26–51.

10. Eileen D. Gambrill and Kermit T. Wiltse, "Foster Care: Prescriptions for Change," *Public Welfare* 32 (Summer 1974):39–47; Sally E. Palmer, "The Decision to Separate Children from Their Natural Parents," *Social Worker* 39 (1971):82–87; Arthur Emlen, Janet Lahta, Glen Downs, Alex McKay, and Susan Downs, *Overcoming Barriers to Planning for Children in Foster Care* (Portland, Ore.: Regional Research Institute for Human Services, 1977), p. 43.

11. Bernice Boehm, "An Assessment of Family Adequacy in Protective Cases," *Child Welfare* 41 (January 1962):10–16; Bernice Boehm, "Protective Services for Neglected Children" in *Social Work Practice: Proceedings of the National Conference on Social Welfare* (conference committee chaired by Arnulf N. Pins) (New York: Columbia University Press, 1967), pp. 109–25.

12. Boehm, "An Assessment of Family Adequacy . . . ," p. 10.

13. Boehm, "Protective Services for Neglected Children," p. 118.

14. Ibid., pp. 119–120.

15. Ibid.

16. Alfred Kadushin, *Child Welfare Services* (2nd ed.; New York: Macmillan, 1974), p. 50.

17. Michael H. Phillips, Ann W. Shyne, Edmund A. Sherman, and Barbara L. Haring, *Factors Associated with Placement Decisions in Child Welfare* (New York: Child Welfare League of America, 1971).

18. Ibid., p. 6.

19. Ibid., pp. 51, 87.

20. Ibid., p. 87.

21. Scott Briar, "Clinical Judgment in Foster Care Placement," *Child Welfare* 42 (1963):161–69.

22. Ibid., p. 168.

23. Mech, op. cit., p. 44.

24. Phillips et al., op. cit., p. 69.

25. Ibid., p. 84.

26. Martin Wolins, *Selecting Foster Parents* (New York: Columbia University Press, 1963).

27. Ibid., pp. 72–73.

28. Theodore J. Stein, "A Content Analysis of Social Caseworker and Client Interaction in Foster Care." Ph.D. diss., University of California, Berkeley, 1974, p. 91.

29. Ibid., p. 278.

30. Naomi Golan, "How Caseworkers Decide: A Study of the Association of Selected Applicant Factors with Worker Decision in Admission Services," *Social Service Review* 43 (1969):289–96.

31. Ibid., p. 294.

32. Donald Brieland, *An Experimental Study in the Selection of Adoptive Parents at Intake* (New York: Child Welfare League of America, 1959).

33. Ann W. Shyne, *The Need for Foster Care* (New York: Child Welfare League of America, 1969).

34. Ibid., p. 59.

35. Ibid., p. 72.

36. Shirley Jenkins and Mignon Sauber, *Paths to Child Placement* (New York: Community Council of New York, 1966), pp. 62–80.

37. Ibid., p. 185.

38. Phillips et al., op. cit., p. 14.

39. Briar, op. cit., p. 168.

40. Martin Wolins and Irving Piliavin, *Institution or Foster Family: A Century of Debate* (New York: Child Welfare League of America, 1964).

41. Boehm, "An Assessment of Family Adequacy . . ."; Bernice Boehm, "The Community and Social Agency Define Neglect," *Child Welfare* 43 (1964):453–64; Maas and Engler, op. cit.; Edward T. Weaver, "Long-Term Foster Care: Default or Design? The Public Agency Responsibility," *Child Welfare* 47 (June 1968):339–45.

42. Brieland et al., op. cit., p. 12.

43. Boehm, "Protective Services for Neglected Children"; Jessica S. Pers, *Government as Parent: Administering Foster Care in California* (Berkeley: Institute of Governmental Studies, University of California, 1976), p. 17.

44. Gruber, op. cit., p. 47.

45. Eileen D. Gambrill and Kermit T. Wiltse, "Foster Care: Plans and Actualities," *Public Welfare* 32 (Spring 1974):12–21.

46. Child Welfare League of America, *Standards for Foster Family Care* (rev. ed.; New York: the League, 1975), pp. 8–9.

47. Ibid.; Kadushin, op. cit., p. 29; Delmer J. Pascoe, *Review, Synthesis and Recommendations of Seven Foster Care Studies in California* (Sacramento: Children's Research Institute of California, 1974), p. 8.

48. Pers, op. cit., p. 83.

49. Henry Maas, "Highlights of the Foster Care Project: Introduction," *Child Welfare* 38 (July 1959):5.

51. Edmund A. Sherman, Renee Neuman, and Ann W. Shyne, *Children Adrift in Foster Care: A Study of Alternative Approaches* (New York: Child Welfare League of America, 1974), ch. 4.

52. Gruber, op. cit., p. 72.

53. Trudy B. Festinger, "The New York Court Review of Children in Foster Care," *Child Welfare* 54 (April 1975):217.

54. David Fanshel and John F. Grundy, *CWIS Report* (New York: Child Welfare Information Services, 1975), p. 8.

55. Kermit T. Wiltse and Eileen D. Gambrill, "Foster Care 1973: A Reappraisal," *Public Welfare* 32 (Winter 1974):8.

56. Nebraska Department of Public Welfare, *Where Are the Children?* (Lincoln: the Department, 1976), p. 7.

57. Maas and Engler, op. cit., pp. 390–91.

58. Jeter, op. cit.

59. Ibid., p. 6.

60. Gruber, op. cit., p. 50.

61. Ibid., pp. 53–54.

62. Brieland et al., op. cit., p. 17.

63. Ibid.

64. Martha L. Jones, "Aggressive Adoption: A Program's Effect on a Child Welfare Agency," *Child Welfare* 56 (June 1977):401–07; Office of Program Evaluation, *Placement in Foster Care: Issues and Concerns* (Oakland, Calif.: the Office, 1977), p. 3; Nebraska Department of Public Welfare, op. cit., p. 7.

65. Gambrill and Wiltse, "Foster Care: Plans and Actualities," p. 15; Robert H. Mnookin, "Child Custody Adjudication: Judicial Function in the Face of Indeterminancy," *Law and Contemporary Problems* 39 (Summer 1975):226–93.

66. Leon W. Chestang and Irmgard Heymann, "Reducing the Length of Foster Care," *Social Work* 18 (January 1973):88.

67. Ibid.; Child Welfare League of America, op. cit., p. 5; Gambrill and Wiltse, "Foster Care: Plans and Actualities," p. 20; Gruber, op. cit., p. 88; Pascoe, op. cit., p. 9; Deborah Shapiro, *Agencies and Foster Children* (New York: Columbia University Press, 1976), p. 140.

68. Shapiro, op. cit., p. 89.

69. Arthur C. Emlen and staff, *Barriers to Planning for Children in Foster Care*, (Portland, Ore.: Regional Research Institute for Human Services, 1976).

70. Ibid., ch. 8, p. 10.

71. Edmund A. Sherman, Michael H. Phillips, Barbara L. Haring, and Ann W. Shyne, *Services to Children in Their Own Homes: Its Nature and Outcome* (New York: Child Welfare League of America, 1973), p. 110.

72. Maas and Engler, op. cit., p. 324; David Fanshel, "Parental Visiting of Children in Foster Care: Key to Discharge," *Social Service Review* 49 (December 1975):513; Festinger, op. cit., p. 224.

73. Paul J. McAdams, "The Parent in the Shadows," *Child Welfare* 51 (January 1972):65.

74. Gruber, op. cit., p. 54.

75. Shirley Jenkins and Elaine Norman, *Beyond Placement: Mothers View Foster Care* (New York: Columbia University Press, 1975), p. 67.

76. Fanshel, "Parental Visiting of Children in Foster Care," loc. cit.

77. Ibid.

78. Shirley Jenkins and Elaine Norman, *Filial Deprivation and Foster Care* (New York: Columbia University Press, 1972).

79. Deborah Shapiro, "Agency Investment in Foster Care: A Study," *Social Work* 17 (July 1972):20–28.

80. Sherman et al., *Services to Children in Their Own Homes*, p. 106.

81. Baltimore County Department of Social Services, "Pilot Project: Experiences with a Specialized Caseload of Natural Parents" (Townsend, Md.: the Department, 1971), p. 6 (mimeographed); Emlen et al., *Overcoming Barriers to Planning for Children in Foster Care*, p.

30; Helen D. Stone, "An Orientation to Foster Care Theory and Values: An Introduction," in Stone, op. cit., p. 6.

82. Shapiro, *Agencies and Foster Children*, pp. 79–82.

83. Ibid., p. 90.

84. Pers, op. cit., p. 87.

85. Gruber, op. cit., p. 27.

86. Edward T. Heck and Alan R. Gruber, *Treatment Alternatives Project* (Boston: Boston Children's Service Association, 1976), p. 196.

87. Public Services Administration, *A Guide: Protective Services for Abused and Neglected Children and Their Families* (New York: Community Research Applications, Inc., 1973), p. 37.

88. Pers, op. cit., ch. 6.

89. Norman Herstein, "The Image and Reality of Foster Care Practice," in Stone, op. cit., p. 174.

90. Alfred Kadushin, "The Social Scene and the Planning of Services for Children," *Social Work* 7 (July 1962):14; Pascoe, op. cit., p. 36; State of California, Department of Health, *Family Protection Act of 1976* (Sacramento: the Department, 1977), "Children's Social Services, Adoptions and Foster Care," p. 7.

91. Gambrill and Wiltse, "Foster Care: Plans and Actualities," p. 14.

92. Elizabeth K. Radinsky, "Provisions for Care: Foster Family Care," in Helen D. Stone, ed., op. cit., p. 61.

93. Gambrill and Wiltse, "Foster Care: Plans and Actualities," loc. cit.

94. U.S. Department of Health, Education and Welfare, Office of Human Development, *The Community Team: An Approach to Case Management and Prevention*, (vol. 3) *Child Abuse and Neglect*, D.H.E.W. publication no. (OHD) 75-30075 (Washington, D.C.: U.S. Government Printing Office, 1975), p. 143; Advisory Committee on Child Development, Assembly of Behavioral and Social Sciences, National Research Council, *Toward a National Policy for Children and Families* (Washington, D.C.: National Academy of Sciences, 1976), p. 84; Nicholas Hobbs, *The Futures of Children* (San Francisco: Jossey-Bass, 1976), pp. 258–60; Anne Minahan and Allen Pincus, "Conceptual Framework for Social Work Practice," *Social Work* 22 (September 1977):348.

95. Pers, op. cit., ch. 2.

96. National Association of Attorneys General, op. cit., p. 3.

97. Jessica Pers and the Staff of the Childhood and Government Project, "Somebody Else's Children: A Report on the Foster Care System in California" (Berkeley: Boalt School of Law, University of California, 1974), p. 73. (Unpublished ms.).

98. Pers, op. cit., p. 87; Office of Program Evaluation, op. cit., p. 54.

99. Gambrill and Wiltse, "Foster Care: Plans and Actualities," p. 18; Office of Program Evaluation, loc. cit.

100. Gruber, op. cit., p. 27.

101. Brieland et al., op. cit., p. 19; M. W. Bryce and R. C. Ehlebt, "144 Foster Children," *Child Welfare* 50 (1971):499–503; Gambrill and Wiltse, "Foster Care: Plans and Actualities," p. 20.

102. Pascoe, op. cit., p. 48; Mary Lewis, "Long-Term Temporary Placement," *Child Welfare* 30 (January 1951):3–7; Gambrill and Wiltse, "Foster Care: Prescriptions for Change," p. 44; Gruber, op. cit., p. 90; Annie Millar, Harry Hatry, and Margo Koss, *Monitoring the Outcomes of Social Services*, vol. 1, *Preliminary Suggestions* (Washington, D.C.: Urban Institute, 1977), p. ix; Marvin R. Burt and Ralph R. Balyeat, *A Comprehensive Emergency Services System for Neglected and Abused Children* (New York: Vantage Press, 1977), p. 82.

103. Fanshel and Grundy, op. cit.; State of California, Department of Health, *Data Matters* (Sacramento: the Department, Report Register no. 342–0395–502, September 30, 1974 [issued June 1975]). John P. Steketee, "The CIP Story," *Juvenile Justice* 28 (May 1977):6.

104. Gruber, op. cit., pp. 22, 35.

105. Emlen and staff, "Freeing Children for Permanent Placement," p. 12; Fanshel and Grundy, op. cit., p. 32.

106. Fanshel and Grundy, loc. cit.

107. State of California, *Family Protection Act of 1976.*

108. Community Research Applications, op. cit., p. 104; Justine Wise Polier, "Myths and Realities in the Search for Juvenile Justice: A Statement by the Honorable Justine Wise Polier," *Harvard Educational Review* 44 (February 1974):112; Office of Program Evaluation, op. cit., p. 56; Burt and Balyeat, op. cit., p. xxvi.

109. Festinger, op. cit.

110. Fanshel and Grundy, op. cit., p. 22.

111. Festinger, op. cit., p. 236.

112. Steketee, op. cit., p. 7.

113. California State Department of Health, *Adoption and Foster Care Study* (Sacramento: the Department, 1973), p. 16; Michael Wald, "State Intervention on Behalf of Neglected Children: A Search for Realistic Standards," *Stanford Law Review* 27 (April 1975):998; Arthur Young and Co., *Final Report: Alameda County Pilot Project on Human Services Planning* (Oakland, Calif.: Arthur Young and Co., 1976), p. V-7; Joint Commission on Mental Health of Children, *The Mental Health of Children: Services, Research, and Manpower* (New York: Harper and Row, 1973), p. 112; Jones, op. cit., p. 403.

114. Gambrill and Wiltse, "Foster Care: Plans and Actualities," p. 18.

115. Brieland et al., op. cit., p. 1; Kadushin, *Child Welfare Services*, p. 462; Michael Wald, "State Intervention on Behalf of 'Neglected' Children: Standards for Removal of Children from Their Homes, Monitoring the Status of Children in Foster Care, and Termination of Parental Rights," *Stanford Law Review* 28 (April 1976):682; Jenkins and Norman, *Beyond Placement*, p. 137.

116. Sherman et al., *Services to Children in Their Own Homes*, p. 110.

117. David Fanshel and Eugene B. Shinn, *Dollars and Sense in the Foster Care of Children: A Look at Cost Factors* (New York: Child Welfare League of America, 1972).

118. California State Department of Health, *Adoption and Foster Care Study.*

119. Ibid., p. 17.

120. Ibid., p. 18.

121. Pascoe, op. cit., p. 31.

122. Gruber, op. cit., p. 27; Shapiro, "Agency Investment in Foster Care," p. 25: Theodore J. Stein and Eileen D. Gambrill, "Early Intervention in Foster Care;" *Public Welfare* 34 (Spring 1976):38–44.

123. State of California, *Department of Health, Comprehensive Annual Services Program Plan: Title XX* (Sacramento: the Department, 1975–76), p. 1.

124. *Community Research Applications,* op. cit., p. 46; John E. Horejsi, Thomas Walz, and Patrick R. Connolly, *Working in Welfare: Survival Through Positive Action* (Iowa City: University of Iowa Press, 1977), p. 9.

125. National Commission on Productivity and Work Quality, *Productivity: Employee Incentives to Improve State and Local Government Productivity* (Washington, D.C.: the Commission, 1975), p. 5.

126. Weaver, op. cit., p. 342.

127. Brieland et al., op. cit.; Fanshel, "Research in Child Welfare"; Gambrill and Wiltse, "Foster Care: Prescriptions for Change"; Mech, op. cit.; Palmer, op. cit.

128. Edward Foy, "The Decision Making Problem in Foster Care," *Child Welfare* 46 (November 1967):502; Boehm, "An Assessment of Family Adequacy . . . ," p. 12.

129. Phillips et al., op. cit., p. 2.

130. Briar, op. cit., p. 167; Phillips et al., op. cit., p. 84; Hillary Rodham, "Children Under the Law," *Harvard Educational Review* 43 (1974):1–28; Mnookin, op. cit.; Wald, "State Intervention on Behalf of Neglected Children: A Search . . . ," p. 1034; Palmer, op. cit., p. 82; Emlen et al., *Overcoming Barriers to Planning for Children in Foster Care*, pp. 43–44; Jones,

op. cit., p. 404; Jenkins and Norman, *Beyond Placement*, p. 137; Irving W. Fellner and Charles Solomon, "Achieving Permanent Solutions for Children in Foster Home Care," *Child Welfare* 52 (March 1973):180.

131. Child Welfare League of America, op. cit., p. 8; Joseph Goldstein, Anna Freud, and Albert J. Solnit, *Beyond the Best Interests of the Child* (New York: Free Press, 1973), p. 31; Rodham, op. cit.; Kathryn Mahoney and Michael J. Mahoney, "Psychoanalytic Guidelines for Child Placement," *Social Work* 19 (November 1974):664.

132. Mahoney and Mahoney, loc. cit.; Goldstein et al., op. cit.; Rodham, op. cit.

133. Arlene Skolnick, *The Intimate Environment: Exploring Marriage and the Family* (Boston: Little, Brown, 1973); Sheldon H. White, Mary C. Day, Phyllis K. Freeman, Stephen A. Hantman and Katherine P. Messenger, *Federal Programs for Young Children: Review and Recommendations*; vol. 1, *Goals and Standards of Public Programs for Children* (Washington, D.C.: U.S. Department of Health, Education and Welfare, 1973).

134. Mech, op. cit., p. 32.

135. Boehm, "Protective Services for Neglected Children," p. 115; Pers, op. cit., ch. 2.

136. Ervin Goffman, *Stigma* (Englewood Cliffs, N.J.: Prentice-Hall, 1963), p. 4.

137. Wald, "State Intervention on Behalf of Neglected Children: A Search . . . ," p. 998; Henry Maas, "Children in Long Term Foster Care," *Child Welfare* 48 (1969):332–33; Boehm, "The Community and Social Agency Define Neglect," p. 459; Boehm, *Social Work Practice*, p. 117; Jenkins and Sauber, op. cit., pp. 12–17.

138. Arnold P. Goldstein, *Structured Learning Therapy* (New York: Academic Press, 1973), pp. 8–14.

139. Boehm "Protective Services for Neglected Children" p. 116.

140. Ibid.

141. Phillips et al., op. cit., p. 10.

142. Jenkins and Norman, *Beyond Placement*, p. 140.

143. Edwin M. Lemert, *Human Deviance, Social Problems and Social Control* (Englewood Cliffs, N.J.: Prentice-Hall, 1967).

144. Thomas J. Scheff, *Being Mentally Ill: A Sociological Theory* (Chicago: Aldine, 1966), p. 74.

145. Edwin M. Schur, *Labeling Deviant Behavior: Its Sociological Implications* (New York: Harper and Row, 1971), p. 41.

146. Ervin Goffman, *Asylums* (New York: Anchor Books, 1961), pp. 155–56.

147. David Fanshel, "Child Welfare," in Henry S. Maas, ed. *Research in the Social Services: A Five-Year Review* (New York: National Association of Social Workers, 1971), p. 88.

148. On case planning, see State of California, *Family Protection Act of 1974*, "Children's Social Services, Adoptions, and Foster Care," pp. 2–3; Victor Pike, Susan Downs, Arthur Emlen, Glen Downs, and Denise Case, *Permanent Planning for Children in Foster Care: A Handbook for Social Workers* (Portland, Ore.: Regional Research Institute for Human Services, 1977), p. 4; U.S. Congress, House of Representatives, *Foster Care, Adoption and Reform Act of 1977*, 95th Cong., 1st sess. (Washington, D.C.: U.S. Government Printing Office, 1977), p. 11; Alfred J. Kahn, "Child Welfare: Trends and Directions," *Child Welfare* 41 (December 1962) 459–76. On intensive services, see Pascoe, op. cit., p. 8; Burt and Balyeat, op. cit., ch. 7. On ancillary community services, see State of California, *Family Protection Act of 1976*, ch. 2; Alfred J. Kahn, "The Social Scene and the Planning of Services for Children," *Social Work* 7 (July 1962): p. 14; Pascoe, op. cit., p. 36.

149. Charles R. Atherton, "Acting Decisively in Foster Care," *Social Work* 19 (November 1974):658, 740, 741; Chestang and Heymann, op. cit., pp. 88–93; Bernice Madison and Michael Shapiro, "Permanent and Long-Term Foster Family Care as a Planned Service," *Child Welfare* 49 (March 1970):131–36; Weaver, op. cit.

150. *Child Welfare League of America*, op. cit.; Madison and Shapiro, op. cit.; David M. Schmidt, "A Commitment to Parenthood," *Child Welfare* 49 (1970):42–44; Hazeltine Taylor,

"Guardianship or Permanent Placement of Children," *California Law Review* 54 (1966):741–47; Wiltse and Gambrill, op. cit., pp. 7–15.

151. Chestang and Heymann, loc. cit.; Madison and Shapiro, op. cit.; Marian V. Peterson, "The Goals of Foster Care," in Stone, op. cit., pp. 165–68; Shapiro, "Agency Investment in Foster Care," Weaver, op. cit.

152. Public Welfare Amendments to the Social Security Act, 1962; State of California, Comprehensive Annual Services Program Plan: Title XX (1975–76).

153. Jeter, op. cit., p. 87.

154. Maas and Engler, op. cit., p. 379.

155. Maas, "Children in Long Term Foster Care," p. 323.

156. David Fanshel, "Status Changes of Children in Foster Care: Final Results of the Columbia University Longitudinal Study," *Child Welfare* 55 (March 1976):145.

157. Deborah Shapiro, "Agency Investment in Foster Care: A Follow-up," *Social Work* 18 (November 1973):3–9.

158. Wiltse and Gambrill, op. cit.

159. Gambrill and Wiltse, "Foster Care: Plans and Actualities."

160. Fanshel and Grundy, op. cit.

161. Nebraska Department of Public Welfare, op. cit., p. 20.

162. Emlen et al., *Overcoming Barriers to Planning for Children in Foster Care,* p. 5.

163. State of California, Department of Health, *Data Matters: Quarterly Report on Children Leaving Foster Care in California* (1974), pp. 67, 75.

164. State of Michigan, Office of Children and Youth Services, *A Temporary Foster Care Program Proposal* (Lansing: the Office, 1976), p. 1.

165. Donald T. Campbell and Julian C. Stanley, *Experimental and Quasi Experimental Designs for Research* (Chicago: Rand McNally, 1966).

166. Jewish Child Care Association of New York, "S.E.E.R. Project" (unpublished report, 1975); Baltimore County Department of Social Services, op. cit.

167. Sherman et al., *Children Adrift in Foster Care,* p. 14.

168. Ibid., p. 15.

169. Florence Hollis, *Casework: A Psychosocial Therapy* (New York: Random House, 1964).

170. Sherman et al., *Children Adrift in Foster Care,* p. 50.

171. Mary A. Jones, Renee Neuman, and Ann W. Shyne, *A Second Chance for Families: Evaluation of a Program to Reduce Foster Care* (New York: Child Welfare League of America, 1976), pp. 13, 18.

172. Ibid., p. 56.

173. Ibid., p. 83.

174. Atherton, op. cit.

175. State of California, Department of Health, *Data Matters;* Fanshel, "Status Changes of Children in Foster Care," loc. cit.

176. Atherton, op. cit.

177. Jones et al., op. cit., p. 83.

178. Sherman et al., *Children Adrift in Foster Care,* ch. 4.

179. Jeter, op. cit., pp. 35, 87.

180. Ibid., p. 91.

181. Maas, "Children in Long Term Foster Care," 321–33.

182. Wiltse and Gambrill, op. cit., pp. 7–15.

183. State of California, Department of Health, *Data Matters.* Report Register no. 242-0395-601 (December 31, 1974).

184. Fanshel, "Status Changes of Children in Foster Care," loc. cit.

185. Nebraska Department of Public Welfare, loc. cit.

186. Atherton, op. cit.

187. Sherman, et al., *Children Adrift in Foster Care,* p. 6.

188. Ibid., pp. 50, 91.

189. Fellner and Solomon, op. cit., pp. 182–85.

190. Festinger, op. cit., p. 237.

191. Steketee, op. cit., p. 7.

192. Fanshel, "The Exit of Children from Foster Care"; Maas, "Children in Long Term Foster Care"; Stein and Gambrill, op. cit.

193. California State Department of Health,, *Adoption and Foster Care Study;* Child Welfare League of America, op. cit.; Madison and Shapiro, op. cit.; State of California, Department of Social Welfare, *Children Waiting* (Sacramento: the Department, 1972).

194. Fanshel and Grundy, op. cit.; Gruber, op. cit.; Patricia G. Morisey, "Continuum of Parent-Child Relationships in Foster Care," in Stone, op. cit., pp. 148–156.

195. Gruber, op. cit., p. 74.

196. Festinger, op. cit., p. 238.

197. Fanshel and Grundy, op. cit., p. 7.

198. Ibid., pp. 20–27.

199. State Charities Aid Association, *Adoptability: A Study of 100 Children in Foster Care* (New York: the Society, 1960).

200. Pascoe, op. cit., pp. 39–40.

201. Gruber, op. cit., p. 20.

202. Emlen and staff, *Freeing Children for Permanent Placement,* ch. 8, p. 5. Fellner and Solomon, op. cit., p. 182.

203. Festinger, op. cit.

204. State of California, *Children Waiting.*

205. Bernice Boehm, *Deterrents to the Adoption of Children in Foster Care* (New York: Child Welfare League of America, 1958); Gruber, op. cit.; Kadushin (1974) op. cit.

206. Kadushin, *Child Welfare Services,* p. 589.

207. California State Department of Health, *Adoption and Foster Care Study,* p. 14.

208. Vivian Hargrave, Joan Shireman, and Peter Connor, *Where Love and Need Are One* (Chicago: Illinois Department of Children and Family Services, 1975); Benson Jaffee and David Fanshel, *How They Fared in Adoption: A Follow-up Study* (New York: Columbia University Press, 1970); Alfred Kadushin, *Adopting Older Children* (New York: Columbia University Press, 1970); Alfred Kadushin, "Adoption Failure: A Social Work Postmortem," *Social Work* 16 (1971):32–38.

209. Kadushin, "Adoption Failure," pp. 32–34.

210. Fanshel and Grundy, op. cit., pp. 21, 28.

211. Emlen and staff, "Freeing Children for Permanent Placement"; Gruber, op. cit.; Fellner and Solomon, op. cit.; Goldstein, Freud, and Solnit, op. cit.; Weaver, op. cit.

212. *Commission on Population Growth and the American Future: Report.* (New York: New American Library, 1972); National Association of Attorneys General, op. cit., p. 39.

213. Correspondence with state of New Jersey, Department of Institutions and Agencies (1976); Hargrave et al., op. cit.; Kadushin, *Child Welfare Services,* p. 599.

214. Kadushin, *Child Welfare Services,* loc. cit.; Correspondence with state of New Jersey.

215. Pike et al., op. cit., p. 68.

216. National Association of Attorneys General, op. cit., p. 37.

217. Fanshel and Grundy, op. cit., p. 21.

218. Gruber, op. cit., p. 21.

219. Emlen et al., *Overcoming Barriers to Planning for Children in Foster Care,* p. 43.

220. Wald, "State Intervention on Behalf of Neglected Children: A Search . . .," p. 988.

221. Cited in Mnookin (1975) op. cit., p. 244, footnote 86.

222. Ibid., p. 245.

223. For a discussion of this act, see Sanford N. Katz, "The Changing Legal Status of Foster Parents," *Children Today* 5, no. 6 (November/December 1976):11–13.

224. U.S. Congress, House, *Foster Care, Adoption and Reform Act of 1977,* pp. 27–31.

225. Wiltse and Gambrill, op. cit., p. 12.

226. State of California, *Welfare and Institutions Code,* sec. 232 of Civil Code; Gruber, op. cit.

227. Mnookin, op. cit., p. 246, footnote 105; State of California, *Welfare and Institutions Code,* sec. 7.

228. Child Welfare League of America, op. cit., p. 23.

229. Kadushin, *Child Welfare Services,* p. 457.

230. Madison and Shapiro, op. cit., p. 135.

231. Emlen and staff, *Freeing Children for Permanent Placement.*

232. Ibid., ch. 4, p. 1.

233. Ibid., ch. 8, p. 9.

234. Emlen and staff, "Freeing Children for Permanent Placement," pp. 1–2; Gruber, op. cit., p. 25; Pascoe, op. cit., p. 41. This issue is discussed extensively in National Conference of Lawyers and Social Workers, *Law and Social Work* (Washington, D.C.: National Association of Social Workers, 1973).

235. Robert H. Mnookin, "Foster Care: In Whose Best Interest," *Harvard Educational Review* 43, no. 4 (November 1973):184–85.

236. State of California, Department of Health, *Data Matters;* Fellner and Solomon, op. cit., pp. 178–87.

237. Fanshel, "The Exit of Children from Foster Care"; Maas, "Children in Long Term Foster Care," pp. 321–33; Stein and Gambrill, op. cit., pp. 38–44.

238. Fanshel and Grundy, op. cit.; Pascoe, op. cit.; State Charities Aid Association, op. cit.; Festinger, op. cit.; Gruber, op. cit.; State of California, Department of Social Welfare, *Children Waiting.*

239. Fanshel and Grundy, op. cit.; Gruber, op. cit.; Festinger, op. cit.

240. Fanshel and Grundy, op. cit.; correspondence with state of New Jersey; Hargrave et al., op. cit.; Kadushin, *Child Welfare Services.*

241. Richard Ergo, Robert Mnookin, and Robert Walker, "Effective Juvenile Court Participation" (Berkeley: University of California Extension, 1974).

242. Mnookin (1975), op. cit., pp. 237–40.

243. Cited in ibid., p. 238, footnote 55.

244. Ibid., pp. 237–40; Schmidt, op. cit.; Taylor, op. cit.

245. State of California, Department of Social Welfare, *Children Waiting,* p. 33.

246. California State Department of Health, *Adoption and Foster Care Study,* p. 22.

247. Pascoe, op. cit., pp. 42–43.

248. Ibid., p. 42.

249. State of California, *Family Protection Act of 1976,* p. 3.

3

DESCRIPTION OF THE ALAMEDA PROJECT

The Alameda Project was a cooperative endeavor of the Children's Home Society of Oakland, California, and the Alameda County Department of Social Services. Its primary objective was to increase continuity of care for children in out-of-home placement. Intensive services were offered to biological parents in order to facilitate their participation in decision making such that more permanent planning for their children would result. Four types of decisions were possible: (1) the child could be restored to the natural parents; (2) the child could be placed for adoption following parental relinquishment or termination of parental rights; (3) an adult could be designated by the court as the child's legal guardian; or (4) it could be decided that the child would remain in long-term foster placement.

A second objective of the project was to compare the effectiveness of a systematic case management procedure, in which behavioral intervention methods were employed to resolve identified problems, with the methods typically employed by the agency staff. Our intention was to develop a decision-making framework that could be employed by practicing child welfare workers in other settings. A third objective was to test the feasibility of having one social worker provide concentrated services to biological parents while another worker served the child and foster parents.

POPULATION

Alameda County, with an estimated population of 1,091,000, is the fifth largest of California's 58 counties and eighth in per capita income ($4,413; range = $3,686 to $9,928).[1] There are approximately 1,800 children in care in the county, including youngsters in foster homes, group homes, and residential treatment facilities.[2] This represents about 6 percent of the estimated 28,883 children in care statewide.[3] The county compiles data for a statewide foster care registry. Statistics are reported describing the demographic characteristics of this population, the length of time children have been in care, the reasons why they were placed, whether placement was voluntary or court-ordered, and the numbers leaving care by various exit routes (restoration, adoption, and so forth).[4] However, the county does not maintain a data bank describing its own foster care population.[5] Therefore, it is not possible to discuss the representativeness of the study sample in terms of the foster care population from which it was drawn.

THE SETTING

When the project began in 1974, there were six placement units at the Alameda County Social Service Department, each consisting of one supervisor and a maximum of seven child welfare workers. Two units were initially selected to participate in the project, one for experimental and the other for control purposes. Acceptance of new cases into the project was contingent upon openings in the caseloads of workers in these units. In the experimental unit, caseload size reached a maximum by the end of the first month and a second experimental unit was added at the beginning of the second month. Thus, for the remainder of the project, there were two experimental units and one control unit. At the end of the first year, the first experimental unit ceased to participate; and one of the remaining units was added as an experimental unit. Thus, over the two-year project period, four of the six placement units were involved, three as experimental units and one as a control unit.

SELECTION OF CASES

Participating workers in both the experimental and the control units were asked to volunteer cases from their active files. These constituted the beginning caseload for the project. Additional cases from intake were randomly assigned, as they became available, to the experimental and control units. Cases meeting the following criteria were acceptable:

1. At least one biological parent had to be present in the county

2. The child must be under 16 years of age; children over 16 were excluded because they were within two years of their majority and frequently planned their own futures

3. The child must be in foster home placement; children in treatment institutions were excluded because other resources were primary treat-

ment agents and because geographic distances would make frequent contact between parents and children difficult

4. A decision as to the child's future must not have been made; such decision making was an objective of the project

Table 3.1 shows the number and percentage of experimental and control unit children entering the project in each year who were categorized as volunteered and new intake. New cases represented the smaller percentage in both units (experimental, 46 percent; control, 34 percent). There was a greater number of new intake cases in the experimental units because there

TABLE 3.1

Experimental and Control Cases
Volunteered for the Project and Those from Intake

	Experimental (n = 227)			Control (n = 201)		
	Volunteered	New	Total	Volunteered	New	Total
Year 1	76	60	136	133	40	173
Year 2	46	45	91	0	28	28
Total	122(54%)	105(46%)	227	133(66%)	68(34%)	201

Chi-square = 6.85 (1 degree of freedom); p $\leq$.01.
Source: Compiled by author.

were two experimental units. New cases were assigned on a 2:1 ratio; that is, the pattern of assignment was experimental unit 1, experimental unit 2, and control. However, whether or not a unit could accept a case depended upon two factors. There had to be an opening in the caseload of a county worker, and the new case had to be in the geographic locale handled by the worker. On some occasions either of these factors precluded case assignment.

The number and percentage of children entering the project in each year are shown in Table 3.2. A significantly greater number of children entered during the first year (p. $<$ .001). This is explained by the fact that the majority of children were volunteered (see Table 3.1) and, hence, entered the project at the start of year 1. The greater number of experimental than control cases in year 2 (91 vs. 28) resulted from the addition of a new experimental unit at the start of that year. These cases consisted primarily of those volunteered by workers in that unit when they entered the project (46 cases [51 percent]; see Table 3.1). The total number of children in the experimental and control units is approximately equal (227 experimental vs. 201 control).

TABLE 3.2

Number of Experimental and Control Unit Children Entering Project, by Year

	Experimental	Control	Total	Percent
Year 1	136	173	309	72
Year 2	91	28	119	28
Total	227	201	428	100

Chi square = 36.33 (1 degree of freedom); p ≤ .001.
Source: Compiled by author.

CASELOAD SIZE

The maximum caseload of Alameda County child welfare workers was 49 children. Caseload for each project worker was 20 families, equaling a maximum of 35 children. Direct comparison of the numbers of children carried by project staff compared with county staff should be made cautiously, since project cases were, by definition, all active (that is, in various states of decision making). Once a case was designated as long-term care or referred for adoption or guardianship, it was closed to the project in order to make room for a new case. While exact data are not available, it is reasonable to suggest that some percentage of the cases of each county worker consisted of children in long-term care, where case activity is less relative to cases where parents are involved in a planning process.

STAFF WORKERS

Three workers with M.S.W. degrees were hired as project staff by the Children's Home Society. Two workers left at the end of the first year, at which time two additional M.S.W. staff were hired. Of the five project workers, one was a 30-year-old male and four were women with a mean age of 34.6 (range = 26–42). A total of 26 county child welfare workers were involved in the project, 10 of whom held B.A. degrees (38 percent) and 16 (62 percent) of whom held M.S.W. degrees. Ten of these either left the Social Service Department or were transferred to nonplacement units over the two-year project period. In addition, seven supervisors were involved, four of whom (57 percent) were either transferred within the department or left it during the two years. Four of the county personnel were males (mean age, 34.5; range = 31–44), and the remaining 39 were women (mean age, 32.2; range = 26–45). The project director also served as supervisor of the project staff.

DESCRIPTION OF CASES

In this section the various circumstances under which children came into care are described, as are characteristics of the children, including their age, sex, racial and ethnic background, and family composition. Data are presented for both the control and the project units.

Circumstances of Entry into Foster Care

Children in foster home care either are voluntarily placed by their parents or enter as dependents of the juvenile court. Section 600 of the *California Welfare and Institutions Code* describes four categories of children who fall under court jurisdiction.* In common parlance these are children who have been neglected (600:a), who are destitute (600:b), who are deemed physically dangerous to the public because of mental or physical deficiency (600:c), or who have been abused (600:d). In California approximately 61 percent of the children enter care under court jurisdiction.[6] In Alameda County, however, this proportion is in excess of 95 percent.

TABLE 3.3

Conditions of Entry into Placement of Project Children

	Experimental		Control	
	Number	Percent	Number	Percent
Neglect (600:a)	195	(86%)	185	(92%)
Abuse (600:d)	1	(1%)	5	(3%)
Neglect and abuse				
(600:a, d)	28	(12%)	10	(5%)
Voluntary	3	(1%)	01	(.001%)
	227		201	

Chi-square = 3.67 (1 degree of freedom) = n.s.

Note: Voluntary placements and 600:d's were not considered separately in testing significance because of the small number of children in these categories.

Source: Compiled by author.

Table 3.3 shows the number and percentage of children in the project by the petition under which they entered foster placement. The great majority

---

*Other sections of the code cover children who are in danger of becoming delinquent (601) or who are adjudicated as such (602).

of children in both units entered care under neglect petitions (experimental, 86 percent; control, 92 percent). Abuse alone accounted for only 1 percent and 3 percent of the experimental and control children, respectively. Twenty-eight experimental (12 percent) and ten control unit children (5 percent) entered care under both neglect and abuse petitions. Only three children in the experimental units and one child in the control unit were voluntary placements. The difference between units was not significant.

In some cases additional problem information was noted in case records. Such data were available for 173 of the 227 experimental (76 percent) and 154 of the 201 control children (77 percent). Seventy-seven of the 173 experimental (45 percent) and 39 of the 201 control cases (27 percent) had two reasons for placement listed. Reasons, by the number and percentage of children in each category, are shown in Table 3.4.

In the experimental section, 53 children (21 percent) were placed because of parental drug abuse, compared with 20 children in the control

TABLE 3.4

Number and Percentages of Children in Each Group, by Reason(s) for Placement

Reason	Experimental		Control	
	Number	Percent	Number	Percent
Alcohol	25	10	20	10
Drugs	53	21	20	10
Parent in psychiatric hospital	27	11	15	8
Parent in prison	21	8	15	8
Condition of household	5	2	5	3
Child left unattended with neighbor or relative	36	14	56	29
Child out of parental control	18	7	15	8
Abuse alleged[a]	28	11	9	5
Parent said to be mentally ill, not hospitalized	20	8	28	15
Miscellaneous[b]	17	7	10	5
Total	250		193	

Chi-square = 30.6 (9 degrees of freedom); p $\leq$ .001.

Note: Since the numbers reflect some children for whom there were two reasons listed, the total n is not equal to that in prior tables.

[a]These are cases where abuse is mentioned in the case record but the child was placed under a neglect petition.

[b]Miscellaneous includes parent hospitalized for physical reasons (experimental = 6, control = 3); child's medical needs not met (experimental = 8, control = 2); and marital problems (experimental = 3, control = 5).

Source: Compiled by author.

section (10 percent); 28 children (11 percent) allegedly were abused, compared with 9 children in the control section (5 percent). In the control unit, 56 children (29 percent) were left unattended with a neighbor or relative, while in the experimental unit 36 children (14 percent) were placed for this reason. The differences between groups in these problem areas are significant (p. $\leq$.001). While some variation existed in the remaining categories, difference between groups was slight.

Demographic Variables

Table 3.5 shows that there is a significant difference between experimental and control units in the ages of children (p. $\leq$.001), with the majority of experimental cases six years of age or less (58 percent, compared with 31 percent for the control unit). There was a slightly higher percentage of control unit children age seven–nine (31 percent vs. 22 percent) and an equal percentage in both units of children ten–twelve years old. The control unit had a greater percentage of children over twelve, than did the experimental (22 percent vs. 6 percent).

TABLE 3.5

Ages of Experimental and Control Unit Children

	Experimental	Control
under 1 year	16 (7%)	3 (1%)
1–3	56 (25%)	26 (13%)
4–6	58 (26%)	34 (17%)
7–9	49 (22%)	63 (31%)
10–12	34 (15%)	30 (15%)
over 12	14 (6%)	45 (22%)
Total	227	201

Chi-square = 42.95 (5 degrees of freedom); p $\leq$.001.
Source: Compiled by author.

Male and female children were approximately equally represented in both units (see Table 3.6), with a slightly higher percentage of males in the experimental units (53 percent vs. 49 percent).

Table 3.7 shows the racial or ethnic background of the children. Caucasian, Mexican-American, and biracial children are almost equally represented in both units. A greater percentage of experimental than control children were black (48 percent vs. 37 percent). Children of American Indian descent accounted for 8 percent of the control unit cases; there were no such children in the experimental units.

TABLE 3.6

Sex of Experimental and Control Unit Children

	Experimental	Control	Total
Male	120 (53%)	98 (49%)	218
Female	107 (47%)	103 (51%)	210
Total	227	201	428

Chi-square = 2.96 (1 degree of freedom) = n.s.
Source: Compiled by author.

The family composition of cases is shown in Table 3.8. The percentages are approximately the same in both experimental and control units, with female-headed families accounting for over 70 percent; two-parent families for 23 percent; and male-headed families for 7 percent of the experimental and 3 percent of the control cases.

PROCEDURE FOR DIVIDING CASES BETWEEN TWO WORKERS

All experimental unit cases were jointly managed by a project worker and a county child welfare worker, whereas one worker (the county worker) was responsible for the entire case in the control section. Project workers were responsible for service delivery to biological parents, while the county staff responsibility was to provide services to the child and foster parents. (An evaluation of this approach to service delivery is presented in Chapter

TABLE 3.7

Racial or Ethnic Background of Children

	Experimental		Control		
	Number	Percent	Number	Percent	Total
Caucasian	76	34	75	37	151
Black	108	48	74	37	182
Mexican-American	21	9	16	8	37
American Indian	0	0	16	8	16
Biracial	22	9	20	10	42
Total	227		201		428

Eliminating American Indian children, the difference between units is not significant: chi-square = 7.68 (3 degrees of freedom).
Source: Compiled by author.

TABLE 3.8

Family Composition

	Experimental		Control		
	Number	Percent	Number	Percent	Total
Two-parent	51	23	46	23	97
Female-headed	161	71	149	74	310
Male-headed	15	7	6	3	21
Total	227		201		428

Chi-square = 4.79 (2 degrees of freedom) = n.s.
Source: Compiled by author.

4.) A set of procedural steps were followed by the workers. If a case was volunteered from the files of a participating county worker, that worker contacted the parent(s), explained the project, and asked them to cooperate as participants. Over the two-year period only one family refused. Once agreement was obtained, the county worker arranged to introduce the parents and the project worker. If a case was referred from intake, a member of the project staff made the initial contact, explained the project, and obtained parental consent. The following procedure for joint case management was then employed:

1. The project worker determined the goal of the parent for the future of the child. If a parent wanted the child returned to his or her care, assessment was initiated to identify what changes, if any, were necessary before this would be recommended. Assessment information was shared with the client, the use of written contracts was explained to clients, and an initial case plan was designed. (See Part II for a detailed description of the case management procedure.)

2. Project and county workers conferred in order to share information collected and to obtain agreement concerning the feasibility of the parent's goal, the relevance of specific objectives to goal attainment, and the intervention plan for each. While workers sometimes disagreed over the probable outcome of a case, with county workers on the pessimistic side, there was never an instance in which they did not agree on providing the parents with an opportunity to work toward restoration.

3. The contract and case plan were put in writing by the project worker and approval was sought from both supervisors. The contract was then signed by both workers and presented to the client for signature.

4. Intervention then began, with conferences between workers on an as-needed basis (but at least once a month). Written summaries were exchanged quarterly regarding the progress of the parents and child.

5. Any changes in contract objectives or goals were discussed by workers, and supervisory approval of any change was obtained. For example, a parent who expressed a wish to obtain employment prior to having a child restored may later decide that he or she doesn't want to work. This differs from a change in an overall goal—for instance, a decision not to have a child restored. Contracts were amended, in writing, as necessary.

6. Differences of opinion that could not be reconciled by the workers were discussed in conferences attended by both workers and their supervisors. Parental behavior, for example, may have indicated that the probability of fulfilling objectives was slight. Perhaps one worker wanted to refer the case for adoption while the other wished to offer the parent a second opportunity.

7. Prior to "report and review hearings" project workers submitted written reports and recommendations to county workers. Both reports were submitted to the court.

8. Ninety days after restoration occurred, project workers prepared follow-up reports. This follow-up period was extended if any problems arose in the parent's home. Usually, if no problems occurred during this time, the court dependency was dismissed. Although in almost all instances county and project workers agreed on actions to be taken, there were some instances in which they disagreed. Examples are instances in which the mother was labeled schizophrenic or lesbian; in both instances county workers felt these conditions rendered the mothers incapable of assuming an adequate parenting role even though data gathered by the project workers indicated the child was doing well in the home. When county workers were asked to supply evidence of inadequate parenting to support their opinion, none was produced. Rather, there was the "feeling" that such persons simply could not be good parents. In two instances the project worker had to inform the county worker that she would go into court against the position of the county worker, since evidence she had gathered demonstrated parental adequacy. In each case, at this point the county worker concurred with the decision, knowing that there was little to support her position in court other than the feeling that the mother was unsuitable.

In cases where a no-dismissal decision was made and no identified problems existed, full case management responsibility returned to the county worker.

DATA COLLECTION FORMS

A number of data collection forms were needed to gather essential information, such as minimal descriptions necessary to determine whether a case met project criteria (See Appendix A, Form 1). Form 1 was used for all new cases, whether volunteered by workers or coming from intake. Both county and project workers recorded the frequency and purpose of contacts with natural and foster parents, the child, and collateral resources on a monthly basis on Form 2. This was the only information required of county workers involved in the experimental units, except for quarterly narratives describing a child's progress.

Two forms were employed by both experimental and control workers to obtain information concerning the decision status of each child. On Form 3, the names of each child in each worker's caseload were listed, and at monthly intervals workers placed a check mark in the appropriate column to indicate the current decision for each child (to be restored, to be referred for adoption or guardianship, or long-term care). Major decision categories, and a number of possible reasons why a given decision was made, were listed on Form 4. Each time a decision was made, the reason was recorded on this form.

Two forms were designed to obtain information regarding contacts with biological parents. On Form 5 the problem areas that were the focus of intervention were noted at the end of each month. In addition, at the close of each quarter, workers were asked to indicate whether identified problems were resolved or unresolved. Following each interview with parents, workers identified the predominant casework method(s) used on Form 6.

A number of forms were used only by project workers in the course of service delivery. Form 7 requested parental consent to tape-record interviews (see Part II). An 11-page assessment form (Form 8) was designed and used for the following purposes: (1) to assess whether objectively dangerous conditions, such as exposed wiring or broken glass, existed in the parent's home; (2) to gather information on certain medical matters, such as proximity of a physician or clinic to the parent's home and parental eligibility for medical assistance; and (3) to direct worker attention to potential problems in parent-child interaction. Questions were organized with a recognition that the areas to be assessed might vary according to the length of the visit as well as by its setting, such as whether it occurred in the foster home or in the natural parent's home.

The notations made on Forms 9 through 15 provided information essential for developing intervention programs, such as specific examples, in behavioral terms, of identified problems (Form 9); environmental resource data, such as reinforcers and names of persons whose assistance might be helpful during intervention (Form 10); description of the method to be employed to gather baseline data (Form 11); summary results of baseline information (Form 12); and beginning case plans (Form 13). The information on Form 13 was formalized into a written contract. (See illustrations of case examples and a description of contracts in Part II.) The effect of intervention was monitored using the following methods, either alone or in combination:

1. In every case, direct observation in the client's natural environment by project staff was employed. The procedure used to collect baseline data was employed during intervention to assess program effectiveness. (See chapter 8, case 1.)

2. Whenever possible, clients were asked to maintain records that were used to supplement the data gathered by project staff. (See chapter 8, case 3, for examples of client-maintained records.)

3. When intervention focused upon resolution of verbal communication problems and when clients were willing to use recorders at home, tapes were employed to supplement written data. An example of their use is provided in chapter 8, case 2.

In-person interviews between workers occurred if they were necessary to clarify any case-related information. An occasion for such an interview might be a sudden shift in decision categories—for example, from "to be referred for adoption" to "to be restored to natural parents."

NOTES

1. U.S. Government, Bureau of the Census. *Current Population Reports: Population Estimates and Projections.* (U.S. Dept. of Commerce: G.P.O.), series P-25, no. 549 (May 1975).

2. County of Alameda, California, Office of Program Evaluation. *Placement in Foster Care: Issues and Concerns.* Alameda, California: (County of Alameda) final report (September 1977).

3. State of California. *Data Matters: Report No. 340-0395-501.* Sacramento, California: (Dept. of Health, 1974).

4. Ibid.

5. County of Alameda, Calif., op. cit., p. 6.

6. State of California, op. cit.

4

RESULTS

Results of the project are reported in three sections. The first describes the outcomes of all project cases. In the second, some characteristics of the process of service delivery are reviewed, and in the last section the relationship between selected variables and case outcome is discussed in order to determine whether these variables are predictive of differential outcomes for children in foster care.

CASE OUTCOMES

Nases were closed in one of three ways: (1) as a result of purposeful planning—for example, following restoration of a child to biological parents; (2) in an unplanned manner, such as a change in court jurisdiction after a parent moved out of the county; or (3) without a decision having been made. Table 4.1 shows the number and percentage of cases closed in each of these three categories. More experimental cases (56 percent) were closed as a result of purposeful planning than was true of control cases (34 percent). In both units the greatest number of these children were restored to their natural parents (56 experimental and 40 control youngsters). Adoption referrals accounted for the second-largest group (35 experimental and 17 control cases). Eighty-nine children in the control unit (44 percent) and 31 in the experimental units (14 percent) were designated for long-term care. In both units the number of cases closed with no decision having been made was small (3 percent of the experimental cases and 2 percent of the control cases). It should be noted that all children for whom no decision was made entered the project in the latter part of year 2.

Unplanned closings accounted for 27 percent of the children in the

TABLE 4.1

Case Outcomes: Planned, Unplanned, No Decision

	Experi- mental	Control	Experimental		Control	
			Number	Percent	Number	Percent
Planned Outcomes						
Restored	56	40				
To be restored	15	7				
Referred for adoption	35	17				
Guardianship being pursued	20	5				
Total children out or headed out of care			126	56	69	34
Long-term care			31	14	89	44
Unplanned Outcomes						
Jurisdiction changed	15	7				
Court-ordered restoration[a]	7	9				
Miscellaneous[b]	40	23				
Total cases closed in unplanned manner			62	27	39	19
No decision			8	3	4	2
Total			227		201	

Chi-square = 58.73 (9 degrees of freedom); significant $p \leq .001$.

[a]Situations where a judge or referee ordered that a child be restored, against the recommendation of the caseworker.

[b]See Table 4.3 for detailed information on miscellaneous closings.

Source: Compiled by author.

experimental units and 19 percent in the control unit. Two factors accounting for these relatively high percentages were changes in court jurisdiction and restorations made by the court against caseworker recommendations. The difference between units in case outcomes is significant ($p \leq .001$).

Effective use of the case management procedures employed by project staff in the experimental units required the learning of new assessment and intervention methods. The use of contracts, for example, was initiated in year 1. Hence, it was expected that the maximum benefits that might result from applying these methods would occur in the project's second year. The data in Table 4.2 indicate that this indeed was the case. Seventy percent of the restorations in the experimental units occurred in the second year, as compared with 30 percent in the first year; in the control unit the figures were 75 percent in the first year and 25 percent in the second. The difference

TABLE 4.2

Restorations, by Year of Occurrence

	Experimental		Control		
	Number	Percent	Number	Percent	Total
Year 1	17	30	30	75	47
Year 2	39	70	10	25	49
Total	56		40		96

Note: Percentages are to n for each group.
Chi-square = 18.62 (1 degree of freedom); $p \leq .001$.
Source: Compiled by author.

between units in the percentage of children restored by project year is significant ($p \leq .001$).

Forty experimental and 23 control unit cases were closed for what were considered to be miscellaneous reasons. Included here are cases where decisions had been made before the project began, instances where a child was already at home with its parents, cases where no parent was available in the community,* and cases in which the child never entered foster care.†
Cases that were inappropriate by project criteria account for 50 percent of the experimental and 91 percent of the control case closings. Seventeen of the 20 experimental cases (85 percent) and all such cases from the control unit were from the first year of the project. Their initial inclusion in the project reflects inexperience with the case selection process.

Some closings occurred after a child was adjudicated a delinquent and the case was transferred from a foster care unit to the probation department. The cases of three experimental unit children were closed by agreement with a collateral resource that the court had designated as primary treatment agent and with which a satisfactory division of case responsibility could not be made. Twelve experimental unit cases were closed at the request of the county. Included in this group are seven cases closed at the end of year 1,

---

*This situation also occurred in year 2. However, at that time it was decided that the experimental worker would keep the case and attempt to locate the parents until the six month period for filing an abandonment petition had elapsed.

†These were cases accepted after the court had assumed jurisdiction over the child but prior to the dispositional hearing. At the subsequent dispositional hearing, a decision was made to leave the child with its natural parents.

TABLE 4.3

Reasons for Miscellaneous Closings

	Experimental	Control
Inappropriate by project criteria		
Child at home when project began	7	11
Case decision already made	3	10
Children never entered foster care	3	
No parent available	7	
Subtotal	20 (50%)	21 (91%)
Child adjudicated delinquent	4	2
Closed by agreement with collateral resource	3	
Parent refused to work with project	1	
Closed at request of county	12 (50%)	(9%)
Total	40	23

Note: Number of empty cells and those with small frequencies precludes a test of significance.

Source: Compiled by author.

when the first experimental unit withdrew from the project, and five cases that had to be transferred because a county worker's caseload exceeded the maximum of 49 children.

Outcome of Adoption and Guardianship Referrals

Decisions had been made to refer 35 experimental and 17 control unit children for adoption (see Table 4.1). For an additional 20 youngsters in the experimental units and 5 in the control unit, guardianship was being pursued. Comparative data showing the status of experimental and control unit children are in Table 4.4. At the end of the second year, 12 of the 35 adoption referrals made by experimental unit workers were completed, nine were awaiting court dates, and eight were in the adoption section, ready to be referred to County Counsel. Four of the 17 control unit adoption referrals were completed, six were awaiting court dates, and one was ready for referral to County Counsel. Guardianship had been established for three experimental and two control children. In an additional six cases in the experimental units (11 percent) guardianship papers had been signed and cases were awaiting court dates. Guardianship was in process for six experimental unit children and one control unit child.

Outcome status changed for 11 experimental (20 percent) and 8 control youngsters (36 percent) who had been referred for either adoption or guardianship. In two experimental cases and one control case, children were

TABLE 4.4

Status of Adoption and Guardianship Cases

	Experimental	Control
Adoption completed	12 (22%)	4 (18%)
Adoption referral awaiting court date	9 (16%)	6 (27%)
Case in adoption unit, ready for referral to County Counsel	8 (15%)	1 (5%)
Guardianship completed	3 (5%)	2 (9%)
Guardianship papers signed, awaiting court date	6 (11%)	
Guardianship arrangements in process	6 (11%)	1 (5%)
Subtotal	44 (80%)	14 (64%)

Outcome changed *	Exp.	Cont.		
Was adoption	6	6		
Was guardianship	5	2	11 (20%)	8 (36%)
Total			55	22

Chi-square = 2.31 (11 degrees of freedom) = n.s. Because of low cell frequency, adoption and guardianship cases, completed and to be completed, were combined for both units for test of significance.

*Status of cases with outcomes changed	Experimental	Control
Restored: Planned (Parents became involved in planning process after case went to court for first hearing on adoption action.)	2	1
Restored by judicial order		2
Jurisdiction changed, misc. closing	4	
Changed to undecided	5	5
Total	11	8

Source: Compiled by author.

restored to parents who became reinvolved in case planning for their children after the adoption referral. Two control unit children were restored by judicial order. Adoption action was terminated in four experimental cases following a change in court jurisdiction. The status of ten children was changed to undecided. Included here are two cases, one from each unit, that County Counsel could not take to court because of insufficient grounds to support a termination action,* and three control unit cases from one family

---

*Neither of these cases met the full six-month time requirement for terminating parental rights under an abandonment petition. Both cases were expected to be referred back to the adoption section when this requirement was met, unless the parents returned to the community.

for which there was a judicial order that the parent be given a "second chance." For the remaining cases from both units adoption action was ended when absentee parents returned to the community and expressed interest in working toward having their children restored to their home. The difference between units in the status of adoption and guardianship cases was not significant.*

Terminating Parental Rights

Children may be freed for adoption after being voluntarily relinquished by their parents or through court-ordered termination of parental rights. Section 232 of the California Civil Code contains seven subsections, each of which describes a different basis for a termination action (see Appendix B). Information required in support of a termination petition varies by each provision of the code. To file an abandonment petition, for example, one must show that the parents' whereabouts are, and have been, unknown for a minimum of six months. Documentation for such a petition may consist of listing the number of occasions on which a worker has tried to locate parents, letters that have been returned by the post office bearing the legend "moved—no forwarding address," and data supplied by a foster parent showing the date of the last contact made by natural parents.

The subsection of the code relating to child abuse requires documentation of a different sort. For example, subsection 7 of the code states:

> . . . the court [must] find[s] beyond a reasonable doubt† that return of the child to his parent or parents would be detrimental to the child and that the parent or parents have failed . . . or are likely to fail in the future, to
> (i) provide a home for said child;
> (ii) provide care and control for the child;
> (iii) maintain an adequate parental relationship with the child.

The intent of this subsection of the code is to make it possible to terminate parental rights even though there is no evidence to support specific allegations, such as abandonment, child abuse, or mental illness. However, a parent must be shown to have demonstrated by his or her behavior over at least a two-year period that there is little or no possibility he or she will be in a position to resume care of the child.

Evidence in support of a petition filed under this section differs

---

* More current data on the status of incomplete adoption and guardianship cases appear in the section of this chapter entitled "One-Year Follow-up."

†The 1976 California Legislature reduced this standard of proof to "clear and convincing evidence."

substantially from that required for an abandonment petition. Evidence is assembled to establish improbability rather than to prove a specific allegation. In effect, this statutory provision shifts the burden of proof on to the natural parent who must seek to establish a different conclusion in the face of convincing evidence of nonperformance over an extended period of time. The support for a charge that a parent is unable to "provide care and control," or is unlikely to "maintain an adequate parental relationship with a child," may be evidence of lack of contact with the child in foster care, as is the case with an abandonment petition. However, the agency's testimony also must show the kinds of services that have been offered to biological parents, the frequency with which they were offered, the goal to be attained through parental participation in service programs, and parental response to these offered services. Unwillingness to utilize rehabilitative services may be construed by the court as a lack of intent to establish a permanent home for the youngster.

The worker's task in gathering evidence in support of an abandonment petition also differs from the task when this provision of the code is the basis of allegations. In abandonment petition cases worker activity often is minimal, consisting of evidence of efforts to locate parents and a record of the lack of success of these efforts. In contrast, cases pursued under this provision are preceded by efforts either to provide services or to arrange for service delivery by others. In addition, data collection is far more extensive, since a parent is present in the community (in contrast with an abandonment action) and parental inability or failure to use rehabilitative services must be documented meticulously.

Project staff were expected to provide intensive services to natural parents in order to systematically collect an array of data.* Hypothetically, they should have been in a position to use diverse provisions of the Civil Code and to have the necessary data to support the petitions they filed. The results indicated that this indeed was the case. Table 4.5 shows the number and percentage of children for whom termination proceedings were pursued under the subsection of the code involved. Ten of 29 experimental cases (34 percent) were referred under 232:7 or on a combination of this provision and 232:1 (abandonment). Ten of the 11 control unit referrals (91 percent) were based on either voluntary relinquishments or abandonment, compared with seven such referrals from experimental units. The remaining 12 referrals (41 percent) made by workers in experimental units utilized provisions of the Civil Code dealing with substance abuse, mental deficiency, or mental illness. Only one control case that went to court was based on any of these Civil Code subsections.

---

*Data collection forms are shown in Appendix A. The kinds of information gathered by project staff can be seen in the case examples in Part II.

TABLE 4.5

Children Categorized by Civil Code Section(s) Under Which Case Was Prepared for Court and Voluntary Relinquishments

	Experimental		Control	
	Number	Percent	Number	Percent
Parent relinquished	2	7	2	18
Civil Code (232)				
232:1 Abandonment	5	17	8	73
232:3 "Controlled substance"				
(alcohol/drugs)	6	21		
232:5 Mental deficiency	3	10		
232:6 Mental illness	1	3	1	9
232:7 "Beyond a reasonable doubt"	6	21		
Combined Petitions				
232:1 and 232:3 Abandonment and				
controlled substances	2	7		
232:1 and 232:7 Abandonment and				
"beyond a reasonable doubt"	4	14		
Total	29		11	

Notes: n = number of experimental and control adoption referrals where final status of case did not change (see Table 4.4). Number of empty cells and those with small cell frequencies precludes a test of significance.

Source: Compiled by author.

It should be noted that section 232:7 of the Civil Code had never been used in the county prior to the project. The basis for the judicial decision to terminate in the first case referred using this section rested largely upon the specificity of a written contract and supportive documentation describing the response of the parents to the case plan described in the contract.[1]

Final Status of Cases

The cases of 60 children in the experimental units (26 percent) and 37 in the control unit (18 percent) had been closed to the Foster Care Department when the project ended (see Table 4.6). They were closed following dismissed court dependencies or after adoption and guardianship actions were completed. Dependencies were to be dismissed in the near future for an additional ten experimental and seven control youngsters who were restored to their biological parents. Forty-four experimental unit children and 15 from control were headed out of the foster care system when the project

TABLE 4.6

Final Case Outcomes

			Experimental	Control
Cases closed: Out of foster care	Exp.	Cont.		
Dismissed dependencies of				
children restored	45	31		
Completed adoptions	12	4		
Completed guardianships	3	2		
Subtotal	60	37		
			60 (26%)	37 (18%)
Children restored, dependencies				
to be dismissed soon			10	7
Subtotal			70 (31%)	44 (22%)
Children headed out of foster				
care	Exp.	Cont.		
To be restored	15	7		
Adoption to be completed	17	7		
Guardianship to be completed	12	1		
Subtotal	44	15		
			44	15
Total children out or				
headed out of foster care			114 (50%)	59 (29%)
Long-term care			31 (14%)	89 (44%)
Undecided[a]			14 (6%)	11 (5%)
Miscellaneous[b]			68 (30%)	42 (21%)
Total			227	201

[a]This category includes eight experimental and four control children shown in Table 4.1, plus five children from each unit who had been adoption or guardianship referrals (see Table 4.4); and one experimental unit and two control children who had been restored to parents and reentered care the second year.

[b]Miscellaneous includes 62 experimental and 39 control cases shown in Table 4.1, plus 6 experimental and 3 control cases that were recategorized from adoption or guardianship referrals (see Table 4.4).

Source: Compiled by author.

ended. Included here are children to be restored as well as those for whom adoption and guardianship were to be completed. Thirty-one experimental unit youngsters (14 percent) and 89 from control (44 percent) were designated for long-term foster care. No decisions had been made for 14 children in the experimental units (6 percent) and 11 in the control unit (5 percent). Sixty-eight experimental (30 percent) and 42 control (21 percent) cases were closed for miscellaneous reasons.

The results of case planning can be more clearly discerned when the categories of undecided and miscellaneous closings are omitted (see Table

TABLE 4.7

Planned Outcomes: Year 2

	Experimental	Control
Closed as of 3/31/76	60	37
Headed out of foster home care	54	22
Subtotal	114 (79%)	59 (40%)
Long-term care	31 (21%)	89 (60%)
Total	145	148

Chi-square = 45.5 (1 degree of freedom); p. ≤ .001.
Source: Compiled by author.

4.7). We then see that 114 experimental children (79 percent) and 59 control children (40 percent) were either out or headed out of foster home placement when the project terminated. Thirty-one youngsters from the experimental units (21 percent) and 89 from the control unit (60 percent) were designated for long-term foster care placement. The difference between units was significant (p ≤ .001).

Summary

A total of 428 children were involved in the Alameda Project, 227 in the experimental units and 201 in a control unit. Of 135 cases, 82 experimental (36 percent) and 53 control (26 percent) closed with outcomes undecided or for miscellaneous reasons. Of the remaining 145 experimental unit children, 114 (50 percent) were either out or headed out of foster placement. Fifty-five of these were restored to their natural parents, twelve were adopted, and three had legal guardians appointed. Forty-four were to be restored or were in the process of having adoption or guardianship actions completed. Thirty-one youngsters were designated as long-term placements. In the control unit, 59 (29 percent) children were either out or headed out of placement, 38 were restored to their natural parents, 4 were adopted, and 2 had legal guardians appointed. Fifteen were to be restored or were in the process of having adoption or guardianship actions completed. The remaining 44 percent were designated as long-term placements. The difference between units in case outcomes was significant (p ≤ .001).

Workers in the experimental sections referred cases for adoption on more diverse grounds than did control staff. This was explained by reference to the frequency with which experimental workers saw natural parents as well as the kinds of information gathered by workers. The latter was seen as providing evidence in support of termination actions under various provisions of the Civil Code.

THE PROCESS OF SERVICE DELIVERY

Several dimensions of service delivery are discussed below, including the frequency of contact by experimental and control workers with natural parents, foster parents, children in foster care, and collateral resources. Other dimensions discussed include casework methods employed, purpose of client-counselor contact, problem areas identified by staff, types of collateral resources employed, and division of case management responsibilities. Throughout this section the family, rather than the individual child, is the unit for analysis unless otherwise noted.

Frequency of Contact with Clients and Collateral Resources

The overall mean difference between units in number of contacts with clients and collateral resources was not great, averaging 4.47 contacts per case. However, there were striking differences in the distribution of specific types of contacts. Experimental staff, including both project and county workers, had an average of 21.53 contacts with natural parents, in contrast with a control average of 13.57, for a mean difference of 7.96. Contacts with natural parents represented the bulk of casework effort for experimental staff, whereas for control workers, contacts with foster parents accounted for the greatest portion of their efforts (an average of 16.64 such contacts, in contrast to 10.56 for the experimental group). Children were seen more frequently by control workers (an average of 9.35 contacts per case; 6.07 for experimental workers). Contacts between experimental workers and collateral resources were more than double those made by control (an average of 10.80 per case; 4.93 for the control group). It is clear that experimental staff directed services to natural parents, while control group services centered on foster parents. The difference between experimental staff contacts with natural parents and control contacts with foster parents was only 4.89 per case. Hence, the major difference between units was in the client group served.

The differential focus in service delivery by experimental and control staff can be seen in the fact that 60 percent of all contacts made by experimental workers were on behalf of children who were eventually restored. An almost equal percentage of control contacts (57 percent) were for children designated as long-term care (see Table 4.8*). Fifteen percent of experimental worker contacts were for cases referred for adoption, compared with 9 percent for control.

---

*Since these data focus on case outcomes, the unit for analysis is the child.

TABLE 4.8

Percentage of Contacts, by Case Outcome

	Experimental (n = 145)	Control (n = 148)
Restored	60	32
Adoption	15	9
Guardianship	4	3
Long-term	21	57

Note: The total number of children reported here is the same as shown in these categories in Table 4.6.
Source: Compiled by author.

There was a statistically significant difference between units in contacts with natural parents and collateral resources for children who were restored, referred for adoption, and classified as long-term care.* Differences were not significant for contacts with children or foster parents in any outcome category or for contacts with any client or collateral resource for children for whom guardianship was pursued.

Casework Methods Employed

During the second year of the project, experimental and control staff were asked to supply information† regarding the casework methods employed in contacts with natural parents and the purpose of such contacts. Following each personal interview with a natural parent, workers completed a form indicating the primary casework method used during the interview. This form listed six categories that Florence Hollis has suggested are descriptive of the "means" used by workers for achieving the ends of a casework interview.[2] An additional category was added for staff to indicate the use of behavioral methods.

The primary method used in almost half of all the interviews between control workers and natural parents consisted of exploratory verbal behavior (see Table 4.9 for definitions of categories). This category accounted for

---

*Analysis of variance for difference in contact between units: natural parent and collateral contacts for children restored and designated long-term care, $p \leq .01$; children referred for adoption, natural parent contact, $p \leq .05$; collateral contacts, $p \leq .01$.

†Experimental staff maintained extensive process data throughout the project. This can be seen in the detailed case studies in Part II. The data described in this section represented additional information supplied by these staff members for the purpose of comparing the approaches used by workers in both units.

TABLE 4.9

Percentage of Interviews with Natural Parents, by Primary Type of Verbal Behavior Used in Interview

	Experimental (n = 254)[a]	Control (n = 106)
Exploration	27[b]	47
Structuring	24	24
Support	11	15
Directive techniques	6	4
Reflective techniques	4	4
Practical help	4	4
Behavioral treatment	25[b]	3

[a]Total number of natural parent interviews; all cases open in year 2.
[b]Chi-square = 33.74 (2 degrees of freedom); $p \leq .001$.

Definitions of Caseworker Activity Categories

Exploration: Worker seeks information about relevant present or past situation, attitudes, and behavior. Although this activity may encourage airing of emotion-laden subject matter, its primary purpose is to gain knowledge rather than to effect a change in the client's behavior or attitudes.

Structuring: Worker explains agency or court functions, requirements, and expectations, so as to structure and clarify the nature of the agency-client and worker-client relationships. The primary purpose is to enhance the client's functioning in the role of client, rather than to affect his or her functioning in life situations.

Support: Worker expresses reassurance, understanding, encouragement, or sympathy with the client's feelings, situation, and efforts to cope with the situation.

Directive techniques: Worker attempts through advice, recommendations, or suggestions to prompt the client to engage in specific tasks such as visits with a child, etc. Such attempts by the worker can range from commands to implicit suggestions couched in the form of questions.

Reflective techniques: Worker raises questions or gives explanation to increase the client's understanding of his or her own behavior and attitudes, his or her situation, the consequences of his or her behavior, and the reactions of others to him or her.

Practical help: Worker arranges for or provides concrete services (such as homemaker service, transportation, money, goods, escort).

Behavioral treatment: All dialogue that relates to a behavioral approach is in this category. The way to determine whether something belongs here, rather than in one of the other categories, is by the content of questions and statements. For example, if you are asking questions to gather information for a problem profile, or to identify reinforcers, even though such questions fit the definition of "exploratory" verbalizations, they would be categorized here because the content relates to a behavioral approach to treatment. Similarly, if you are purposefully verbally reinforcing a client for participating in a program, it would likewise go here even though it could fit the definition of "support."

Source: Compiled by author.

27 percent of content in contacts between project workers and clients. The difference in the use of exploratory verbal behavior in the two types of units was significant (p ≤ .001). Structuring techniques and provision of support accounted for a similar percentage of interview content in both units. Workers in the experimental units used behavioral methods in 25 percent of their interviews, whereas control staff reported the use of such methods only 3 percent of the time (p ≤ .001). Directive, reflective, and practical help techniques were rarely employed by workers in either control or experimental units.

Purpose of Client-Counselor Contact

The majority of contacts with natural parents by control staff was to arrange for parent-child visits (37 percent; see Table 4.10), whereas this purpose accounted for only 4 percent of the interviews held by experimental staff. Workers in the experimental units identified monitoring parent-child interaction and discussing progress toward case objectives (that is, supervisory visits) most often (34 percent). When in-person supervisory contacts are combined with supervisory phone calls, this reason for contact accounted for 43 percent of all interviews between experimental staff and biological parents, whereas it accounted for only 16 percent of all contacts made by control staff. Routine case management tasks, such as dealing with eligibility for financial or housing assistance, accounted for 24 percent of experimental workers contacts but only 12 percent of control staff contacts. These tasks

TABLE 4.10

Percentage of Interviews with Natural Parents
Devoted to Various Purposes

	Experimental (n = 254)	Control (n = 106)
Arrange for visits with child	4	37
Routine case management	24	12
Supervisory visits: personal	34	10
Supervisory phone calls	9	6
Problems related to foster home	1	6
Parent's personal problems	7	12
Parent-child problems	15	9
Decision making for child's future	2	4
Discussing forthcoming court hearing	4	5

Source: Compiled by author.

commonly were dealt with just prior to restoring a child, so the high percentage for experimental cases would be expected.

Discussion of client problems accounted for similar percentages of the interview content in both experimental and control units, representing 23 percent of interviews held by experimental staff and 27 percent of those held by control staff. Difficulties in parent-child interaction was the most frequently discussed area reported by experimental workers, accounting for 15 percent of all experimental interview content. For the control group this category accounted for 9 percent, with discussion of parents' personal problems ranking highest of the three problem categories (see Table 4.10). Control workers reported that 6 percent of all interview content dealt with issues related to problems in the foster home, whereas in experimental worker interviews, this was reported as only 1 percent. The percentage of interviews devoted to decision-making issues and forthcoming court hearings was small in both units.

Problems Identified by Workers

In the first year of the project, control workers did not maintain records reporting the types of problems identified for families in their caseloads.* Only in the second year did staff in this unit record information describing problems that were the focus of casework intervention. Data were supplied for year 1 cases that were open at the start of year 2 and were recorded for cases entering the project units in year 2. Experimental staff reported such information throughout the two project years.

A total of 52 experimental and 23 control families form the basis of this part of the report. Information concerning experimental cases that were closed during the first year are not included. In addition, three cases from the experimental units and two from the control unit are not included because there was no contact between worker and parent.

Number of Problems

All families were "multiproblem," having two or more identified problems. Thirty-five percent of experimental cases and 43 percent of control cases had six or more identified problems (see Table 4.11).

---

*The reporting issue here refers to problems that were the focus of casework intervention. Hence, the fact that certain problems may not be identified should not be taken to mean that no such problems existed. Rather, the likelihood is that families with such difficulties were not seen by workers, in which case the problem could not be dealt with during intervention.

TABLE 4.11

Percent of Families with One-Six Problems Identified

Number of Problems	Exp. (n = 52)	Cont. (n = 23)
One	0	0
Two	15	26
Three	17	9
Four	19	4
Five	13	17
Six	35	43

Note: Because of the small number of control cases with three and four identified problems, these categories were combined in order to do a test of significance. Chi-square = 6.57 (3 degrees of freedom) = n.s.

Source: Compiled by author.

Types of Problems

Eleven different problem areas were identified (see Table 4.12). Since the majority of families were multiproblem, the totals indicated in Table 4.12 are greater than the actual numbers of families for whom data were maintained. While the percentage of families in problem areas varies by unit, there were no significant differences. The majority of all families had problems in the area of hard services. Sixty-nine percent of the control unit families and 83 percent of the experimental unit families were reported as having financial and/or housing difficulties. Problems in parent-child interaction were identified almost twice as often by control (83 percent) as by experimental staff (44 percent). Experimental workers reported fewer problems in parent-child visiting (42 percent) than did control workers (57 percent). Legal issues were reported for experimental families four times as often as for control families (17 percent vs. 4 percent), while parents' personal problems were reported three times more often by control (61 percent) than by experimental workers (23 percent). Difficulties with relatives, in keeping appointments with counseling resources, with decision making for a child's future, and with alcohol use were noted with almost equal frequency by the staffs of both units. Drug use was not identified as a problem in control cases, but, it was reported for five experimental families (10 percent). Problems with a marital partner or unrelated adult with whom the parent was living were identified more frequently in experimental (27 percent) than in control cases (17 percent).

TABLE 4.12

Percent of Families with Each of 11 Identified Problems

Problem Area	Experimental (n = 52)	Control (n = 23)
* Hard services[a]	83	69
* Visiting with child	42	57
* Parent-child interaction	44	83
** Legal[b]	17	4
* Parent's personal problems[c]	23	61
** Problems with relatives	12	13
* Problems with counseling services[d]	31	39
* Decision making for child's future	21	26
Evidence of		
** Drug use	10	0
** Alcohol use	10	13
* Problems with marital partner or nonspouse[e]	27	17

* Chi-square = n.s.

** Numbers are too small for a test of significance.

[a]Hard services includes determining eligibility for financial assistance, job training, housing, or locating employment.

[b]Legal includes custody issues and warrants for a client's arrest for parole violation or a suspected felony.

[c]Although all workers were asked to provide specific information on the type(s) of personal problems, this was not done frequently enough to create separate categories. In those instances when information was provided, "depression" was the most frequently cited problem.

[d]This refers to failure to keep appointments with counseling services.

[e]"Nonspouse" refers to a person with whom the parent was living but to whom the parent was not legally married.

Source: Compiled by author.

Collateral Resources

As in most areas of social work, collateral resources constitute an important part of service delivery. Ths is especially so with multiproblem families. Staff in both experimental and control units were asked to keep track of collateral services to which clients were referred over the two-year project period. Examination of these records revealed that nine types of collateral services were used (see Table 4.13). These services included assistance with housing and employment problems, legal aid and counseling services, and programs directed to resolving drug and alcohol problems. While the total frequency with which contact with collateral resources was made is three times greater for experimental than for control staff (1,490 for experimental, 488 for control), the percentages are quite similar in each category. The difference between units in frequency of contact is significant (p ≤ .001).

TABLE 4.13

Frequency and Percentage of Caseworker Contact with Collateral Resources

	Experimental		Control	
	Fre-quency of Contact	Percent-age of All Contacts	Fre-quency of Contact	Percent-age of All contacts
Legal aid	252	17	99	21
Locating housing	166	11	56	11
Medical aid	169	11	43	9
Employment counseling	101	7	9	2
Child's school	157	11	66	14
Community social service centers	130	9	25	5
Counseling resources[a]	152	10	69	14
Counseling programs[b]	176	12	53	11
Financial aid	187	13	68	14
Totals	1,490		488	

Note: Chi-square = 35.62 (8 degrees of freedom); significant at p ≤ .001.
[a]Psychiatric or psychological counseling resources.
[b]Counseling programs such as those for alcohol or drug abuse.
Source: Compiled by author.

Division of Case Management Responsibilities

A significant dimension of service delivery in the Alameda Project was the joint case management of experimental unit cases.[3] One of the two workers assigned to each case was the county child welfare worker, who bore primary responsibility for service delivery to the child in the foster home. The second worker (referred to as the project worker) was hired expressly for the experimental period and was not a county employee. This person was charged with providing services to biological parents. The procedure employed for sharing case management responsibilities was described in chapter 3. Given the relative novelty of this case management arrangement, it is of interest to examine important characteristics of the process, such as time involved in contacts between project and county workers involved in the same cases and caseworkers' and supervisors' perceptions of the advantages and disadvantages of this "case-sharing" approach.

Duration and Purpose of Contacts Between Workers

One possible objection to case sharing is the time involved in joint contacts. It is thus important to examine carefully the duration of such contacts. To this end, project workers were requested to keep track of the amount of time spent in joint contacts and to note the purpose of such contacts over four different one-month periods spread over 18 months. Table 4.14 shows the total number of cases, total time devoted to project-county worker contacts, and the mean number of contacts (range 2.4-3.0) and minutes per case (range 18-44). The mean number of contacts for 18 months is 2.6. It should be noted that the total amount of time spent on collaboration decreased sharply during the second year of the project even though the number of project cases increased. The mean number of minutes per case also decreased substantially from year 1 to year 2 (40.5 vs. 19.5).

TABLE 4.14

Contacts Between Project and County Workers
for Four Time Periods

	Time periods						
	First Year		First 6 months of Second Year				Difference Between Means
Total no. of contacts	One (n = 98)	Two (n = 106)	Three (n = 139)	Four (n = 155)	Year 1	Year 2	of Year 1 and Year 2
Total cases	41	45	54	52	43	53	+10
Mean no. of contacts per case	2.4	2.4	2.6	3.0	2.4	2.8	+0.4[a]
Total amount of time[b]	30:11	27:26	15:51	17:47	28:49	16:49	−12:00[c]
Mean no. of minutes per case	44	37	18	21	40.5	19.5	−21

[a]Not significant.
[b]Time is reported in hours and minutes.
[c]$Z = 5.19$; $p \leq .001$.

Source: Compiled by author.

Thus a relatively modest amount of time was consumed by contacts between project and county workers.

The highest percentage of contacts in any time period was either for "case discussions" or "updating" case progress (see Table 4.15). The percentages of contacts devoted to each purpose changed in year 2 relative to year 1 in four categories. There was an increase of 45 percent in updating and decreases ranging from 20 percent to 67 percent in discussing court hearings and court reports and in joint home calls. Time spent in joint home calls, each of which lasted an average of one hour, greatly exceeds time spent in updating, although the latter occupies a much higher percentage of total contacts. With the exception of updating, where there was an increase of 44 seconds, time reductions ranging from 2 hours, 27 minutes (collateral meetings) to 8 hours; 2 minutes (case discussion) occurred in all other categories. Personal contacts decreased from year 1 to year 2 (56 percent vs. 34 percent), phone contacts increased (44 percent vs. 66 percent), and the percentage of brief contacts (five minutes at most) increased in year 2 (Table 4.16).

Perceptions of Supervisors and Workers

Eighteen workers (15 county, three project) and five supervisors (four county, one project) were asked to cite advantages and disadvantages of dividing case management responsibilities.* Responses were received from 13 of 19 county staff (68 percent) and all four project staff. The majority of comments fell in three areas: intensive services, communication between workers, and decision making. Project and county staff did not differ on either the issues cited or their evaluations.

Intensive Services. Thirteen respondents (76 percent) commented on this area and were unequivocal in evaluating it as an advantage of dividing case management tasks. Eight specifically stated that such services facilitated early case planning, which resulted in rapid case movement.

Communication. Seven staff members (41 percent) commented on the role of communication. The division of tasks was considered viable by three respondents "only insofar as communication was good." The remaining reactions focused on disadvantages that included time involved, communication problems, and a "personal loss of information, since data on one of the clients is provided 'second-hand' through another worker."

---

*This survey took place in the second year of the project. Only staff members employed by the project or county at that time were surveyed.

TABLE 4.15

Purposes of Contacts Between Workers and Time Devoted to Each

Purpose	Mean Pecentage[a]		Total Time (hours and minutes)		Percentage Increase or Decrease in Contacts from Year 1 to Year 2	Time Difference Year 1 versus Year 2
	Year 1 (n = 204)	Year 2 (n = 294)	Year 1	Year 2		
Case discussion[b]	39	39	15:48	7:46	0	-8:02
Update case progress	31	45	7:21	8:05	+45[c]	+0:44
Discuss court report	12	4	8:16	0:44	-67	-7:32
Discuss court hearing	5	4	4:13	1:03	-20	-3:10
Joint home call	8	4	14:07	10:35	-50	-3:32
Collateral meeting[d]	3	3	7:52	5:25	0	-2:27
Total			57:37	33:38		-23:59

[a]Percentages are of the total number of contacts in each time period. The data gathered in each period in each year were similar. Hence, both time periods in each year were combined.

[b]See steps 2 and 3 under procedure for dividing case management responsibilities.

[c]Figures obtained by dividing the difference between the mean percentage of contacts in the first and second years by the mean percentage of contacts in the first year.

[d]Collateral meetings included project and county workers, as well as a worker from an ancillary community resource.

Source: Compiled by author.

75

TABLE 4.16

Percentage of Time Spent in Personal and
Phone Contacts over Six Time Categories

	Year 1 (n = 204)		Year 2 (n = 294)	
Time Category	Personal (n = 114;56%)	Phone (n = 90;44%)	Personal (n = 100;34%)	Phone (n = 194;66%)
5 minutes	31	60	54	91
10 minutes	13	21	10	8
15 minutes	11	14	10	0
16–30 minutes	21	5	7	1
31–60 minutes	15	0	11	0
1 hour or more	9	0	8	0

Source: Compiled by author.

Decision Making. Dividing case management tasks was seen by 15 respondents (88 percent) as producing separate parent and child advocates. Four positions were stated unequivocally, two stressing an objectivity in decision making when a worker "isn't involved with the entire family" and two taking the opposite position, noting that "the gestalt of the family unit is lost," a loss that negatively affects decisions. The remaining responses were equivocal, suggesting that separate parent and child advocates may or may not cause conflict in decisions that are made. Ten staff members (59% percent) commented on two aspects of dividing case tasks that relate solely to the structure of the project: responsibility to the court and separate supervision of project and county workers. The first issue concerned retention of court responsibilities by the county worker while sharing decision-making tasks with the project worker. Three respondents suggested that "the process of dividing case management tasks would run more smoothly with equal responsibility to the court and a single supervisor." Dual supervision also was seen as producing "process delays, since each worker must obtain supervisory approval for major decisions and contacts." Two county and one project staff member saw a noncourt-related person as an advantage, stating that the "client does not transfer his or her distrust of the court respresentative to the project worker"; two saw the process as disadvantageous, one county worker suggesting that it was unfair, since "If a bad decision were made she would have to deal with the problems it presented."

Time and Purposes of Contacts

Much of the time cost in year 1 is explained in terms of procedural issues. County workers must resolve feelings about losing case management and decision-making autonomy and must develop trust and confidence in a project worker whose information they are asked to accept. Part of the time in each "purpose of contact" category is devoted to learning each other's methods of working with clients and developing confidence in each other's judgment. If the process were implemented within an agency, this aspect of time cost could be expected to vary as a function of how familiar workers were with each other's approach. Unequal responsibility to the court initially increased anxiety that should be absent during implementation.

Another concern was to establish procedures to delineate the tasks of each worker and direct the process of dividing cases. The guidelines presented earlier were not fully developed until the beginning of the second year of the project; and new procedures, such as the use of written contracts (introduced during the first year), required a period of socialization for all concerned. It is worth noting that three of the four workers citing communication problems were involved in the project only during its first year.

Increased familiarity with the process of dividing cases, and growing confidence and trust between workers, can explain the reduction in time spent in case discussions, joint home calls (some of which initially were made as a means of gaining reassurance that all was going well), and the increase in brief contacts. The reduction in time spent on discussion of court reports and hearings reflects project workers' increased familiarity with court-related matters. Additional time spent in orientation to handling court procedures at the beginning of the project would have avoided this subsequent overinvestment.

Personal Advocacy

The problem of decision making based on individual worker discretion has been noted in the foster care literature and has been related to an absence of decision-making guidelines, as well as to vagueness in agency philosophy, goals, and policies.[4] Optimally, such decision making should be guided by a framework established in accordance with agency objectives, not by workers separately advocating the rights of parents or of children (and thus being free to exercise biases resulting from personal values and responses to individual clients). The worker's primary task is to gather objective data demonstrating that the initial problems requiring placement have been resolved and that a child may be returned to his or her parents or, in the absence of such resolution, that alternative planning for the child should occur.

The problems presented when decision making is guided by an advocacy stance will exist whether cases are managed by one worker or two workers. In the former situation, separate advocacy results in decisions as to which member of the parent-child dyad receives services; in the latter, it culminates in unnecessary delays in decision making while workers focus on resolving the differences created by their separate positions. Where client advocacy may be a concern—for example, with an older child whose parents wish his return when the child does not wish to be returned—the issue is appropriately dealt with in court.

Practical Aspects of Case Division

The separation of parent worker and worker for the child and foster parents is in part theoretical. Assessment of parent-child interaction occurs in every case; and if problems are identified, treatment involves both clients. Hence, project staff members become involved with children, although children are the county workers' clients. This involvement becomes more extensive as a case moves toward the child's return home and the child begins to have overnight and weekend visits with parents, during which project staff members visit and assess for longer periods of time. County workers likewise become involved with natural parents. Joint home calls are made, and natural parents telephone and drop in on county workers.

When a child is quite young, client decision making can be done unilaterally by the parents and treatment is concerned primarily with either modifying the parents' problems or teaching them new ways to interact with their children. However, the older the child, the more both parents and child are involved in decision making and treatment programs; and it becomes dysfunctional, if not impossible, to have complete division of the client consultation between two workers. Justification for adopting a case-sharing procedure would have to rest on empirical demonstration that such a process was necessary in order to provide intensive services to parents. If a single worker can manage the entire case and provide intensive services to biological parents, there seems little to recommend a division of labor.

Summary

It is clear that workers in experimental and control units directed services to different client groups. Workers in the former focused their attention on natural parents, while those in the latter centered on foster parents. This is reflected in the mean number of contacts per case with each client group, as well as in the data showing that the greatest percentage of experimental worker contacts were made on behalf of children restored, while for control they were on behalf of long-term care cases. Interview methods employed by workers were distinguished by the use of exploratory techniques by the control staff, and by the use of behavioral methods by experimental group workers.

The experimental and control staff members cited different for their contacts with natural parents. Control staff reported visits between children and parents most frequently, whereas s case progress toward specific goals was the primary purpose noted by experimental workers. Workers in both units spent similar amounts of time discussing client problems; however, the problem areas most often discussed were different. Discussing parent-child difficulties was reported with greatest frequency by experimental staff members, while control workers gave their major attention to discussing the parents' personal problems.

All families were multiproblem. The percentage with financial and/or housing difficulties was very high in both units. Other frequently cited difficulties were parent-child interaction and parental visiting behavior. Personal problems of parents were reported in over 60 percent of control families but in only 23 percent of experimental group cases. Although the percentage of contact with various types of collateral resources was similar in both groups, the frequency of contact with such resources was significantly greater for experimental workers. A wide range of collateral resources was involved in all cases.

The case-sharing procedure employed in the Alameda Project, with project workers concerned primarily with the natural parents and county workers primarily with foster parents, resulted in a mean of 40.5 minutes of contact per case between project and county workers the first year and 19.5 minutes the second year (Table 4.14). Thus, this method of providing services was not costly in terms of worker time, nor did it create severe case management problems. Comparative data showing the effects on case outcome when one worker manages the entire case are needed before this approach can be recommended. However, the fact that the major difference between experimental and control units was in the methods employed and the client groups served, rather than in the amount of service provided, suggests that one worker could manage the entire case. We would hypothesize that a single worker, directing attention to biological parents and children, using methods similar to those employed by the experimental staff, could achieve results not unlike those reported for experimental cases.

A SEARCH FOR PREDICTOR VARIABLES

The issue in this section is to identify variables that might predict differential outcomes for children in care. The cases considered here include those in which decisions had been made when the project ended (see Table 4.17). Cases categorized as miscellaneous and undecided were omitted. In several instances, when outcomes were viewed in relation to selected variables, such as the child's age or reason for placement, cell frequencies became too small for tests of significance. Hence, different combinations of

TABLE 4.17

Number of Children, by Outcome Category, in Each Group

	Experimental	Control
Restored	55	38
To be restored	15	7
Adoption	29	11
Guardianship	15	3
Long-term care	31	89
Total	145	148

Source: Compiled by author.

categories are used in the following discussion, in order to minimize this problem.

As can be seen in Table 4.18 regardless of the variable considered, when the number of children restored, to be restored, and referred for adoption or guardianship are combined, most experimental unit children were either out or headed out of foster placement by the end of the project. In contrast, nearly a majority of control unit children were designated for long-term care. Exceptions to this were children placed under combination neglect and abuse petitions—they had similar percentages in the "restored" or "to be restored" and in the "long-term care" categories—and children four to six years of age and those of biracial parentage—more of them were restored or to be restored than were headed for long-term care.

There was no significant difference in outcome between units for children from two-parent families or in the age categories birth to three years, four to six, or ten years or older. Because of the small number of cases involved, tests of significance could not be conducted for three of the categories related to the child's racial or ethnic background or for youngsters who entered placement under combination abuse and neglect petitions. For all remaining variables displayed in Table 4.18, more experimental than control children were out or headed out of care ($p \leq .01$ to $\leq .001$).

Despite these exceptions, only one predictive relationship emerged, that between the type of placement and the outcomes of adoption and guardianship for experimental unit children. Children placed with relatives were unlikely to be adopted (7 percent) but were likely to have the relative assume guardianship (26 percent) (See Table 4.19). The reverse was true for children in nonrelative placements: adoption occurred for 27 percent and guardianship for only 1 percent (lambda = .70).* Correlations between type of outcome and other variables ranged from zero for age of child to .38 for ethnicity.

---

*Guttman's lambda is the measure of association used throughout, unless otherwise noted.

TABLE 4.18

Percentage of Children in Three Outcome Categories, by Six Demographic Variables

	Restored/ To Be Restored		Adoption/ Guardianship		Long-Term		Total	
	Exp. (n = 70)	Cont. (n = 45)	Exp. (n = 44)	Cont. (n = 14)	Exp. (n = 31)	Cont. (n = 89)	Exp. (n = 145)	Cont. (n = 148)
Sex								
Male[a]	49	27	28	8	23	64	83	70
Female[a]	48	33	32	11	19	56	62	78
Total							145	148
Type of placement								
Relative[b]	39	29	33	12	28	60	54	42
Nonrelative[b]	54	31	28	9	17	60	91	106
Total							145	148
Family composition[d]								
Two-parent[c]	75	34	0	13	25	53	24	32
Female-headed[a]	44	30	35	9	22	62	112	113
Total							136[d]	145[d]
Petition								
Neglect[a]	49	30	29	9	23	62	124	135
Neglect/abuse[e]	55	46	40	8	5	46	21	13
Total							145	148
Age								
0–3[c]	52	18	30	36	18	45	49	22
4–6[c]	42	58	42	0	17	42	36	19
7–9[a]	55	21	19	8	26	70	31	47
10+[c]	45	33	27	4	28	63	29	60
Total							145	148
Race/ethnicity								
Caucasian[a]	71	34	15	6	15	61	48	57
Black[a]	29	14	41	13	29	74	68	57
Mexican-American[e]	42	25	50	13	8	63	12	16
Biracial[e]	70	67	12	17	18	17	17	12
American Indian[e]	0	100	0	0	0	0	0	6
Total							145	148

Note: Percentages are of horizontal totals.
[a]$p \leq .001$.
[b]$p \leq .01$.
[c]Not significant.
[d]Male-headed families were excluded because of the small number of cases.
[e]Cell frequencies too small for significance test.
Source: Compiled by author.

TABLE 4.19

Percentage of Experimental Group Children in Relative and Nonrelative Placements, by Outcome

	Restored (n = 55)	To Be Restored (n = 15)	Adoption (n = 29)	Guardianship (n = 15)	Long-Term Care (n = 31)	Total
Relative	30	9	7	26	28	54
Nonrelative	43	11	27	1	17	91
Total						145

Source: Compiled by author.

TABLE 4.20

Reason for Placement, by Case Outcome

Reason for Placement	Percent out or Headed out of Care		Percent Long-Term		Total	
	Exper. (n = 111)	Cont. (n = 59)	Exper. (n = 31)	Cont. (n = 88)	Exper. (n = 142)	Cont. (n = 147)
Alcohol	86	55	14	45	21	11[a]
Drugs	77	55	23	45	26	20[a]
Psychiatric problems	45	30	55	70	15	20[a]
Parent in prison	100	46	0	54	6	13[b]
Child left unattended	79	30	21	70	24	23[c]
Child out of parental control	80	58	20	42	5	12[b]
Abuse alleged	64	0	36	100	17	5[b]
Neglect	94	39	6	61	16	38[c]
Abuse	100	20	0	80	12	5[b]

Notes: Four children (three from the experimental group and one from the control group) who were placed because of parental hospitalization for physical illness were omitted. The three experimental children were restored and the one control unit child was headed for long-term placement.

"Neglect and abuse" categories contain those cases where no specific reason for placement was noted in case records. The neglect category includes four children from control for whom "condition of household" was listed as the reason for placement and one experimental unit child for whom "medical needs not being met" was noted.

[a]Not significant.

[b]Cell frequencies too small for test of significance.

[c]$p \leq .001$.

Source: Compiled by author.

Reason for Placement, by Outcome

With the exception of youngsters placed because of psychiatric problems of the parents, most children in the experimental units were out or headed out of care. For control unit children placed because of parental use of alcohol or drugs, because a parent was in prison, or because the child was said to be out of parental control, outcomes were almost evenly divided between those out of or headed out of care and those designated for long-term placement. The majority of children placed for other reasons were designated for long-term care.

The difference between units is significant for only two of the nine placement categories noted in Table 4.20. These are children who were left unattended by their parents and those in the general category of neglect ($p < .001$). No predictive relationships were found between reason for placement and case outcome. Correlations ranged from zero for children out of parental control to .45 for children left unattended.

Age, Outcome, and Time in Care

Since age was the only demographic variable for which there was a significant difference between groups (see Table 3.5), this variable was examined further, controlling for length of time in care. If age is predictive of outcome, one would expect that a majority of long-term cases would consist of older children who have been in care for long periods of time. This was not found to be the case. All control children in care for one year or less who were under one year of age or between 10 and 12 years of age were reported as long-term cases (see Table 4.21). All control children who were over age thirteen and who were in care one year or less were referred for adoption. Of control children in care two to three years, those one to three years old account for the highest percentage of long-term cases (100 percent), followed by those seven to nine years old (69 percent); children over 13 are almost equally divided between restoration (45 percent) and long-term care (55 percent). Children 10 to 12 years old represented the majority of long-term cases for control children in care for three years or more (82 percent), followed by those seven to nine years old (73 percent). Once again, we see a relatively small percentage difference between the restoration (43 percent) and long-term care (57 percent) for children 13 or older. The only instance in which children over 13 constitute the greatest percentage of long-term cases are those in care between one and two years (88 percent).

In the experimental group, the highest percentage of children in any age group said to be long-term cases were over 13 and in placement less than one

TABLE 4.21

Length of Time in Care, By Age and Outcome.

Case Outcome	Age Under 1 Year		Age 1-3 Years		Age 4-6 Years		Age 7-9 Years		Age 10-12 Years		Age 13+	
	Exp.	Cont.	Exp.	Cont.	Exp.	Cont.	Exp.	Cont.	Exp.	Cont.	Exp.	Cont.
In Care One Year or Less (experimental n = 52; control n = 34)												
Restored	40%	—	39%	17%	33%	25%	55%	—	67%	—	33%	—
To be restored	20	—	15	—	8	13	18	—	22	—	—	—
Adoption	40	—	15	42	25	13	—	15%	—	—	—	100%
Guardianship	—	—	8	—	25	—	9	8	—	—	—	—
Long-term care	—	100%	23	42	8	50	18	77	11	100%	67	—
In Care More Than One Year but less than Two Years (experimental n = 44; control n = 39)												
Restored	25%	—	41%	25%	42%	80%	20%	15%	—	17%	—	—
To be restored	—	—	4	—	25	—	40	23	—	33	—	12%
Adoption	25	—	41	50	25	—	—	8	—	—	—	—
Guardianship	25	—	—	—	—	—	20	8	50	—	100%	—
Long-term care	25	—	14	25	8	20	20	46	50	50	—	88

In Care Two to Three Years (experimental n = 29; control n = 41)

Restored	—	50%	20%	38%	33%	31%	—	50%	50%	45%
To be restored	—	—	—	—	17	—	—	13	—	—
Adoption	—	30	40	25	17	—	100%	—	—	—
Guardianship	—	—	20	—	17	—	—	—	—	—
Long-term care	—	20	20	38	17	69	—	38	50	55

In Care Three Years or More (experimental n = 20; control n = 34)

Restored	—	—	100%	25%	9%	33%	9%	43%
To be restored	—	—	—	—	—	—	—	—
Adoption	—	17%	—	25	—	22	—	—
Guardianship	—	50	—	17	18	11	9	—
Long-term care	—	33	—	33	73	33	82	57

Source: Compiled by author.

85

TABLE 4.22

Case Outcomes, by Time in Care

	Restored/ to be Restored		Adoption/ Guardianship		Long-Term		Total	
	Exper. (n = 70)	Cont. (n = 45)	Exper. (n = 44)	Cont. (n = 14)	Exper. (n = 31)	Cont. (n = 89)	Exper. (n = 145)	Cont. (n = 148)
Less than one year	60%	15%	22%	18%	17%	68%	52	34[a]
One year but less than two	50	38	34	13	16	49	44	39[b]
Two to three years	38	39	41	7	20	54	29	41[b]
Three years or more	30	26	25	0	45	74	20	34[c]

Note: ·Percentages are of horizontal totals.
[a]Chi-square: $p \leq .001$.
[b]Chi-square: $p \leq .01$.
[c]Not significant (restored/to be restored and adoption/guardianship combined for chi-square because of cell frequency).
Source: Compiled by author.

year (67 percent). Of the remaining children in care for the same time period, a majority have been restored, regardless of age. Fifty percent of those 10 to 12 years old and in care for one to two years have been referred for guardianship and an equal percentage designated for long-term care. Likewise, 50 percent of those children over 13 and in foster homes for two to three years have been restored and an equal percentage designated for long-term placement. Thus, in general, it can be stated that a child's age has no predictive value even when length of time in placement is controlled.

Length of Time in Care

Most experimental unit youngsters in care for less than two years were restored or to be restored to biological parents. Forty-one percent of those in care for two to three years were referred for adoption or guardianship, and 38 percent had been or were to be restored (see Table 4.22). Following three years in care, forty-five percent were in long-term placements, 30 percent had been restored or were to be restored, and 25 percent were referred for adoption or guardianship.

There was a relationship between the length of time in care and the outcomes restored/to-be-restored and adoption/guardianship for experimental unit cases in care less than three years. The percentage of children restored or to be restored decreases (from a high of 60 percent for children in care less than one year to a low of 38 percent for children in care two to three years) as the length of time in care increases. As the percentage in the restored/to-be-restored category decreases, there is a concomitant increase in the percent referred for adoption or guardianship action. The percentage of such referrals is lowest for children in care less than one year (22 percent). This increases to 34 percent for youngsters in placement one year but less than two, and is highest for children who have been out of their homes for two to three years (41 percent). The percentage of children referred for adoption or guardianship decreases to 25 percent following three years in foster placement.

Regardless of the length of time in care, most control children were designated for long-term placement. The pattern of adoption/guardianship referrals and children restored or to be restored was the reverse of that found for the experimental cases. Most adoption or guardianship actions occurred for children in care less than one year (18 percent), decreasing to a low of 7 percent for children placed two to three years. Restorations were highest for children in care between two and three years (39 percent), with only 15 percent of those in foster homes less than one year either restored or to be restored.

That experimental unit children in care less than 36 months will move out of foster placement can be predicted within a range of .59 (in care two to three years) to .68 (in care one year but less than two). (See Table 4.23.) Outcome is not predictable for children in care three years or more (lambda = .10). No predictable relationships were found for control unit children. Correlations ranged from a low of .05 (in care two to three years) to a high of .47 (in care three years or more).

For both experimental and control units, children out or headed out of care is markedly reduced once a child has been in placement three years or more (see Table 4.24). For experimental youngsters the reduction is from 82 percent (less than three years) to 55 percent, and for control, from 44 percent to 26 percent. Long-term cases constitute a very small percentage in the experimental unit when the child has been in care less than three years (18

TABLE 4.23

Correlations Between Length of Time in Care and Outcomes

Correlation*	Experimental	Control
Less than one year	.66	.35
One year, less than two	.68	.26
Two to three years	.59	.05
Three years or more	.10	.47

*Restored/to be restored and adoption/guardianship combined.
Source: Compiled by author.

TABLE 4.24

Relationship Between Case Outcome and Time in Care

| | Less Than Three Years | | | |
| | Experimental (n = 126) | | Control (n = 114) | |
	Number	Percent	Number	Percent
Headed out of foster care	103	82	50	44
Long-term care	22	18	64	56

| | Three Years or More | | | |
| | Experimental (n = 20) | | Control (n = 34) | |
	Number	Percent	Number	Percent
Headed out of foster care	11	55	9	26
Long-term care	9	45	25	74

Chi-square, less than three years = 30.36 (1 degree of freedom).
Chi-square, three years or more = 9.81 (1 degree of freedom).
Source: Compiled by author.

percent vs. 56 percent for control). This increased considerably after three years (experimental, 45 percent; control, 74 percent). However, regardless of the time period considered, a significantly greater number and percentage of experimental than control children were either out or headed out of foster placement (less than three years, $p \leq .001$; three years or more, $p \leq .01$).

The only predictable relationship found was for experimental unit children in care three years or less; movement out of foster placement can be predicted at .65. Other correlations range from a low of .11 (experimental, in care three years or more) to a high of .47 (control, in care three years or more). There were no predictable relationships across the two time categories of less than three years compared with more than three years in care.

Identified Problems by Outcome

No relationship was found between the number of problems and case outcome (see Table 4.25). Even when many problems were identified, half or more of the children in both units were restored or to be restored to their parents. In the experimental section between 88 percent and 90 percent of the families with two to four identified problems had their children returned to their care. This decreased to 71 percent for families with five identified problems and to 56 percent for families with six or more problems. The distribution is more random in the control section. Children whose parents had two or five identified problems were just as likely to be restored as not, and there was an increase in restorations for families with six or more problems. All children in the control group whose parents had three or four identified problems were restored.

In three categories (parent-child interaction, personal parental problems, and problems with spouse) problems were resolved for a significantly greater number of experimental than control families.* (See Table 4.26.) Seventy-five percent of the total number of identified problems were reported as resolved by experimental workers, whereas for control the split between resolved and unresolved was almost 50-50. This difference is statistically significant ($p \leq .001$).

In both units the probability of restoration, given problem resolution, was high, with 91 percent of the experimental children (n = 92) and 83 percent of the control children (n = 34) being restored under these conditions. Alternative outcomes were very unlikely when problems were resolved, occurring for only 9 percent of the experimental and 17 percent of the control children. For experimental cases (n = 30), the majority of children were not restored if identified problems remained unresolved (90

TABLE 4.25

Number of Families, by Number of Identified
Problems and Outcome

| Number of Problems | Experimental (n = 52) | | | Control (n = 23) | | |
	Restored or to Be Restored	Alternative	Total	Restored or to Be Restored	Alternative	Total
One	0	0	0	0	0	0
Two	88%	13%	8	50%	50%	6[a]
Three	89	11	9	100	0	2[a]
Four	90	10	10	100	0	1[a]
Five	71	29	7	50	50	4[a]
Six	56	44	18	60	40	10[b]
Total			52			23

[a]Fisher's exact test not significant.
[b]Chi-square not significant.

Source: Compiled by author.

*There were no identified drug problems in the control unit; hence no test of significance could be run on this problem area.

TABLE 4.26

Identified Problem Areas: Resolved or Unresolved at the End of Year 2

	Resolved		Unresolved		Total	
	Exper.	Cont.	Exper.	Cont.	Exper.	Cont.
	(n = 92)	(n = 34)	(n = 30)	(n = 35)		
Visiting with children	67%	69%	33%	31%	21	13[a]
Parent-child interaction	91	33	8	67	23	18[b]
Legal	67	100	33	0	9	1[c]
Parent's personal problems	100	36	0	64	12	14[d]
Problems with relatives	67	33	33	67	6	3[c]
Problems with counseling service	75	63	25	37	16	8[c]
Decision making for child's future	64	67	36	33	11	6[c]
Evidence of						
Drug use	40	0	60	0	5	0[e]
Alcohol use	40	100	60	0	5	2[c]
Problems with marital partner or non-spouse	86	25	14	75	14	4[f]
Total	75	49	25	51	122	69[g]

Notes: Percentages are of horizontal totals.

"Total" column affected by lack of information on problem resolution for one experimental and three control families.

"Total" row is total percentage of resolved/unresolved problems by units.

[a] Not significant.

[b] Chi-square = 15.07 (1 degree of freedom); $p \leq .001$.

[c] Fisher's Exact Test not significant.

[d] Fisher's Exact Test = $p \leq .005$.

[e] Absence of control cases precludes test of significance.

[f] Fisher's Exact Test = $p \leq .05$.

[g] Chi-square = 12.82 (1 degree of freedom); $p \leq .001$.

percent). This was not the case for control youngsters (n = 35). Forty-three percent were restored when problems were not resolved, and for 57 percent alternative outcomes occurred. The difference between units concerning lack of problem resolution and outcome was significant ($p \leq .01$).*

---

*Chi-square = 8.71 (1 degree of freedom).

Source: Compiled by author.

TABLE 4.27

Relationship Between Contracts and Outcome in Foster Care

	Restored	Adoption	Guardian-ship	Long-Term	Total
Yes: signed	42 (70%)	3 (5%)	7 (12%)	8 (13%)	60
Yes: unsigned	3 (43%)	—	—	4 (57%)	7
No	10 (16%)	26 (41%)	8 (13%)	19 (30%)	63
Total	55	29	15	31	130

Eliminating the "yes/unsigned" category, chi-square = 46.4 (3 degrees of freedom); $p \leq .001$.

Source: Compiled by author.

For experimental unit cases, the predictability of outcome, given knowledge of problem resolution, is quite high (67 percent). For control it is substantially lower (31 percent).

Contracts and Outcome

Written contracts between workers and their clients were employed by experimental staff only. An examination of the relationship between contract use, including whether it was a signed or unsigned contract, and case outcome revealed that a far greater percentage of children were restored to families who signed restoration agreements (70 percent) than to those who did not (16 percent) ($p < .001$). (See Table 4.27.) Most children whose parents verbally agreed to, but did not sign, contracts were designated for long-term foster care (57 percent). The remaining three children were restored. Fifty-three children (84 percent) whose parents would not consider a written or verbal contract were either referred for adoption (41 percent) or legal guardianship (13 percent) or designated for long-term placement (30 percent).

The relationship between contract status and case outcome can be seen even more dramatically by combining the outcomes of adoption, guardianship, and long-term care into a single category of alternative outcomes (see Table 4.28).

The probability of children being restored when parents sign a contract is significantly greater than when they refuse ($p < .001$); 70 percent are restored with a signed contract and 84 percent head for long-term care when there is no contract. The predictability of either outcome, given information as to whether a contract was signed, is 57 percent.

Summary

With a single exception, outcome was not related to any demographic variable, reason for placement, the child's age (even when time in care was controlled for), or the number of identified problems. The exception noted was for experimental unit children, by type of placement in relation to the outcomes of adoption and guardianship. Those placed with relatives were unlikely to be adopted but likely to have a relative assume the role of legal guardian. This relationship was reversed for youngsters in nonrelative placements, where adoption was the likely outcome and guardianship was not likely to occur.

A pattern was observed between length of time a child was in care and case outcome in the experimental group. The greatest percentage of children were restored during the first year in care (60 percent). Restorations decreased as time in care increased up to the third year in placement (38 percent restored). Adoption, which was lowest during the first year (22 percent), increased to a high of 41 percent at the end of three years. This pattern was reversed for children in the control unit. Adoptions were highest during the first year (18 percent) and restorations lowest (15 percent). At the end of three years, restorations increased to 39 percent and adoptions decreased to 7 percent. For all children in care three years or more the greatest percentage appear as long-term care (experimental, 45 percent; control, 74 percent). There was no predictable relationship between outcome and time in care for control unit children. For experimental unit youngsters in care up to three years, it was predictable within a range of .59 to .60 that a child would move out of care. The critical relationship between time in care and outcome is well illustrated by these data. Children in care less than three years are most likely to move out of placement. Following the third year, such movement is unlikely.

Seventy-five percent of the identified problems of experimental unit families were resolved, in contrast with 50 percent for control families. In both units the majority of children were restored if problems were success-

TABLE 4.28

Contract Status and Case Outcome: Verbal Contract Omitted

	Contract		
	Yes	No	Total
Restored	42 (70%)	10 (16%)	52
Alternative	18 (30%)	53 (84%)	71
Total	60	63	123

Chi-square = 36.88 (1 degree of freedom); $p \leq .001$.
Lambda = .57.
Source: Compiled by author.

fully resolved. Alternative outcomes occurred for 90 percent of experimental unit children if family problems were unresolved, whereas in the control cases, 43 percent of the children were restored whether or not problems were resolved, with alternative outcomes occurring for 57 percent. For experimental cases, outcome was predictable with 67 percent accuracy, given knowledge of problem resolution. There was no predictable relationship for control children.

Seventy percent of the experimental unit youngsters were restored if a parent signed a written contract, whereas alternative outcomes occurred for 84 percent of those whose parent would not sign a written agreement. There was a predictable association between contracts and outcomes (n = .57). (Written contracts were not employed by control unit staff.)

LIMITATIONS OF THE STUDY

The design of the study precluded identification of the relative contributions to outcome of method and frequency of contact. Restructuring service units in order to tease out the relative contribution of these factors is not easily accomplished in a public bureaucracy. Important implications for social work education and practice could have been drawn had it been possible to structure such an experiment. Attempts to conduct such research in the future are warranted by the positive results reported here for the experimental units. It also would be useful to compare outcomes by contrasting a condition of one worker managing the entire case with the division of case management responsibilities employed in this study. Actually, the framework for case sharing often broke down in practice in the Alameda Project.

Responsibility for services to the child initially was viewed as the task of county workers. However, because of the need to observe parent-child interaction and to resolve difficulties in this area, these services often became the responsibility of project staff. Hence, conclusions must be drawn with extreme caution. Case assignment to units did not meet the ideal of a purely random model. Some cases that should have been in the project had to be rejected when the caseloads of county workers reached maximum. Others could not be taken because there was no room in the caseload of a worker covering the geographic locale where a child was placed. However, we do not think our sample was seriously distorted. Except for the child's age, cases were comparable across units on all other demographic variables.

ONE-YEAR FOLLOW-UP

Cases were followed up one year after the project ended. The question addressed in this section is where the children were one year later.

Before considering this question, we remember from our earlier discussion of the procedure for dividing experimental unit cases between two workers that Alameda Project workers had been hired expressly for the experiment. These workers received training in behavioral methods of intervention and bore the responsibility for providing intensive services to natural parents. Their employment terminated when the project ended. The second person assigned to each project case, the county child welfare worker, did not receive the special training provided to project staff. Thus there could be no follow-up on the continued efficacy of the treatment methods employed during the experimental period, because the methods were no longer being employed.

No doubt the process of collaborating on cases resulted in some informal learning for county personnel. However, several of these workers left the department or were transferred out of foster care units during the follow-up year. The result of this change in staffing is that many of the cases in the follow-up period were not carried by county workers who had any part in initial decision making. Because of these overall changes in staff composition, follow-up data are not presented separately for experimental and control units. Reporting data by units would suggest that we were comparing casework methods used. Such a view would have meaning only if staff composition in the units was the same as in prior years. Since the units no longer existed insofar as county staff was concerned, it would be misleading to report data in such a manner. Reference is made to the units in which children had been only when appropriate.

Three interrelated questions are addressed in this one-year follow-up report: Did the children who left care during the project period remain out of placement; that is, did any of them return to foster care? Were plans completed to move children out of foster care; that is, plans that were in process at the end of the project period? What was the status of children classified for long-term placement at the end of the project period; that is, did this remain their status at the end of the follow-up year?

The Sample

At the end of the project, decisions had been made for 293 children, 145 in the experimental unit and 148 in the control. (This figure excludes cases classified as undecided and those closed for miscellaneous reasons. See Table 4.8.) Seventy experimental unit (48 percent) and 44 control unit children (30 percent) had moved out of foster care. A total of 179 children remained in placement. Of these, 44 in the experimental (30 percent) and 15 in the control group (10 percent) were headed out of placement. Thirty-one in the experimental unit (21 percent) and 89 in the control unit (60 percent) were designated for long-term placement. Cases were closed during the follow-up year for 7 of these 179 children for miscellaneous reasons, such as change in court jurisdiction,* leaving a total of 172 children for whom follow-up data are discussed.

Data Collection

Records were reviewed to determine the current whereabouts of children who were headed for restoration or for whom guardianship was being pursued at the time the project ended, and to ascertain the current decision status of children classified as long-term. If records did not contain the necessary data, casework or supervisory staff were interviewed. Information regarding the current status on incomplete adoptions was obtained from the supervisor of adoptions.

Results

Two children who had been restored to their natural parents (one from experimental and one from control) reentered care during the follow-up year. New decisions had not been reached for these youngsters at the time of follow-up.

The remaining 172 children fall into two groups, based on decisions made during the project years: 59 children (34 percent) were headed out of placement and 113 were designated for long-term care (66 percent). Case movement during the first follow-up year for the 59 children is shown in Table 4.29. Decisions were completed in 64 percent of the cases, changed in 25 percent, and unchanged in 10 percent. Cases that had been referred for adoption accounted for the highest percentage of completed decisions. Thirteen of the 22 youngsters headed for restoration (59 percent) were restored, and guardianship actions were completed for 6 of 13 children (46 percent). Initial decisions were changed for 15 children. Five who were headed for adoption were referred for guardianship, and one child who was a guardianship referral was in the adoption unit. The six remaining youngsters for whom guardianship was being pursued, plus two who were to have been restored, were classified as long-term placements.† The one

---

*Six of these had been experimental unit children, and one was from control. All had been designated long-term cases.

†Five of these children were from the same family and were to have become the wards of their maternal aunt, in whose care they had been for over five years. Changing the aunt's relationship from that of foster mother to guardian would have resulted in a substantial financial loss, since she would not have been eligible to receive the boarding home rate provided to foster parents. For this reason the action was terminated.

TABLE 4.29

Decision Status of Children Headed out of Placement, One Year Later

Decision Status at End of Project	No of Children	Status One Year Later		
		Completed	Unchanged	Changed
To be restored	22	13 (59%)	6 (27%)*	3 (14%)
Incomplete adoption	24	19 (79%)		5 (21%)
Incomplete guardianship	13	6 (46%)		7 (54%)
Total	59	38 (64%)	6 (10%)	15 (25%)

Note: Percentages are of horizontal totals.

*Categories of unchanged and changed were combined for chi-square test because of the empty cells in the "unchanged" category.

Source: Compiled by author.

additional child who was headed for restoration was reported as undecided. The difference between completed, unchanged, and changed decisions was not significant (chi-square = 4.43 [2 degrees of freedom]).

Case outcomes for the 113 children classified as long-term placements* are shown in Table 4.30. For 54 percent of the children, there was no change in decision status. However, changes did occur for 46 percent. Sixteen percent of the children from this latter group were restored to their natural parents and twenty-eight percent are now headed out of placement. No new decisions were reached for two youngsters.

Discussion

An essential goal of foster care administration identified by several authors is consistent implementation of decision-making procedures that achieve continuity of care for children.[5] Movement toward continuity of care begins when a decision is first reached, and continues as progress is evidenced by approximations to a clearly identified objective. Approximations to restoration, for example, might include parental compliance with a visiting plan or location of new housing. The goal is accomplished when the child has remained in a stable living situation for a predefined period of time, such as one year.†

---

*Twenty-five of the 113 children in the long-term category were from experimental units, the remaining 88 from control.

†There is no established minimum time period for continuity. Hence, any decision is somewhat arbitrary. The one-year minimum used here seems reasonable.

TABLE 4.30

Decision Status of Children Categorized as
Long-Term Placements, One Year Later

		Long-Term
Status unchanged		61 (54%)
Decision changed		
Restored	18 (16%)	
To be restored	12 (11%)	
Adoption	6 (5%)	
Guardianship	14 (12%)	
Undecided	2 (12%)	52 (46%)
Total		113

Note: Percentages are of the total number of children.
Source: Compiled by author.

It has been recognized that planned long-term placements are an appropriate living situation for some children.[6] However, certain issues must be resolved for this to be a viable option; specifically, deciding on a minimum length of time that a child must be in placement before designation as long-term, and arranging the legal safeguards for foster parents that are accorded to adoptive parents and legal guardians.[7] The frequent references to children drifting in unplanned long-term care suggests that some may be assigned haphazardly to this category. The need for guidelines is recognized in the Foster Care and Adoptions Reform Act of 1977, which delineates criteria for this designation.[8] Viewing goal attainment in this manner, what can be said with reference to the children in the Alameda Project?

It seems reasonable to suggest that continuity was achieved for the 112 out of the 114 youngsters (98 percent) who left placement before the experimental period ended.* These children have remained in stable home environments for periods ranging from one to three years. Fifty-nine children were headed out of placement when the project ended (Table 4.29). A number of successful approximations to goal attainment were made for 38 of these children, all of whom left care during the follow-up year. It is difficult to evaluate progress in positive terms for the six who were still headed for restoration. If movement through each of the steps specified for accomplishing this objective was monitored within a set period of time, the goal should have been either accomplished or changed. Whether such

---

*The two youngsters who reentered care were classified as undecided when follow-up data was collected.

monitoring occurred is questionable, since the status quo had been maintained for over a year. Examples of altering decisions contingent on monitoring progress toward specific goals are suggested by the 15 youngsters for whom changes did occur. If changes are assumed to reflect attempts to achieve continuity via alternative routes, it is possible to evaluate the progress of these children in a more positive light. However, definitive statements cannot be made without a follow-up in the second successive year.

Our data suggest that long-term care decisions are the least likely to result in continuity of care. Proof that stability and continuity are accomplished for a child through planned long-term placement is established only as this decision does not change over time. It is possible to argue that approximations to this goal are evident at follow-up for 61 of the 113 youngsters so classified. However, the fact that changes occurred for almost half of those for whom this was an initial decision (46 percent) diminishes our feeling of certainty. Additional changes might well follow a careful case review. We suggest, however, that the real reason for greater probability of changes in designated long-term care cases is that this category includes cases other than those resulting from specific long-range planning, such as those remaining in long-term care simply because of a failure to press for other outcomes. Such misuse obviously negates the accomplishment of real stability for the child.

The variety of reasons that eventuate in a decision for long-term care is illustrated by a review of the process of reaching decisions on project cases. In experimental unit cases, natural parents were given the opportunity to work toward having their children restored to their care. If restoration could not be accomplished, a decision for long-term care might follow as a second choice if a youngster had been in the same foster home over a number of years. If such was not the case, adoption would be the alternative to restoration as the path to maximum stability, with the appointment of a legal guardian as a third choice, and long-term care as the last. There were cases, however, in which adoption was prevented by parents who refused to relinquish a child, there were insufficient legal grounds for terminationn and there was no adult willing to assume the role of guardian. This is an example of a long-term decision based upon the lack of alternatives. A different example is the children categorized as long-term placements because their parents are designated temporarily unavailable through being in prison or residing in a drug or alcohol treatment facility. In such instances, a decision for long-term placement is not clearly a result of long-range planning; hence, there would be a greater likelihood of change than in the case of decisions that follow a careful assessment of the child's placement history, an assessment that establishes the virtual impossibility of restoration.

Long-term decisions also may be made for the purpose of "banking" cases.[9] Banking may be seen by workers as one functional approach to managing large caseloads. It may occur because workers lack a framework for decision making or lack skills for resolving client problems.[10] Control unit data from the second year of the project suggest that banking does occur, and at an early point following a child's entry into care. Out of a total of 28 new cases, 13 were designated long-term. This decision was reached within two months after entry for six children and within four months for an additional four.* Several issues are raised by this kind of decision making. First, when decisions are reached soon after a child enters placement, they are likely to be based on data in case records or court reports rather than on following up on a thorough assessment of the probabilities of alternative outcomes. Given the poor quality of records and the absence of a shared definition of neglect, the value of case or court documents as a basis for decision making is questionable.[11] The result of reliance on such records may be that children are needlessly detained in placement simply because alternatives are not vigorously sought. In view of the available data showing how length of time that a child is in care affects case outcome, this kind of decision making can only be considered irresponsible.[12] Another concern is that once classification occurs, a mind-set tends to be established that limits consideration of alternatives.[13] The worker responsible for the initial decision may fully intend to reconsider the options, but the chances of this happening are reduced by the high rate of worker turnover.[14]

A way to minimize some of the problems is to establish two programs of long-term care.[15] One would be for children whose parents were temporarily unavailable; it would have a definite end point, such as when the parent returns from prison. Children expected to remain in placement indefinitely would be placed in the second long-term program. Cases in the latter group then could be assigned to special units in which staff would carry caseloads larger than prevailing agency standards, since these cases require less worker activity than do new cases or cases where movement is expected. Caseloads for other staff then could be reduced, making it possible to provide intensive services where there is the greatest probability of moving children out of placement. If banking of cases results from skill deficits, these deficits must be addressed through in-service training in decision making and problem solving. With supervisory personnel monitoring the basis upon which decisions are made and progress toward identified objectives, concerted attention to those cases in which movement is possible will certainly yield the largest payoff.

---

*This could not have occurred for experimental unit cases, which were continually monitored. Workers reaching a decision in such a manner would have to defend a position that would prove untenable.

Summary

Progress toward decisions made during the project period for a group of 172 children in foster care was examined one year after close of the project. The results revealed a good "batting average" in decision making for children who were headed out of the foster care system (to be restored, incomplete adoption and guardianship actions). Decisions for long-term care were twice as likely to have been altered within one year compared to decisions to move a child out of a foster home. Possible reasons for the greater instability of long-term care decisions were discussed in terms of the reasons why children are placed in this category; specifically, it is a way to manage a large caseload, which is itself a consequence of a lack of decision-making and problem-solving skills. It was suggested that long-term placements be divided into two categories, one containing cases where no immediate alternatives exist and a second where foster care seems permanent. The latter long-term placements could be assigned to a special unit in which workers carry higher caseloads, thereby freeing staff to focus on cases in need of intensive services.

NOTES

1. Information obtained in telephone conversation with William Rundstrom, County Counsel for Alameda County.

2. Florence Hollis, *Casework: A Psychosocial Therapy* (New York: Random House, 1965), chs. 3, 4.

3. See Theodore J. Stein, Eileen D. Gambrill, and Kermit T. Wiltse, "Dividing Case Management in Foster Family Cases," *Child Welfare* 56 (May 1977): 321–31, for our previously published analysis of this issue.

4. Arthur C. Emlen and staff, "Freeing Children for Permanent Placement" (Portland, Ore.: Regional Research Institute for Human Services, 1975).

5. See, for example, E. V. Mech, "Decision Analysis in Foster Care Practice," in H. D. Stone, ed., *Foster Care in Question* (New York: Child Welfare League of America, 1970), pp. 26–51; Eileen D. Gambrill and Kermit T. Wiltse, "Foster Care: Plans and Actualities," *Public Welfare* 32 (Spring 1974): 12–21; J. Koshel, *Deinstitutionalization—Dependent and Neglected Children* (Washington, D.C.: Urban Institute, 1973), pp. 48–51; E. T. Heck and A. R. Gruber, *Treatment Alternatives Project* (Boston: Massachusetts Department of Welfare, 1976), p. 247.

6. See W. E. Claburn, S. Magura, and W. Resnick, "Periodic Review of Foster Care: A Brief National Assessment," *Child Welfare* 55 (June 1976): 395–405.

7. Conflicting opinions as to the minimum length of time that a child should have been in placement before being designated for long-term may facilitate indiscriminate assignment of children to this outcome. See, for example, S. Jenkins, "Duration of Foster Care: Some Relevant Antecedent Variables," *Child Welfare* 46 (October 1967): 450–55; H. B. M. Murphy, "Predicting Duration of Foster Care," *Child Welfare* 47 (February 1968): 76–84.

8. See United States 1st Congress, House of Representatives, Bill no. 5893, 95 Cong., sess. (March 1977), pp. 15–16.

9. J. S. Pers, *Government as Parent: Administering Foster Care in California* (Berkeley: Institute of Governmental Studies, University of California, 1976), pp. 87–88.

10. On the framework for decision making, see note 5.

On lack of skills, see L. W. Chestang and I. Heymann, "Reducing the Length of Foster Care," *Social Work* 18 (1973): 88–93; Child Welfare League of America, *Standards for Foster Family Services* (New York: The League, 1975), p. 5; R. H. Mnookin, "Child Custody Adjudication: Judicial Function in the Face of Indeterminancy," *Law and Contemporary Problems* 39 (Summer 1975): 226–93.

11. See, for example, S. N. Katz, *When Parents Fail* (Boston: Beacon Press, 1971), p. 57; Juvenile Rights Project of the American Civil Liberties Union, *Children's Rights Report* (New York: ACLU, 1977), Vol. 1, no. 7, p. 2; Gambrill and Wiltse, op. cit.

12. A majority of children who leave care do so within the first year. See, for example, T. S. Stein and E. D. Gambrill, "Early Intervention in Foster Care," *Public Welfare* 34 (Spring 1976): 38–44; H. S. Maas and R. E. Engler, *Children in Need of Parents* (New York: Columbia University Press, 1959); D. Fanshel, "The Exit of Children from Foster Care: An Interim Research Report," *Child Welfare* 50 (February 1971): 65–81. Following three years in placement, the probability of movement out of care is unlikely. See Theodore J. Stein and Eileen D. Gambrill, "Facilitating Decision Making in Foster Care" *Social Service Review* 51, no. 3 (September 1977): 502–13; Henry Maas, "Children in Long-Term Foster Care," *Child Welfare* 48, no. 6 (June 1969): 321–33; Fanshel, op. cit., p. 80.

13. See, for example, N. Hobbs, *The Futures of Children* (San Francisco: Jossey-Bass, 1976); T. J. Scheff, ed., *The Labeling of Madness* (Englewood Cliffs, N.J.: Prentice-Hall, 1975); E. M. Lemert, *Human Deviance, Social Problems and Social Control* (Englewood Cliffs, N.J.: Prentice-Hall, 1967).

14. During the two years of the project, 10 of 26 line workers and 4 of 7 supervisors either left or were transferred out of foster placement units. D. Shapiro, *Agencies and Foster Children* (New York: Columbia University Press, 1976), p. 83, reports that children in care for up to 17 months were more likely to be discharged when there was no change in worker. Lack of information in case records regarding case objectives and the plans developed to accomplish them compounds difficulties resulting from high turnover of staff. In addition, new staff is subject to the time pressures that initially led to the banking of cases.

15. See D. J. Pascoe, *Review, Synthesis and Recommendations of Seven Foster Care Studies in California* (Sacramento: Children's Research Institute of California, 1974), p. 6.

5

IMPLICATIONS OF THE STUDY

The Alameda Project addressed a number of issues that have been highlighted as major problems in the provision of foster care services. These include a need for a decision-making framework to guide child welfare workers in making necessary choices, deficits in case planning for children in care, and a lack of services to biological parents.[1] This study demonstrated that significant numbers of children can be moved out of foster home placement when these issues are addressed. The value of this work is highlighted by the fact that this is the first study to achieve such results. Two prior investigations employing experimental designs in which the aim was to reduce the number of children in out-of-home placement reported either minimal or no success in achieving this goal. In one study a higher percentage of restorations was reported for control than for experimental units.[2] Results of the second study showed that the percentage of children restored to their homes was greater for experimental than for control groups. However, the difference was not significant.[3]

It is important to consider the procedures employed in the Alameda Project in more detail, including implications for child welfare workers, supervisors, administrators of child welfare agencies, and social work education.

IMPLICATIONS FOR CHILD WELFARE WORKERS

The results of the Alameda Project have a number of implications for child welfare workers in terms of guidelines for service delivery decisions. Major service delivery decisions are reviewed in this section, relating factors such as caseload size, worker competence, and worker attitudes to service delivery. In addition, the relationship between predictor variables in foster care and case outcome is discussed as this association bears on service delivery decisions.

Service Delivery Decisions

The central task of project workers* was to arrange for continuity in the living arrangements of children in their caseloads. This outcome could be achieved by restoring children to their biological parents, by arranging for an adoptive home or legal guardian, or through planned long-term foster placement. The final disposition of each case was based on a series of prior decisions, each of which followed from an initial case plan. Two considerations guided planning activities. First, natural parents were seen as having the right to work toward restoration of their children to their care if that was their wish. The wishes of children with respect to returning home also were considered. Objections were raised by children in less than a dozen cases. When this occurred, we asked only that youngsters agree to visit with parents, deferring final decision until these visits could be observed. Our hypothesis was that if interaction between parents and children was positive, objections to restoration would diminish. This assumption was borne out in all but two cases. Second, available data on the relationship between length of time a child is in care and case outcome show that most children who leave placement do so within their first year, and that the likelihood of leaving care is markedly reduced as time in care increases.[4] Thus, it is essential that social workers adopt an active decision-making stance in the early stages of planning a child's placement career.†

The first decision reflecting parents' desires for their children's future preceded a written case plan. In response to the question "Do you wish to have your child returned to your care?" 95 percent of all parents responded affirmatively. No attempt was made at that point to assess parental motivation for working toward this goal. Subsequent data documenting parental involvement in planning were viewed as the best evidence of intent. The second decision constituted the first step in a formalized plan. This step required workers to establish a schedule for parent-child visiting and for a method of collecting necessary assessment information. Careful observation during visiting periods allowed workers to identify any problems that needed

---

*The term "project worker" refers to staff hired specifically for the experiment, and does not include the county workers with whom cases were shared.

†Ideally, planning occurs as soon as a child enters placement. This was possible with new intake during the project. With older cases, which constituted a high percentage of the caseloads (See Table 3.1), this took place as soon as the case came into the project.

resolution before restoration could occur, and provided essential data for selecting specific programs to resolve problems identified during assessment.

Assessment provided the worker with information to substantiate that there were, or were not, sufficiently severe conditions in the parental home to threaten restoration if not alleviated before the child was returned. This point directs attention to an essential criterion guiding decision making. The focus of worker attention during assessment was on minimal standards of parenting. Each time a worker stated that a problem required resolution before a child could be restored, he or she was explicitly answering the question "What is the connection between parental behavior I see as a problem and the child's well-being?" Stated otherwise, this question asks "What would be the negative consequences to the child if the problem were not ameliorated prior to restoration?" If this connection between the child's well-being and the issue of concern could not be established, it was not considered appropriate to make restoration contingent upon resolution of the problem noted. This does not mean that clients were left with unresolved difficulties. What it does mean is that if issues were not directly related to restoration, referrals were made to community resources for assistance. (See chapter 7 for further discussion of this point.)

If no problems were identified during assessment, the immediate decision was to accelerate visiting and hasten restoration.* Establishing a schedule for parent-child contacts required decisions as to the frequency with which parents and children would meet, where visits would take place, and the duration of visits. Current visiting behavior served as the reference point for these choices. Most parent-child visits occurred once a week. Contraindications to weekly visiting derived from evidence that parent-child interaction during visits was not positive. In some situations initial visits were for very brief periods, perhaps only ten minutes, because the worker observed that parent-child interaction remained positive only for a brief period. Such visits were carefully planned to insure that a positive interchange would take place. Variations in both the duration and the locale of visits often revealed problems that were not visible in brief visits in a single locale.

Each visiting plan included worker observation of parent-child interaction during all or part of the visit. The plan included a discussion between the worker and the client immediately after the visit. The worker's observations of parent-child interaction were shared with the parents as they bore on issues of restoration.

In many instances, additional decisions can be made at this early stage

---

*An absence of identified problems refers to the absence of difficulties in any area for which the project worker would assume treatment responsibility. Many of the problems that resulted in classification of cases as multiproblem involved financial, housing, or legal assistance, for which community resources provided the major service.

of assessment. For example, plans can be made to locate new housing, obtain financial assistance, or start parents in programs in which their participation was mandated by the court. (For additional details describing such early planning and the conditions related to it, see chapter 7.) All decisions made at this point—specifically the parents' wishes regarding the future living arrangements of their child, the frequency, place, and duration of parent-child visits, and a schedule for assessment of parent-child interaction—were then formalized into a written contract signed by both the project and the county worker and by the parents. (See chapter 7.)

If problems were identified during assessment, a plan had to be made for their resolution. Whether problems were identified during early or later phases of assessment, similar decisions directed toward resolution were necessary. At the beginning of the project, the workers were not familiar with sociobehavioral treatment methods. The project supervisor offered guidance in choosing the most efficacious method for dealing with the problem at hand, and suggested relevant literature to buttress their learning. As familiarity with these methods increased, project staff relied increasingly on learning from prior experiences to make treatment decisions. In brief, as methods were identified and their application understood, treatment decisions followed upon this new understanding. When multiple difficulties in parent-child relationships were identified, decisions had to be made as to order of resolution followed by a specific plan for engaging the persons significant to each problem. (See chapter 7.) Workers learned new techniques for engaging parents in a treatment regime, for example, using role playing to increase positive verbal interaction between parent and child.

The use of collateral resources was a major area of social worker decision making. In some cases a court order required the parent to participate in a program of therapy. Except for situations in which a parent was directed to work with a specific child abuse program, court orders for therapy typically were stated in very general terms. Court directives ordered therapy with a psychologist or psychiatrist, not with the caseworker. In some instances special legal, medical, financial, or housing problems called for the use of collateral resources.

When collateral resources were involved, decisions as to frequency of contact and method of treatment were made by the collateral agent. The project worker's role was that of service coordinator. He or she had to reach agreement with the collateral resource as to the expected outcome of client participation, clarify the respective roles of worker and collateral to avoid duplication of services, agree upon time limits within which resolution was expected to occur, and arrange for an exchange of information. The decisions reached on each of these aspects were written into the client-worker contract.

Community counseling resources were used for help with problems of a personal nature, such as depression or substance abuse, only when ordered by the court or if the conditions maintaining drug or alcohol problems could not be altered by the worker. Using a residential treatment program to remove a client from the pressures of the home environment is an example. Except in instances in which the court ordered parental participation in a certain treatment program, project staff assumed direct responsibility for all treatment.

Deciding who in the case situation was to be the primary recipient of casework services often was a crucial first step. Cases drift into long-term foster care through lack of determined or consistent efforts to involve parents. Unless parents appeal directly to the court to have their children returned to their care (a highly unlikely circumstance), restoration is quite unlikely to occur. Staff in the experimental units had a much higher average number of contacts per case with biological parents, compared with staff in the control units. In the two years of the Alameda Project, experimental staff contact with natural parents remained constant, ranging from an average of 21.7 contacts in year 1 to 21.5 in the second year. Control worker contacts also remained constant, averaging 13.5 during the first year and 13.6 during the second. This is remarkably similar to the figures reported by Mary Ann Jones, Renee Neuman, and Ann Shyne—an average of 20.1 personal contacts for experimental staff and 12.2 for control workers.[5] Other data bearing upon frequency of contacts with parents are presented in terms of number per month, and include contacts with agencies, supervisory conferences, letter writing, and reports. For example, Deborah Shapiro reports caseworker activity on behalf of parents as averaging "one action per month directed to or concerning clients."[6]

Control staff devoted far more attention to foster parents than did staff in the experimental units. This distinct difference in focus is shown by the fact that control staff had an average of 16.64 contacts per year with foster parents, compared with 10.56 for experimental staff. It should be clear that devoting primary service attention to foster rather than to natural parents reflects a pattern of case planning that is at odds with the objectives of foster home placement—namely, that it be of short duration and have the aim of reuniting children with their families. Sixty percent of all experimental worker contacts were on behalf of children who ultimately were restored to their parents. An almost equal percentage of control contacts (57 percent) were made in relation to children categorized as long-term placements. This raises an interesting question of the relative contribution to outcome of frequency vs. content of contact. This issue is discussed in detail later.

Indicators of Systematic Case Planning

Regularly gathered information describing case activity reflects the presence or absence of systematic case planning in several ways. It is first apparent in the types of decisions made. For example, if purposeful planning is taking place, it is unlikely that the majority of children will be designated for long-term care, regardless of length of time in care, as was the case in the control unit. If planning were taking place, one would expect case outcomes to follow a pattern. To illustrate, let us consider the data on outcome in relation to the length of time a child was in care (see Tables 4.22 and 4.23). Past research indicates that the probability of a child leaving care is greatest in the first year and that the likelihood of such movement decreases as time in placement increases. After three years, movement out of placement is substantially reduced. On the basis of this information, one could predict the outcome pattern that in fact occurred for experimental unit children: the greatest percentage of children restored or to be restored to their parents were those in care less than one year (60 percent). Percentage reductions occurred in subsequent years to a low of 38 percent by the time a child had been in out-of-home placement for three years. The percentage of experimental unit youngsters leaving placement decreased from a high of 82 percent for those in care less than three years to a low of 55 percent for those in care more than three years.

The difference between units in planning activities also is apparent from an examination of the purpose of contacts with natural parents. Case planning activities included arranging for parent-child visits, gathering data describing parent-child interaction, sharing such information with clients, and discussing issues related to case progress. As might be expected, as cases move closer to the point of restoration, issues such as finances and housing become critical concerns for discussion and planning. For experimental workers the extent of these activities can be seen in the fact that 43 percent of all contacts were for "supervisory" purposes, in contrast with 16 percent in the control unit. This category included monitoring of parent-child interaction and discussion of case progress. Routine case management included such tasks as helping with finances and housing. These tasks account for twice the percentage of contacts made by experimental staff in comparison with control staff (24 percent and 12 percent, respectively). It is of interest to note that arranging for parental visits with children represented 37 percent of control worker contacts and only 4 percent of those made by experimental staff. Such arrangements were formalized in contracts for experimental families, thus reducing or eliminating the necessity to discuss the topic.

Factors Related to Service Delivery Decisions

Three salient factors bearing on service delivery in foster care are caseload size, worker competence, and worker attitudes.

Caseload Size

There is abundant evidence that in the natural parent-foster parent-child triad, natural parents receive the least amount of attention from caseworkers.[7] One of the most frequently cited reasons offered to account for service deficits to natural parents is caseload size and resultant time constraints.[8] It is argued that given reduced caseloads, the provision of intensive services to natural parents would be possible.[9] Although we do not suggest that no relationship exists between caseload size and time available for service delivery, it should be clear that caseload size alone is not a significant determinant in decisions concerning who will receive services. There is no a priori reason why any given number of cases should dictate that services be directed to one client group rather than to another.

Advocates for reduced caseloads are unable to specify an optimal size. For example, in four California counties (Riverside, Alameda, San Francisco, Los Angeles) the number of cases carried by workers responsible for children under court jurisdiction range from a low of 33 (San Francisco) cases to a high of 68 (Riverside), with workers in the two remaining counties responsible for between 38 (Los Angeles) and 49 cases (Alameda).[10] In all probability, workers in the county with the highest number of cases would settle for a caseload like that of their colleagues in counties with the median size caseloads—who, in all likelihood, would be satisfied with the number carried by staff in the county with the lowest number of cases.

It is our position that arguments to reduce caseload size are spurious because type of activity, not size per se, is the crucial dimension.[11] To illustrate this, let us consider the caseloads carried by experimental and control staff in this project. Experimental workers carried a total of 20 families, with a maximum of 35 children. Control staff were responsible for 49 children. All of the cases of project workers were active, that is, in various stages of decision making. Once a case was referred for adoption or guardianship, or designated long-term care, it was closed to the project so as to make room for a new case. This was possible because the project worker could return the case to the county staff person with whom the case had been shared, or it was moved to the adoption section. Control staff had to continue carrying guardianship and long-term care cases. While data are not available, it seems reasonable to suggest that long-term care and guardianship cases require less service than do those in various stages of decision making. Therefore, caseload size alone cannot be cited as the significant determinant of the intensity of services offered to natural parents.

Furthermore, Shapiro has shown that workers with the smallest and the largest caseloads were more apt to move children out of care than were those with medium caseloads.[12] We would agree with her statement that "High caseloads do not always lead to slow decision making, as is commonly supposed. The size of the caseload may mean a different approach to its management, not necessarily diminished efficiency."[13] It is reasonable to conclude that decisions as to who will receive services involve issues other than the number of cases carried. If workers continue to argue for reduced caseloads, suggesting that this alone will resolve problems of deficient service delivery, they may create a situation not unlike that prevailing in the 1960s, when professionals argued that simply increasing services, with no concern for the types of services or evidence regarding their effectiveness, would reduce the size of welfare rolls.[14]

It is suggested in the literature that frequency of contact, by itself, contributes to the movement of children out of foster home placement.[15] The design of the Alameda Project precluded factoring out the relative contributions of frequency from specific methods employed. It is likely that there are some families for whom frequent contact alone will be sufficient to engage parents in planning. The major purpose of this discussion is to alert the reader to the limits inherent in directing too much attention to hypothesized relationship between caseload size and frequency of contact as explanatory of case outcome.

Worker Competence

As Eileen Gambrill and Kermit Wiltse suggest, "Contact, per se, without meaningful skills being available must have an upper limit of utility far below contact accompanied by relevant skills."[16] In a similar vein, Leon Chestang and Irmgard Heymann note that "It is crucial to develop approaches to the child's natural parents" and that a failure to do so "perpetuates extended foster care."[17] Edmund Mech states that "Practice theory is so limited, inconsistent and fragmented that it provides little in the way of guidelines for the practitioner in his efforts to help a child."[18] Bernece Simon echoes this opinion. In her review of casework theory, she states: "In general, these approaches [to casework treatment] do not provide a complete statement of treatment methodology. Insofar as this is true, it might be said that there is only rudimentary treatment theory in social casework."[19] The possibility that skill deficits are a crucial variable in decisions as to who will receive services cannot be overlooked. Gambrill and Wiltse, for example, report that workers participating in their study were "unclear as to what changes had to be brought about in order to facilitate restoration."[20] The types of skills considered necessary to resolve problems will vary according to the definition of the problem and to the caseworker's favored intervention model.

Let us consider in more detail the issue of caseworker skills. Data are presented in Table 5.1 comparing the use of the Hollis classification system by Alameda Project staff (see Table 4.9) with seven studies, four of which were reviewed by Edward Mullen, that used this system for describing

TABLE 5.1

Comparison of Major Types of Caseworker Verbal Behavior

| | Alameda Project | | Sherman | | | |
	Exp.	Cont.	1973 Study	1974 Study	Stein	Mullen
Exploration	27%	47%	23%	24%	37%	36–50%
Structuring	24	24	12	11	—	—
Support	11	15	28	26	22	2–8
Directive	6	4	14	21	13	1–5
Reflective	4	4	11	4	13	31–45
Practical help	4	4	11	11	8	—
Behavioral	25	3	—	—	—	—
Other*	—	—	1	3	7	7

*All verbal behavior not fitting into any of the defined categories.
Source: Compiled by author.

casework methods.[21] An additional investigation used a categorizing system that differs somewhat from those shown in Table 5.1, thus preventing direct comparison.[22] Exploration was the form of verbal behavior most commonly used by experimental and control workers in the Alameda Project (experimental unit, 27 percent; control 47 percent). However, for experimental staff, use of this technique differed only slightly from the use of structuring (24 percent) and behavioral methods (25 percent). Exploration also was found to be the most commonly used method in conducting interviews in a public foster care agency and in the studies reviewed by Mullen in which data were gathered in psychiatric settings.[23] It ranked second in use in two studies reported by Edmund Sherman et al., which were conducted in public foster care agencies.[24] Mary Ann Jones et al. gathered data in both public and voluntary child welfare agencies and found use of the comparable category "information seeking" predominant for a few interviews in every case. However, it ranked third in total use, following "advice, guidance, and direction" and "emotional support, reassurance."[25] The high use of exploratory techniques is somewhat surprising. This form of verbal behavior is aimed at information gathering; and, while recognizing the importance of information gathering at various stages of casework activity, heavy reliance upon such an approach would be less likely to move cases toward goal attainment than would its use together with directive, practical, or behavioral methods.

Sherman suggests that one possible reason for the extensive use of this method is that in public agencies interviews are infrequent, requiring the worker to bring himself or herself up to date about changes in family circumstances, and that this updating may account for the high percentages of this type of worker activity.[26] The extensive use of questioning might indicate that workers were seeking to identify important areas for discussion or that there was a lack of planning of the content to be discussed during an interview.[27] Suggestive of such reasons was the median number of seven changes in the topic of conversation per 30-minute period during interviews between clients and carrying workers in a public foster care agency.[28]

The use of structuring techniques by workers in both our experimental and control units was the same (24 percent). This category includes exchanges of information in which the worker describes or clarifies issues related to court and/or agency functioning. Its high rate of use may be explained by the large number of court-dependent children (over 95 percent) in project cases. In the Sherman studies, as well as in Theodore Stein's dissertation, support techniques were used at an almost equal rate (Sherman 26 percent and 28 percent, Stein 22 percent). The percentage of interviews reported by Sherman in which structuring methods were used (11 percent and 12 percent) is almost equal to the percentage of reported use of support techniques by project workers (experimental, 11 percent; control, 15 percent). Neither Stein nor Mullen reports information in this category, and there is no comparable classification in the Jones investigation.

As suggested above, we would have expected that directive, practical, and behavioral techniques would be the methods most likely to move a case toward a goal attainment. Behavioral methods were used by project experimental unit workers 25 percent of the time. Sherman reports an almost equal percentage of directive techniques for workers in his 1974 study (21 percent). This method was employed less frequently in his 1973 study, accounting for only 14 percent of interview content. Stein reports a similar figure of 13 percent. Giving "advice, guidance, and direction" was the most predominant method reported by Jones et al. "Practical help," which was rarely used by workers in either unit in our project (4 percent each), was reported for 11 percent of the interviews from both of Sherman's studies and in 8 percent of the interviews analyzed by Stein. No data were reported in this category by Mullen. Jones et al. did not use any directly comparable category. Studies reviewed by Mullen were the only ones in which a high percentage of "reflective or analytic" methods were used (31 to 45 percent of all interview content). Since these data were gathered in psychiatric settings, this finding should not come as a surprise.

The 1974 Sherman study and the work by Jones et al. were both concerned with moving children out of foster care. As such, these two studies are of the greatest interest for our purposes. Sherman et al. reported that their control unit workers* had a higher rate of return of children than did their special worker group, while Jones et al. report a nonsignificant difference in children returned to their homes in favor of their experimental units.[29]

---

* Interview content data reported in Table 5.1 are only for the special worker segment. No data were reported for control workers.

The data discussed above suggest skill deficits as partial explanation of why workers elect to offer services to foster rather than to biological parents. There is no basis for expecting that use of exploration or questioning with the latter client group, which accounts for almost 50 percent of control worker interview content, would move a case toward problem resolution. Further support for directing attention to skill deficits is found in the difference between the experimental and control units in resolved and unresolved problems at the project's conclusion. The percentage of problems that control staff reported as resolved or not was no better than chance, with 49 percent in the former category and 51 percent in the latter. In contrast, 75 percent of all problems were reported as resolved by experimental workers.

Worker Attitudes

One possible basis for deciding to focus service attention on foster parents is that biological parents are viewed as having severe problems. This assumption is implicit in the suggestion that intensive services are required, and is supported by the fact that parents are alleged to have done something wrong in order for the court to assume jurisdiction over their children. Thus, work with natural parents may be seen as more time-consuming than work with foster parents.

The possibility that service delivery to biological parents may be limited by perceived severity of problems is one of the unfortunate outcomes of what Margaret Rosenheim and others refer to as the "pathological" view that prevails in most approaches to treatment.[30] Shirley Jenkins and Elaine Norman point out that this approach "de-emphasizes strengths and highlights weaknesses," creating an antitherapeutic climate by means of the stigma that such a view assigns to clients.[31] Addressing the same issue, Arthur Emlen noted that conditions diagnosed as "irremediable" often were found to be in error, and that parents responded to proper evaluation and treatment.[32] He found that the "general climate of attitudes in the particular county where the worker practices, strongly determined the worker's permanent planning decisions."[33] Concern that one lacks skills may be heightened by the prevailing pathological orientation toward client problems. The result of this is summed up by Ronaele Whittington, Katarina Digman, and John Digman. They note that parents most in need of help are those least likely to receive it.[34]

Prediction and Decision Making

Ideally, decision making should be guided by knowledge of predictable outcomes. For example, each time a child is removed from the home of its biological parents, an explicit or implicit decision is being made that the youngster will be better off in foster placement. This issue of prediction has concerned investigators since the late 1950s. During this time many efforts have been made to identify variables that could be used to predict the probabilities of differential outcomes for children in foster home care. The repeated finding that the longer a child is in placement, the greater the probability that he will grow to maturity in out-of-home care has encouraged attempts to identify variables that could be used to make such predictions at an early point in a child's placement career.[35] Research efforts for the most part have produced equivocal results. Some studies suggest that demographic characteristics of the child, such as age, sex, and ethnicity, can be employed to identify children who drift into long-term care, whereas others have not found this.[36] The initial reason for placement of a child also has been viewed relative to outcome, once again producing equivocal results. For example, it has been suggested that the children of abusive and neglectful parents are less likely than children placed for other reasons to have permanent plans made for their futures, whereas others contend that such children are underrepresented in long-term care cases.[37] A number of studies have indicated that children who exhibit behavior and/or emotional problems, or whose parents have emotional problems, are the most likely candidates for long-term care.[38] Other investigators have concluded that these latter presenting problems do not relate to this outcome.[39] Jones et al., using a multiple-regression analysis, correlated 16 independent variables with case outcome.* This analysis yielded a cumulative correlation ratio indicating the variance accounted for by all 16 items. In combination, these variables explained only 26 percent of the variation in case outcome.[40]

In his final report of a five-year longitudinal study in New York, David Fanshel examined an array of independent variables in an effort to identify those associated with outcome. The variables studied included the child's age, birth status (in or out of wedlock), ethnicity, reason for placement, parental visiting, casework contact rate, and worker's evaluation of the mother. The results, insofar as their predictive value was concerned, were disappointing. Multiple correlations varied from a low of .42 to a high of .55. The total variation explained when these variables were considered in combination ranged from a low of 18 percent at the end of the child's first and fourth years in care to a high of 31 percent at the end of the youngster's third year in placement. The correlation for parental visiting, which Fanshel describes as having the strongest relationship to discharge status of the child, at the end of the youngster's first and third years in care yielded a correlation

---

*The variables considered in this analysis fell into three major categories: "Background," which included the number of children in the family, mother's age, and ethnicity; "Problem Situation," which included variables describing the reason for placement, plus the mother's functioning on a number of dimensions; and "Service," which included the number of interviews, number of different services provided, and predominant worker role.

of only .32 (Time 1) and .39 (Time 3), accounting for 10 and 15 percent of the variance (times 1 and 3, respectively).[41]

Our data essentially confirm the findings from previous research. Few variables have much predictive utility. Difficulty in identifying predictor variables is not unique to social welfare research, but reflects a more general state of affairs in social science knowledge. Our limited ability to make more accurate predictions is understandable, in view of the myriad factors that may be related to a given outcome. Studies conducted in the natural environment cannot exercise control over all the variables, nor does any study gather data on every issue that might be relevant. Also, we may have been looking in the wrong places. There is no a priori reason to expect age, sex, family composition, or race to be predictive of case outcome. It might be more reasonable to conclude that the reason for placement would be of greater value in this regard, particularly immediately after a child's entry into foster care. This expectation would diminish over time, given the possibility that some problems may be resolved with the passage of time. In addition, some parents may have received outside assistance with certain problems. One reason related to the absence of any relationship between reason for placement and outcome may be the lack of uniformity in defining key terms, such as neglect and mental illness. These terms are ill-defined, and undoubtedly encompass a wide array of dissimilar behaviors. Perhaps, as Jenkins and Norman suggest, many problems resulting in foster placement are of a crisis nature. Since evidence indicates that such difficulties are likely to resolve themselves, or to decrease in severity with the passage of time, the absence of a relationship is understandable.[42]

While predictability is limited, it is important to consider the extent to which known relationships are ignored by workers. The most obvious example of this is the association between length of time in care and outcome. The implications of this relationship for decision making about service delivery are clear. Services must be provided as early as possible in the child's first year in placement, and planning for services should begin prior to the child's entry into care. The impact of service delivery efforts can be expected to diminish over time. Shapiro highlights this issue by noting that "The opportunity to exploit high quality [service] is optimal in the first year."[43] The failure of workers to heed this information is evident in the fact that a large percentage of control unit youngsters in the Alameda Project in placement one year or less already were designated as long-term care cases.

Whether or not parents are willing to sign a written agreement does have utility for predicting the probabilities of their continued involvement in case planning. The use of written agreements at the earliest stages of placement would facilitate planning at the time when it is most important. Awareness of this probability of continued parental involvement would aid workers in making decisions as to where their services would have the greatest impact.

In addition to their predictive value, contracts provide a framework within which case plans are carried out. Parental objectives (such as having the child returned to their care), visiting, and assessment schedules were put in writing. Plans developed to resolve problems and each step to accomplish these plans were documented and attached to the contracts. Alternative sources of action, such as referring a case for adoption should parents not follow through with plans, were noted, as were time limits within which each part of a plan was to be accomplished. Contracts embody decisions made, and guide additional decision-making tasks by informing workers of those temporal points when alternatives must be confronted. A change of plan may be to seek an alternative approach to solving the problem if there is evidence the current methods are not working, or perhaps only to modify the existing plan to accord with experience. As previously noted, parents were afforded a second and even a third opportunity to work toward their goals if they chose. In these instances, contracts were renegotiated to clarify new time limits. From a case management perspective, project workers remained clearly focused on their responsibility to achieve case movement. Since most contracts were written to cover a period of 90 days, and were initially negotiated within 45 days after the case came into the project, alternatives could be pursued well before the end of the child's first year in placement.

Contracts serve two additional functions. Because of the specificity with which they state client objectives and document progress toward objectives, they can facilitate the transfer of a case to a new worker. The high turnover of public welfare personnel as well as the poor quality of case records have been noted in the literature, and may be viewed as contributing to the problems of extended care.[44] In addition, in the same way that contracts provide a framework for case planning, they are of great assistance to supervisors who must monitor the progress of each child in care. Of those clients who signed contracts, the response, while hesitant at first, was overwhelmingly positive. Clients often remarked that the content of the contracts was the first specific information they had received on precisely what had to be done in order to work toward having their child returned. And having a copy of the contract at home provided a ready reference point for regular checks on what was expected of them on a daily or weekly basis. The specificity and the minimum conditions set forth for restoration were very positively received by court personnel, particularly where termination of parental rights was subsequently pursued.

The value of contracts for case planning, decision making, and prediction derives primarily from the specificity with which they are written. If this value is to be realized, precise guidelines for writing contracts must be employed (see chapter 8). Likewise, identifying predictive relationships in order to forecast differential outcomes for children in care requires uniform and specific definitions of key terms. The behavioral referents of a term such as "neglect" are not contained in the term itself. The basis for an allegation of neglect may differ widely among different jurisdictions. When the meaning is spelled out, as is sometimes the case in a court report, there is no greater agreement as to consequences of neglect. An additional example is supplied by Sherman, who concluded that the global concept of a mother's emotional adjustment was not significantly related to implementation of a case plan; but the somewhat more specific behaviors of drug use, excessive drinking, and sexual promiscuity were significantly related to final disposition.[45] A similar association between drug use and outcomes has been reported by Fanshel.[46] Unless concepts can be uniformly defined and these definitions consistently employed, there is little reason to expect the search for predictive variables to be any more fruitful in the future than it has been in the past.

Summary of Implications for Social Work Staff

In this chapter we have outlined the service delivery decision-making processes pursued by experimental staff. The positive effects of their use for children in care were documented by the results of the Alameda Project. In contrast, an absence of systematic case planning was found in the control units. This was highlighted by the numbers of children classified as in long-term care while still in their first year of placement. The fact that children were classified as being in long-term care during the earliest stages of their placement careers is particularly troublesome, since this is the period during which intensive services are likely to have maximum effect in moving children out of placement. We believe that this early classification allows workers to divert attention from providing timely services to biological parents.

Several factors may be related to this finding. First, workers may not be aware of the relationship between length of time in care and case outcome, and thus not recognize the consequences of allowing cases to drift at this early stage of foster care. Second, decision making may be guided largely by personal values and attitudes toward natural parents. Third, workers tend to bank cases for purposes of case management.[47] By classifying a certain percentage of cases as long-term care, workers can direct their attention to cases where they think their services will have the greatest impact. However, designating new intake cases as long-term care is likely to result in a self-fulfilling prophecy.*

Our data support previous findings that casework staff direct services to foster parents and children rather than to biological parents. It is important

---

*The implications of this practice were considered in detail in the discussion following the report of one-year followup data (chapter 4).

to stress, however, that while the bulk of services are offered to the foster parents and foster children, natural parents are not ignored. Therefore, we must ask why contacts with natural parents do not result in plans being made for greater numbers of children. We think that this is primarily the result of not knowing how to make a case plan and follow through with it. Our data strongly suggest that this outcome results from deficiencies in assessment and problem solving. Strong support for this statement is the extensive and repetitive use of "exploratory" techniques to conduct interviews with natural parents.

The pathological view inherent in most approaches to treatment may lead workers to conclude that problems are more severe than is actually the case. This in turn leads a worker to conclude that he or she does not possess requisite skills for dealing with the issues at hand. A "normalizing" view that seeks to identify and build on client strengths would lead staff to very different definitions of problems, and consequent reevaluations of their ability to act as change agents. If this occurred, patterns of service delivery and case planning, and subsequent results for children in care, would be radically different. The truth of this statement is an empirical question, and one deserving of exploration.

Thus far we have focused exclusively on the individual caseworker. Child welfare personnel are part of large bureaucratic organizations, and many of the cases they manage fall under court jurisdiction. They do not operate in isolation from the systems of which they are a part. Therefore, suggested solutions to problems must take into account the actions of agency administrators, courts, and the immediate supervisors of child welfare units.

IMPLICATIONS FOR SUPERVISORS

Mechanisms must exist for reviewing cases and monitoring their progress toward objectives. Three approaches to case review are in current use: review at the court, at the agency, and at the supervisory levels.[48] In a recent survey of 48 states, the District of Columbia, and Puerto Rico, it was found that court and administrative review substitute for each other.[49] Either full court or agency review was required in 26 jurisdictions, whereas in 8 only limited court or supervisory review was required.* In no state were both full court and agency reviews required. Seventeen states have no review requirements. The review procedures implemented tend to be new. Seventy-

---

*The term "limited" refers to states that permit county-by-county variations in their reporting requirements. In full review, requirements are consistent throughout the state in accordance with statute.

five percent of the court reviews, 79 percent of the agency reviews, and 70 percent of the supervisory reviews were established after 1970. Review by the court generally is mandated by statute and requires that agencies submit periodic reports justifying the status of children in care. Agency review is an administrative process in which persons within a state system regularly review the cases of children in care. Supervisory review also is an internal procedure.

Review must begin at the supervisory level. This is not to suggest that additional review by administrators and the court should not take place. In fact, additional checkpoints are critical ways of furthering movement toward goals. However, careful monitoring of cases is an "inescapable function" of supervisors.[50] Exercise of this function is essential if the practice of discretionary decision making by individual workers is to be held in check. It also is necessary to assure that case plans are made and implemented for each child in care.

There are several reasons for taking the position that review must begin at the supervisory level. First, persons in this position provide a direct link between line staff and administration.[51] They bear major responsibility for interpreting agency objectives to workers, and for insisting that staff do whatever is necessary to attain these objectives. It is the supervisor who is in close contact with line workers, and hence can monitor the quality of their work. It is the supervisor who is in the best position to ascertain that the data gathered are accurate and describe each facet of the agency's service to higher-level administration.

Manageability is yet another reason for suggesting that review begin with supervisors. The concern here is a dual one: First, the further up in the bureaucratic hierarchy that this process occurs, the more likely cases are to get lost in the review process. Second, direct communication between administrators and line workers, particularly in large bureaucracies, is at best tenuous, thus causing unnecessary delays and aggravating, rather than remedying, the problem of deficits in early planning.

The high turnover of public welfare workers is an additional reason for supervisory review. Ideally, supervisors can bridge the gap between old and new staff, thereby providing continuity in case planning. This bridging is a critically important function, especially since cases are not reassigned until after the departure of the worker who was carrying the case. We say "ideally" because it is not clear that turnover of supervisory personnel is any less frequent than that of line staff. There is scant information on this issue. Shapiro reports that only 13 percent of the public agency workers in her study had the same supervisor for two years or more, the remaining 87 percent having experienced at least one change.[52] Our own data support her findings. Over the two years of the project, four out of seven supervisors (57 percent) either left or were transferred within the department.

No matter how effective available procedures for line staff may be, high-quality casework services will be offered on a regular basis only when supervisors monitor the quality of services provided and offer incentives to workers to maintain high quality. Given that any supervisor is responsible for reviewing a large number of cases, a pertinent question is how he or she is to maintain a review process that achieves continuity of care for children. How often should cases be reviewed, and what data are most pertinent to this process? Increased burdens have been placed upon child welfare supervisors by moratoriums on hiring new staff and by the increased use of B.A.-level workers in positions previously held by graduate social workers. Problems created by these conditions are compounded by a trend toward moving eligibility workers with no training for, or experience in, child welfare into positions once held by trained staff. In addition, child welfare workers are barraged by diverse casework practice methods, held by their agencies to greater accountability for effectiveness of methods chosen, and admonished by the literature to find alternatives to home placement. In this welter of confusing demands, the supervisor must somehow help workers of various persuasions and levels of preparation find a way to deliver services effectively.

Case Review Management

If children are not to become lost in the shuffle with regard to continuity of care, all cases must be reviewed periodically by supervisors. As stated above, the time involved in this task is a critical issue that must be considered in the framework of the many demands on supervisor time. The time involved in supervisory review can be shortened considerably by asking line workers to provide data critical to the review process, data that are at the same time seminal to their own case management processes. Thus, it is essential that workers be asked to maintain records pertinent to their work with clients as well as to supervisory review. Case data gathered by line workers will help supervisors keep track of each child in their unit, as well as monitor the quality and timeliness of services provided.

Keeping Track of All Children

At monthly intervals each worker should indicate the number of children he or she has in each outcome category: restoration, long-term care, headed for termination, guardianship, or no plan. Periodic review of this information enables the supervisor to insure that there is a plan for each child in placement. Except for cases newly transferred from intake, in which some delay is understandable, regular monitoring should detect those cases where plans are not being made promptly. Simply by examining the relative number of cases each worker has in each outcome category, supervisors can balance caseloads. Restoration cases, for example, usually require much more work than do other types, such as children in stable long-term foster homes.*

Reviewing the Quality of Casework Services

A breakdown by case plan provides no information on either the appropriateness of the plan chosen for each child; neither does it reveal anything of the quality or timeliness of service provision. In order to establish that high-quality services are being provided in a timely manner, case records must contain certain essential information on each child. Information of critical importance includes the following:

Time of entry into care
Plan for the child, and estimated date of accomplishment
Changes required to achieve the plan, and anticipated achievement date for each
Sources of critical assessment information, such as parental self-report, observation of parent-child interaction
Precise objectives in each area
Clear description of an intervention plan in relation to each objective and intended outcome, including identification of persons or resources that will help the client to achieve each intended change
A clear means of evaluating progress in each area of intended change
A description of how services are to be coordinated, when ancillary services are to be relied upon
Results achieved in each area to date.

If it is not possible to review all cases each month, a specified number of cases from each outcome category can be randomly selected for detailed review. Such a process is already in effect in some community mental health centers.[53]

A second source of information is case management check lists. Here a series of items listed for each outcome category serve as a guide for the worker in completing different types of plans. Workers are required to check the status of each case on each item. Whether responses are affirmative or negative can assist in the supervisory review process. For example, in reviewing cases to be referred for adoption, important questions include: Has the adoption unit accepted the case? If so, has it been referred to County Counsel? Has a court date been set? The response to any item directs

---

*We recognize that there may be barriers to caseload balancing. For instance, case assignment by geographic locale may prevent the most efficient balancing, but it may be necessary to minimize travel costs.

attention to additional data needed. For example, an affirmative response to the first question would lead to inquiries regarding progress in preparing documents for court, and to asking the worker if he or she is prepared to offer testimony. Negative responses may suggest a need for immediate follow-up.

Cases awaiting court dates should be reviewed regularly to determine if a date has been assigned. For cases bogged down in some state of the adoption process, the ideal frequency of follow-up depends upon the reason for lack of progress. Our practice during the project was to check on the progress of these cases at least once each week. Sometimes a phone call was sufficient to obtain the needed information or to remind the adoption worker to attend to a certain matter in order to move the case along. In instances of prolonged delay for no clearly established reason, group meetings that included foster care and adoption staff as well as County Counsel were called in order to detect the specific obstacle.

New cases need constant attention. The project used written contracts to facilitate supervisory review as well as to help both worker and client review progress. If a written and signed contract did not emerge within two weeks of a worker's receiving a case, the supervisor determined the reason for delay. For example, if parents could not be located, what efforts had been made to find them? Were these attempts sufficient? If parents would not make themselves available to the worker, was it time to obtain a subpoena ordering them to appear in court to explain the refusal or reluctance to participate in planning?

Since the written contracts spelled out those worker and client tasks to be completed and the time limits for completion, these documents contained the most pertinent review items. Each step necessary to attain a case goal was viewed as an item on a check list. Case management check lists developed for each outcome category facilitated both case management and supervisory review.[54] The questions posed are intended to give the supervisor a way to determine the client's progress in each area. Use of this check list supplied the content of supervisory sessions, facilitating an immediate focus on areas where progress was slow and alternative approaches might need to be found. The frequency of review during the project was a function of the progress being made in each case. When cases were new, they were reviewed each week, or more frequently if the worker requested. Once it was established that progress was being made at a reasonable pace, regular review occurred every other week.

Summary

Supervisors provide a direct link between line staff and administration. They are thus in a position to monitor the quality of casework methods employed by workers and to make certain that the objective of continuity of care is aggressively pursued. Only if the quality of services is monitored and incentives for appropriate staff behavior are arranged, is it likely that high-quality casework services will ensue. The importance of tracking all children in care was emphasized to make sure that none are "lost in the shuffle." Detailed review of a randomly selected number of cases from each worker's caseload each month was suggested to insure that each worker's perfor-mance level was maintained after it was no longer necessary or possible to review every case. Check lists for each outcome category, identifying the steps in systematic case management, were recommended both as a supervi-sory tool for reviewing service quality and as a means to help workers focus their attention on the critical aspects of each case.

IMPLICATIONS FOR ADMINISTRATION

In the first part of this chapter we described the case management procedures and identified control staff deficits in case management. The overriding problem identified with reference to case management by control workers was a failure to engage in systematic case planning, with a consequent delay in decision making that resulted in children languishing in out-of-home placement. In the following pages, we discuss suggestions that might help administrators of social service agencies to improve case manage-ment. These suggestions are directed to goal setting, worker training, and the use of incentives to increase the probability that staff will direct their efforts to attaining agency objectives. In addition, we will discuss data collection and ways to increase staff utilization of data, first to define goals and then to measure their attainment.

Goal Setting

Specifying the objectives of foster care services is an administrative responsibility. A number of investigators have pointed to the failure of administration to fulfill this task.[55] The absence of goals is viewed by the federal government as the "major defect" of the foster care system.[56] It is suggested that "until agencies assume responsibility for establishing objec-tives, the current situation [lack of planning] will remain as it is."[57]

Resolution of the most critical problems highlighted by this study begins with a clear description of agency objectives. The process of selecting goals is not a difficult one. It is informed by the rationale for providing substitute care services. There is consensus that such services should provide stability and continuity of care for children by obtaining the most appropri-ate permanent home situation for each child. (A central purpose of the proposed *Foster Care Adoption and Reform Act of 1977* is to "establish the fundamental right of each child to a suitable permanent home."[58] If this legislation is passed by Congress, the issue of agency administrators establishing goals will become moot. This will not, of course, absolve administrators of their responsibility to inform staff of this objective and to provide mechanisms for its attainment.) This is accomplished by restoring children to their biological parents, or by arranging for an adoptive home or legal guardian, or establishing a permanent long-term foster care arrangement. The frequency with which this objective is cited in the literature is equal only to the frequency with which failure to attain it is noted.

Goals are of little value unless stated in terms specific enough to inform the process for attaining them. Establishing clear goals, however, does not resolve problems. While this step is essential, it is only a first step. Decisions must be made as to the type of staff training needed, plans developed for supportive services and resources, and incentives designed that reinforce goal-directed worker behavior.[59] Finally, systems must be established for monitoring worker decision making.

Worker Training

We suggested that workers often lack needed problem-solving skills. This has been noted by other investigators, as has the absence of in-service training programs for social work staff.[60] If they lack effective problem-solving skills, workers cannot be expected to attain agency goals without training. The discussion of training needs is complicated by a lack of agreement on the central role of public child welfare workers.[61] Some see it as primarily administrative,[62] with treatment offered by other professionals, especially psychologists and psychiatrists. Some conceive of it as a consultative role, with the service objective being to "empower" parents to seek their own services.[63] (Nicholas Hobbs suggests that workers "empower" parents to become "advocates" for their own children if they actively involve parents in case planning and inform them of their rights and those of their children.[64]) Others see it in inclusive terms—that is, child welfare staff should provide whatever direct treatment is needed.[65] There is, however, agreement on two issues: first, that the job setting greatly affects (some say determines) the role accepted; and, second, that providing indirect services is common to all child welfare settings.[66] Tasks involved in providing indirect services include making referrals and consulting with other community resources, as well as coordinating the delivery of services offered by others.

Training in Coordination of Services

Services must be coordinated to insure that all efforts on behalf of clients contribute to goal attainment and that duplication is avoided. There are frequent references in the literature to the failure of caseworkers to act as service coordinators.[67] While it seems clear that training for service coordination is required, models that serve to guide this process are absent. When the Alameda Project first began, we did not anticipate the type and extent of problems we ultimately confronted in coordinating services. One difficulty we encountered frequently was the lack of clarity on the part of a collateral resource as to the exact outcome to be expected from its involvement with a client. For example, it was not uncommon for a court to order that a client "participate in a program of therapy" as a condition for the return of a child. However, precisely what was to be different as a result of participation was not defined. Was the child to be restored if the parent simply attended therapy sessions regularly? Or was the resource to report that the client's personality had changed in ways that rendered him or her able to parent the child? Or was the resource to document that specific changes in parental behavior had occurred, such as increased use of praise and decreased reliance on physical punishment?

A second problem was the duplication of services. In one case, for example, a father was receiving counseling from an eligibility service worker, a public health nurse, and the project worker.

Exchanging information required for court reports was a third concern. Not infrequently, collateral resources refused to provide information that was needed to make recommendations to the court. We recognize the need to respect a client's confidentiality. However, refusing to share information necessary to make recommendations regarding a parent and child can hardly be viewed as being in the client's best interest. It is generally agreed that social agencies have a responsibility to share, when appropriate, information to facilitate provision of client services.[68] Lacking information from collateral resources, the court often would not accept a worker's recommendation that a child be returned to its parents.

We found the following steps helpful in resolving these difficulties. First, using his or her description of the problems to be resolved prior to restoration, the worker was able to write fully specified objectives, stating what must be different following therapy. As noted previously, a collateral resource was used only when the client was ordered by the court to engage in a program of therapy. In selecting among collateral resources, the worker's first task was to ascertain whether a particular resource could bring about the specified change. This was not difficult when the intervention procedure used by a collateral resource for a particular problem was matched against evidence of effectiveness documented in the empirical literature. The project worker made certain the counselor was willing to work toward the objective specified and within a time limit. Next, the resource must agree to share information, in writing, on a regular schedule. We were able to develop a "referral list" of persons with skills in certain areas and a willingness to work within the framework established by the project. Whether or not the resource person worked with the client on problems other than those related to restoring a child was a matter between the client and resource worker. Should this occur, we made certain it did not take precedence over work on the problem for which a referral was made, thereby delaying resolution of the problem that prevented restoration. In all cases clients were asked to sign consent forms covering exchanges of information between project workers and collateral resources.

If, despite the above constraints, it became evident the counselor was duplicating the project worker's efforts, a meeting of all persons involved in a case was set up. The purpose was to clarify any misunderstanding regarding the respective roles of each person involved and to reaffirm the agreement that the collateral resource counselor would not involve himself or herself in client problem areas other than those specified in the referral. The project worker assumed responsibility for calling and chairing subsequent meetings, and for assembling and summarizing all information supplied by collateral resources.

These procedures resolved a great many difficulties in the use of collateral resources. We suggest that contracts between agencies be used as a framework for coordination of services. These contracts should describe the responsibilities of each professional, criteria for evaluating progress, and expected dates of accomplishment.

It is important to recognize that often both intra-agency and interagency coordination problems exist. The absence of coordination among intake, placement, and adoption units has been pointed out in the literature.[69] Marvin Burt and Ralph Balyeat developed a system for interagency coordination in Nashville, Tennessee, that was tested over a three-year period.[70] Their system relies on a computerized data bank in which is stored socioeconomic, diagnostic, and service delivery information on each child receiving protective services. This system is linked to all service delivery resources. By having each resource supply information on services provided, they are able to track each child's movement and services received through the entire system. Hence, duplication can be detected and eliminated, and unmet service needs identified.

Training in Legal Procedures

Training in legal procedures also is necessary.[71] Social workers are said to view the court as an obstacle to planning options.[72] Cynthia Bell noted that such lack of knowledge is reciprocal, in that attorneys know little about the constraints within which social workers must act.[73]

Workers should be familiar with the state neglect and abuse statutes, as well as with laws governing guardianship and termination of parental rights. They should know what constitutes evidence acceptable in court and know how to document such evidence.[74] The increase in statutes that require reporting suspected neglect and abuse, and the expectation·that workers will be equipped to exercise all planning options, make training imperative.[75]

> No professional group, other than lawyers, come in contact with so many "pigeon holes" of law, such as domestic relations, criminal law, real property, evidence, procedure, and contracts, as do social workers . . . for the most part, however, the caseworker lacks the necessary preparation or skill for handling these problems effectively, and sometimes he even fails to recognize the existence of a legal problem.[76]

Training in the Provision of Direct Services

We view training in the areas discussed above as essential for all staff. If training is provided, a crucial concern is what type of intervention methods workers will be trained to use. When casework services are discussed in the literature, they are described in terms such as "supportive" or "directive" services.[77] We believe these descriptions are too general to be useful.

In view of the lack of evidence that traditional casework methods are effective, their continued use contributes to diminished confidence that publicly supported social services can attain their intended objectives.[78] Selection of methods should be based on empirical evidence that they are effective. It is for this reason that behavioral approaches have been increasingly utilized by social workers.[79] It is why the Alameda Project staff were trained to use behavioral methods.

Project workers were trained in behavioral methods of assessment, intervention, and evaluation. Training materials included assigned reading drawn from the behavioral literature.[80] Training included three components: directed reading, individual supervisory conferences, and group meetings. Brief seminars were held for all staff prior to their beginning work in the project. There was a continuing reliance upon available empirical literature over the course of the project, particularly with reference to the selection and implementation of intervention methods. Training during supervisory sessions was the most concentrated, in that sessions took place at least once weekly on an individual basis. Group meetings were held at least once a month. Supervision also was available on an as-needed basis. The training materials developed over the course of the project, together with examples of how these methods were applied in specific cases, are described in a manual developed by Theodore Stein and Eileen Gambrill.[81] (See also Part II.)

One of the project workers had been a child welfare worker for a number of years before participating in the project. His perception of the helpfulness of the new methods with which he became familiar during training was that they provided much more specific guidelines for service delivery and more specific evaluation procedures compared with the traditional procedures he had learned. The clarity of objectives and the readiness with which degree of progress toward their attainment could be assessed, in his opinion, rendered confrontation of parents making minimal progress a much less painful task. Parents could readily see their lack of participation in the process.

Provision of Appropriate Incentives

Mandates for change in worker behavior will be effective only if incentives are offered for compliance.[82] Workers often are overburdened with administrative tasks, such as completing local, state, and federal reports, and those required for court review. Accomplishment rarely is rewarded, and in fact may have the opposite result, in that the worker will receive a new and perhaps more difficult case each time a child moves out of care. Insofar as a new case requires more work than one designated as long-term, staff are in effect punished for pursuing case movement.

If agency goals are clearly identified, incentive structures can be designed to support staff for attaining them. A system of incentive payments for workers was recommended in a 1973 California study. This recommendation was rejected as unnecessary, the study group asserting that the goal of returning children to their homes or achieving permanent placements could be reached through better organization of services and reduced caseloads.[83] Neither better organization nor reduced caseloads has been accomplished statewide since this recommendation was made. It also is clear that the goal of moving more children out has not been reached in most areas.

There is evidence of increased attention to the importance of incentives to reward staff for attaining agency goals due to abundant evidence that incentives are critical to task performance.[84] Edward Heck and Alan R. Gruber recommend a compensation system that would pay workers on the basis of effort expended and results achieved.[85]

A recent survey covering 41 states, with responses from 93 percent of the 41, revealed that 84 percent of the local jurisdictions in the states responding had used at least one form of incentive.[86] At least three principal types of positive incentives were identified as being in use: monetary rewards, increased vacation time, and merit increases. There was some use of special nonmonetary rewards, such as allowing staff to vary work schedules or rotate job assignments. A type of incentive labeled "quasi or indirect incentives" also was used in some agencies; these incentives included time off for educational advancement, tuition reimbursement, and opening paths for career advancement to persons whose positions had been considered dead-end.[87]

We recognize that fiscal constraints are likely to preclude or limit the use of monetary rewards. However, nonmonetary incentives are a reasonable alternative. For example, staff could be relieved of some caseload responsibilities by providing workers with case aides. Student trainees could be engaged for this purpose. In the Alameda Project, students provided valuable assistance to project staff, particularly in observing and monitoring parent-child interaction and in providing transportation for parents to visit their children. Senior citizen volunteers have been used in case review procedures.[88]

Permitting staff to select work assignments, recognizing that some will prefer work with natural parents while others prefer to work mostly with children, is another potential incentive. In-service training in areas selected by staff is yet another option. The availability of Title XX training funds make this a viable alternative. Encouraging staff to select areas in which they would like to have consultation is an additional way to encourage desired worker behavior.

Cuing Appropriate Behavior

Identifying clear objectives, the means of attaining them, and arranging an incentive structure for supporting their accomplishment may not be sufficient to increase the probability of appropriate worker behavior. Some of the more effective case management and supervisory procedures will be quite novel to staff; and, as with acquiring new behavior, it may be easy to forget to perform them. Thus reminders or cues may have to be arranged. The existence of case management check lists for different outcome categories will provide one source of cues for new worker behaviors. In addition, a check list should be provided to workers that they can use to scan the completeness of their case records.[89] Administrators also will have to arrange cues as well as incentive systems to encourage appropriate supervisory behavior. Periodic call for a selected small number of cases overseen by each unit supervisor for administrative review could function as one such cue.

DATA COLLECTION

Thus far we have given attention to the importance of setting clear agency objectives, of providing training in areas related to goal attainment, and to the use of incentives and cuing systems. Each of these is an essential component of a program to change the foster care system. A data collection system is an additional component. The term means simply a method, most likely computerized in all but the smallest agencies, designed to generate and bank appropriate data. Information in data banks generally is descriptive in nature. It may include, for example, demographic characteristics of the children in foster care, the length of time they have been in out-of-home placement, the number of re-placements, and current case plans.

For many years child welfare literature has noted the need for data collection systems and consequences of not having them.[90] Deficits in methods of compiling local or statewide information regarding youngsters in care are cited as a "major factor contributing to today's social welfare crisis."[91] Heck and Gruber go so far as to suggest that it is impossible for the people responsible for agency administration to exercise control of the foster care program because of the amount of information that has to be managed without an adequate data system.[92] Many agencies lack even such basic information as data describing how long children in care have been in placement or changing trends in populations served and the kinds of problems requiring services.[93] The severity of the problem is illustrated by the situation in California. Each county in California supplies data to the state describing its foster care population on a number of dimensions.[94] However, none of it is maintained by the county in which this study was conducted for its own use![95] All the information that is available at the county level is that maintained in case folders.[96] Therefore, it is not possible to describe how long children have been in placement, and demographic characteristics of the foster care population are unknown.[97] No data are maintained describing the success or failure of placements; hence the cost of re-placing children cannot be calculated. No information is available on the effects of serving children in their own homes or the numbers of these children eventually placed in foster homes. In addition, the costs of the court process through which the majority of these youngsters enter placement cannot be assessed.

Only in recent years has widescale implementation of data collection systems begun.[98] Recognition of their importance is highlighted by a bill currently before the U.S. House of Representatives calling for data systems in each state to provide information on all children in foster care, the services provided prior to the child's entry into placement, and transactions occurring after entry.[99] An adequate data system also would show the number of times a child's placement changes, the legal status of the child, the expected date of return to the natural parents or an alternative plan in process, and the number of children moved out of placement each year.[100] This legislation also calls for yearly reports to the federal government by each state. The reports must contain descriptions of current foster care and adoption programs and recommendations for improvement.

It is our opinion that information gathered for the state should be retained in the county. The utility of information to stimulate change is partly a function of its accessibility to local administrators.

The Process of Data Collection

The process of gathering information begins at the caseworker or clerical level. There are limits to the quality and quantity of information if case records are relied on as the primary source. (The issues raised below also are pertinent to the use of case records for supervisory review.) Missing data are of immediate concern. For example, in discussing case records as a source for case reviews, Len Trout noted that identifying characteristics of children were missing in over 60 percent of the cases reviewed.[101] David Fanshel and John Grundy report gaps in the information provided to the central data bank on forms completed by New York City workers.[102] Martha Jones also highlighed the poor quality of case records. She stated that those reviewed did not contain any information on case planning, nor was it possible to establish that any efforts had been made to rehabilitate families or to locate missing parents.[103] A second difficulty is the manner in which available data are described in case records. A recent report on planning for service delivery stated that the "reports relating to social services delivered were such as to make it difficult or impossible to describe adequately what services social workers were actually providing."[104]

In order to yield useful information, the language of case records must be descriptive, not inferential. For example, it would be helpful if the various reasons why parents seek foster home services could be analyzed from the assembled data as a basis for allocating resources. When vague concepts such as "mental illness" are used, each administrator must interpret the data in his or her own way, a situation contributing little to an informed match of resources to effective methods of preventing placement. However, if data are descriptive, accurately reflecting the reasons for out-of-home placement, funding can be matched to proven preventive services. For example, emergency housekeeper services could be available to avoid placement in cases of physical illness or short-term parental incapacity.

Another obstacle to reliance on case records for assembling data is the infrequency of recording. Project workers found the most recent information in case records typically was a year old. No doubt workers had more recent information in their log books; but so long as it remains there, records are not updated. It is not certain that log book material ever found its way into case records, especially in view of worker turnover. Shortages of clerical staff contribute to information deficits in case records. However, as Hobbs states, "Record keeping is often regarded [by workers] as a chore to be done only after more important work has been completed."[105] The consequences of tardy case recording for case planning are particularly apparent when a case must be prepared for court presentation. It is impossible to establish grounds for a termination action without current and detailed information on the case.

The source of information must be firmly controlled in order to produce accurate data for a statewide system. Record keeping systems must be standardized. Timely information on all areas deemed essential for obtaining agency goals must be recorded regularyy. The language used cannot be subject to varying interpretations, but must be clearly descriptive.

Formats for standardized record keeping are available.[106] Examples of those used during the project appear in Appendix A.

Utilizing Data

Child welfare agency administrators can use data collected to articulate objectives, to direct attention to needed resources, to evaluate the effectiveness of interventions, and to monitor trends. Supervisors can use data collected in their case review process. First we will discuss administrative uses.

When fully specified, a social work objective describes the population expected to benefit from its attainment and the type and direction of expected change. In addition, it specifies the interventions necessary to achieve the objective. A major goal of foster care services is to prevent, whenever possible, the removal of children from their own homes. Carefully compiled data will identify the populations at risk of being removed from their homes and the social conditions that put the children at risk, and will suggest the interventions necessary to reduce or eliminate risk. Goal attainment is then reflected in a reduction in the number of children entering care each year relative to prior years,* and eventually in a reduction in total number of children in foster care. The reduction is accomplished by more children having been returned to natural parents or adopted into new homes.

It is important to note the limitations of available data for pinpointing groups at risk. Concepts such as neglect and mental illness are vague and are employed differentially. Each encompasses such a range of dissimilar referents that their value is limited when used to name a category of children. For example, "neglected" is commonly used to name a category of children at risk. As such, it is too global a term to give direction to treatment planning.

Three groups of "children at risk of out-of-home placement" are those whose primary caretaker requires hospitalization or is incapacitated at home; those whose caretaker is deficient in child management skills; and

---

*One should examine the data over several past years to be sure that a diminishing trend has not already begun.

those whose single parent lacks respite (through day-care or sitter service) child care. Flexible and imaginative use of homemaker services, visiting public health nurses, parenting and nutrition classes, and day care or baby-sitting services can be expected to avoid out-of-home placement in many instances. With data to connect the provision of each service to prevention of placement, agency administration can show that the reduction in numbers of children in foster care is attributable to the service given.

Size, characteristics, and causes of populations of children-at-risk are in constant flux. Data sensitive to these changes are needed. The eventual goal is methods for monitoring the process of service delivery that connect specific services to problem reduction. As a beginning step, ranking problems from most tractable to least tractable would provide a basis for increased availability of those services shown to have the largest impact, and for eliminating those least effective. Measuring the effect of multiple interventions requires an even more sophisticated data collection and analysis process. The end goal is allocation in accordance with established connections between specific services and problem resolution. In the context of foster care, we mean problems that lead to out-of-home- placement.

Periodic Review

The second principal use of computerized data is to facilitate review at the supervisory level by providing each supervisor with a printout of the cases in his or her unit. For example, since we know the significance of time in case planning, computers could be programmed to identify each child in care less than one year in each unit, each child designated for long-term placement soon after entry, and those classified as undecided (no plan) and remaining in this category beyond a specified period. Likewise, cases that have a plan but no written contract could be identified. This would help supervisors to focus on cases where planning or implementation is delayed.

The goal of court review is similar to agency review, that is, to achieve permanence for children in care. The concern of reviewers in either context is similar. The format for presenting information for court review may differ from that of supervisory or administrative review, since court regulations may stipulate the manner of presentation. The issue of which type of review is the more effective in moving foster care systems toward this overall goal is an important one. We noted earlier that most states have one or the other of these review mechanisms. Since the literature suggests there is a trend toward establishing higher-level reviews, which one is chosen is a significant issue.

Arguments for court review seem more persuasive than those for agency review. Objectivity is maintained when procedures are external to the agency. If review occurs internally, subjectivity may be minimized by having non-agency personnel participate in review panels. Michael Wald suggests that parents are more likely to respond to proferred help if ordered to do so by the court and more likely to share complaints with the court than with the social agency. The court's authority to terminate parental rights and to return a child at a hearing is cited as a dynamic that influences parental involvement.[107]

The court as the locus for review is favored in federal legislation that calls for review by an "experienced and objective person [who is] not involved in the provision of services."[108] Unresponsiveness of social work as a profession to the problems of children drifting in care and the frequently noted deficits in services to natural parents have contributed to the increase in the number of states implementing court review. W. Eugene Claburn et al. point out that "failing to implement administrative review procedures renders states vulnerable to the institutionalization of judicial review systems."[109]

It has been suggested that review at the court level will provide an incentive to social workers to conform to court expectations in order to avoid criticism at hearings.[110] Court review also may have a positive effect on the quality of case record keeping. Records are more likely to be maintained in compliance with court standards for documenting evidence. Hobbs believes that review provides a mechanism for monitoring agency performance. For example, he suggests that it can overcome problems of therapists keeping children in care longer than necessary because they are "striving for perfection," that is, working for improvement beyond minimum requirements for a child's effective functioning.[111] Agency review could be available to parents on an as-needed basis between court review periods. This would give parents a forum in which to present concerns arising between scheduled court appearances.[112]

Whether or not periodic review in either form is effective will depend upon at least two conditions. First, it should take place at close intervals, preferably with no more than three to six months between reviews. Second, appropriate resources must be available if all alternatives are to be considered for each child. Included here are both problem-solving resources and specialized foster and adoptive homes.[113]

The effectiveness of any review procedure is partly a function of the quality of information used to reach decisions. If objectivity is to be maintained and consensus reached when review occurs, reviewers must have access to specific material to guide their endeavors. If vague concepts must be interpreted—for example, emotional illness—the process will not result in reliable outcomes. Decision making will remain discretionary, reflecting the individual values and prejudices of the reviewers. Written and signed contracts, as used in the Alameda Project, proved a valuable tool for judicial review. Members of the bench commented on their value in furthering decision making because of the specificity of information they contained.

We lack evidence of the effectiveness of review systems.[114] One project designed to test the effects of court review as a means of promoting permanent planning for children in placement has been underway since November 1974 in 12 states.[115] It recognizes that a key part of any review is pertinent data describing each child in placement. In each of these 12 states, "concerned citizens" serve as volunteers. The project operates out of the court, and the project director is responsible for recruiting volunteers and coordinating their work. A special unit of these volunteers evaluates cases and recommends the early return of children or the termination of parental rights.[116] (Further discussion and evaluation of the effectiveness of court review procedures is presented by Trudy Festinger.[117]) For each case, the reason a child is in care, how long it has been in care, the child's legal status, how frequently it has been moved, the frequency of contact with biological parents, and current treatment plans are reported to the judge.[118] Project outcomes have not been fully evaluated. It is noted that in one state, adoption actions increased 100 percent in one year.[119]

Social workers, expressing a preference for agency-controlled procedures, have raised objections to court review, stating that "administrative review within the agency is preferable."[120] "They claim that court review is unnecessary, time consuming, and threatening to parents."[121]

We believe it is unfortunate that review is not viewed positively as a collaborative effort between the court and child welfare agencies that insures the well-being of children in care. As long as social workers view the court as an obstacle and as a barrier to social work treatment, a negative perception will continue.[122] Misunderstanding occurs on both sides; court officials and social workers often fail to see that they share the same goals for children. We believe that carefully planned educational experiences to address this important issue should be provided jointly to court and social work personnel.

Confidentiality

Data collection systems are necessary to manage the quantity of data generated by public welfare systems. Statutes of nearly every state require that cases of abuse and neglect be reported.[123] The United States Department of Health, Education and Welfare requires that both suspected and actual abuse and neglect be reported.[124] Information is maintained on large numbers of families in these data banks, a fact that has given rise to concern about confidentiality.[125] Some of this concern stems from documented abuse of records maintained on youngsters adjudicated as delinquent.[126]

There are two central issues with respect to confidentiality: who will have access, and the language used to describe cases (specifically, labeling that stigmatizes the adult or child named).[127] Agency administrators bear ultimate responsibility for assuring confidentiality of records. Abuses within the juvenile justice system have stimulated two types of recommendations, one that addressed client rights and the other, administrative mechanisms for controlling data dissemination.[128]

Items in the first category include the client's right to inspect records and to correct inaccuracies. Implementation of this recommendation would require establishing appeals panels and providing clients with legal assistance. It is suggested that clients be informed of records kept on them and of each time information is released, and that records be expunged when allegations are not confirmed in reported cases of suspected neglect or abuse.

The need for record control mechanisms recognizes the fact that information must be released to persons within the system. Safeguards include requirements that the identity of each person requesting information be confirmed, and that there be agreements precluding dissemination of information to a second party without prior authorization from the agency initially providing the data. It also is recommended that committees of citizens and public officials be established to monitor information management and assure that client rights are protected.

The responsibilities of public agency administration were discussed in the preceding sections. Clearly established goals and training to enable staff to work toward these goals were identified as of first importance. While recognizing that worker tasks may vary from agency to agency, we have recommended training for coordinating services and in management of legal issues. We highlighted the importance of selecting empirically validated treatment methods when workers are trained to provide direct services. Provision of incentives to facilitate task-oriented behaviors was seen as essential. Finally, data collection systems were discussed in terms of the value of data systems for case review and for evaluating goal attainment, while noting that strict confidentiality must be assured in the maintenance of data banks.

IMPLICATIONS FOR SOCIAL WORK EDUCATION

A repetitive theme in the child welfare literature is the need to train social workers specifically for child welfare. Training in legal issues, case management, direct treatment, and coordination of services are areas highlighted.[129] Restructuring curriculum to train students in child welfare poses a challenge for social work education. A framework to guide curriculum development has not been developed. We are not optimistic that educators can look to the world of practice for the necessary answers, despite continued reference in the literature to the value of "practice theory."[130] Current practice is responsible for the fact that children drift aimlessly in foster care placement. We know that many child welfare workers employ effective methods in working with their clients. The fact is, however, that effective practice rarely is documented in a way that is informative to educators. Bernece Simon, reviewing a series of papers presented at a symposium on social work practice, sums this up well: "[there is a lack of] clarity as to what it is that social workers do or should do in their day-to-day work."[131]

The methods employed by the Alameda Project staff give direction to this effort. Our approach to assessment, case planning, and decision making addresses deficits in case management and provides a framework for developing a practice curriculum.

Some practitioners and educators will take issue with the procedures employed by project staff. We did not focus on aspects of the parent's situation vaguely related to quality of life. Our concern was to establish minimal standards of parenting and to provide continuity of care for children within reasonable time limits. A persuasive case can be made for the philosophy underlying our approach to practice, regardless of one's individual stand on the issue of aspiring to reach only minimal standards. Central to the philosophy is an appreciation of the parent's rights-child's rights dilemma, and the belief that state intervention should occur only when there is clear and convincing evidence of harm to the child. It should not be construed that qualitative issues are of no concern to us; indeed, they are. However, it is our belief, supported by data from longitudinal studies, that we have limited ability to predict qualitative outcomes for children, given the present level of knowledge of parenting behavior.[132] The majority of cases with which child welfare workers deal fall into a "gray" area between extremes of abuse and neglect. It is here that we run the greatest risk of imposing middle-class values on clients and engaging in discretionary decision making under the guise of scientific practice.

Social Work and the Courts

At present the working relationship between social workers and juvenile court judges is not a good one. It has been described as one of "mutual mistrust."[133] Social workers are said to perceive the courts as a barrier to permanent planning, and the courts to view social workers as responsible for many of the problems of children in care.[134] Judges have cited the bias workers have against some families and the conviction of some social workers that the interests of children are better served in foster care than in their parents' homes.[135] There is no single training need of social workers mentioned more frequently in the literature than that for legal training.[136]

Some of the difficulties contributing to the mutual mistrust between social workers and judges derive from a lack of understanding on the part of each regarding the work of the other. Partial resolution would be achieved if law school curricula included more social science information. Neglect and dependency statutes not only vary from state to state but also are imprecise in wording and subject to diverse application.[137] Judges can, and do, exercise great latitude in interpreting these laws.[138] Legal consultation and training at the child welfare agency level will be necessary to assist social workers in learning specific techniques of collaborating with the court.[139] Social work curriculum can, at most, communicate an appreciation of legal reasoning and legal ethics, plus some general concepts of family and children's law that bridge state-by-state differences. Some of the changes called for the role of the court are discussed below, as a background against which to consider curriculum change.

Earlier we discussed the increased reliance on the judiciary for reviewing the status of children in out-of-home placement. Social workers have criticized this enlarged court role.[140] However, statutes placing review responsibility on the courts came about through a perceived failure of child welfare agencies to resolve the problems of children in foster care. This enlarged role of the courts will have a significant impact on current practice because the changes induced go beyond perfunctory review. Existing and pending legislation requires that specific case plans be presented to the court, and that efforts to provide services and the clients' responses to these efforts be clearly documented.[141] Two changes are of particular significance: the movement away from the best interests of the child to the least detrimental alternative as a standard for decision making, and the mandate that permanent plans be made within a child's first or, at the most, second year in placement.[142] Accommodating to the "least detrimental" standard will require social work educators to rethink current views of minimal acceptable parenting; and insistence on prompt planning and aggressive implementation of plans will require more emphasis on accurate assessment followed by proven intervention procedures.

Curriculum Change: Summary

A basic change that must occur is to move away from the pathological view of human behavior that historically has dominated practice courses in schools of social work. Overemphasis on the pathological has been an obstacle to case planning and service delivery. The fact that social workers are trained to identify pathology is one of the reasons why many children enter care without due consideration of alternatives.[143] Problems are perceived as so complex as to preclude their resolution with such basic approaches as public health education, the use of homemakers, parenting classes, day care, and the like. When neglect is viewed in pathological terms, it is "regarded as a willful act of uncaring parents for which removal of the child is just punishment."[144] This is a perspective incompatible with effective service delivery.

A focus on individual dysfunction diverts attention from the relationship between parental behavior and its effects on a child, a view that leads to a reliance on long-term approaches to treatment antithetical to the early case planning called for in recent legislation. In addition, it detracts from analysis of the effects of numerous environmental variables that impinge on the parent's life, and diverts attention from a search for client assets. When pathology is the focus, it inevitably appears severe. Workers often discourage visits by parents because their pathology is viewed as harmful to the child.[145]

Deficits in services to natural parents may stem from the worker's perception of the severity of a client's problems. When so viewed, the worker's skills appear minimal and community resources insufficient. Workers naturally tend to avoid contact with "sick" parents.

Workers must receive training in effective methods of assessment. Currently used approaches make unsubstantiated assumptions about the consequences to children of certain parental behavior.[146] It is inferred, for example, that drug or alcohol abuse is evidence that a parent is not fulfilling his or her responsibilities. This inference is reinforced by neglect laws that focus on parental behavior rather than on the specific effect of this behavior on the child. Drug-addicted or alcoholic parents may be quite able to meet the physical needs of their children.[147] Workers should be trained to assess whether or not basic needs are being met, in order to justify intervention, under a standard that is set at minimal parenting skills. Child welfare workers may ignore valuable sources of assessment information—observation of parent-child interaction, for example—relying instead upon client self-reports and case records.[148] The assessment procedures employed by project staff are discussed in chapter 7, and are illustrated with case examples in chapter 8.

Assessment data have value only insofar as they direct attention to appropriate interventions.[149] Vague concepts such as neglect, abuse, and mental illness are of little use in this regard. We must employ methods that enable us to identify both environmental variables and personal variables as sources of client problems. If we are to justify demands that resources be expanded and new ones developed, we must be clearer as to precisely how these resources will reduce the pervasive social problem.

We do not know the extent to which child welfare workers provide direct services in problem solving as opposed to marshaling community resources.[150] It probably varies as a function of agency policy, caseload size, individual worker skill, and the availability of community resources. Careful observation and analysis of practice perhaps would reveal a continuum along which approaches to service delivery could be ranged.

In the child welfare literature, discussion of direct intervention covers a broad spectrum ranging from traditional psychosocial methods to behavioral methods of social work treatment.[151] Increasingly, reference is made to short-term, goal-oriented approaches to service delivery.[152] Treatment within this framework is most congruent with early case planning and prompt decision making.

In accordance with a deemphasis on individual pathology, and in recognition of the diverse environmental sources of client problems, there is increasing use of multidisciplinary teams for service delivery.[153] Teams generally are composed of psychiatrists, psychologists, public health nurses, attorneys, and social workers. Social workers are the case managers in these teams.[154] The case manager assumes responsibility for coordinating and monitoring all services received by a client.[155] Social work education is derelict when it fails to prepare students to fulfill this role.

We must remain cognizant of the limited empirical evidence of most social work methods. This evidence guided our selection of behavioral methods for use in the project. The concern about deprofessionalization of social work, and the increasing reliance on courts to solve social problems, can be seen as a failure to demonstrate the effectiveness of methods we employ.[156]

NOTES

1. On the need for a decision-making framework, see Arthur Emlen, Janet Lahti, Glen Downs, Alex McKay, and Susan Downs, *Overcoming Barriers to Planning for Children in Foster Care* (Portland, Ore.: Regional Research Institute for Human Services, 1977), p. 43; Edmund V. Mech, "Decision Analysis in Foster Care Practice," in Helen D. Stone, ed., *Foster Care in Question*, (New York: Child Welfare League of America, 1970), pp. 26–51; Temporary State Commission on Child Welfare, *The Children of the State: Barriers to the Freeing of Children for Adoption* (New York: Department of Social Services, 1976) p. xvii; Eileen D. Gambrill and Kermit T. Wiltse, "Foster Care: Prescriptions for Change," 32, no. 3 *Public Welfare* (Summer 1974):39–47; Nicholas Hobbs, *The Futures of Children* (San Francisco: Jossey-Bass, 1976), p. 246.

On deficits in case planning, see Temporary Commission on Child Welfare, op. cit., p. 106; Victor Pike, Susan Downs, Arthur Emlen, Glen Downs, and Denise Case, *Permanent Planning for Children in Foster Care: A Handbook for Social Workers* (Portland, Ore.: Regional Research Institute for Human Services, 1977), p. 4; Kenneth Kenniston and the Carnegie Council on Children, *All our Children: The American Family Under Pressure* (New York: Harcourt Brace Jovanovich, 1977), p. 190.

On services to biological parents, see Alan R. Gruber, *Foster Home Care in Massachusetts* (Boston: Governor's Commission on Adoption and Foster Care, 1973), p. 50; Temporary State Commission on Child Welfare, op. cit., p. 92; Martin Rein, Thomas E. Nutt, and Heather Weiss, "Foster Family Care: Myth and Reality," in Alvin S. Schorr, ed., *Children and Decent People* (New York: Basic Books, 1974), pp. 24–52.

2. Edmund A. Sherman, Renee Neuman, and Ann W. Shyne, *Children Adrift in Foster Care: A Study of Alternative Approaches* (New York: Child Welfare League of America, 1974), p. 50.

3. Mary Ann Jones, Renee Neuman, and Ann W. Shyne, *A Second Chance for Families:*

Evaluation of a Program to Reduce Foster Care (New York: Child Welfare League of America, 1976), p. 83.

4. Theodore J. Stein and Eileen D. Gambrill, "Early Intervention in Foster Care," *Public Welfare* 34 (Spring 1976):38–44; Henry S. Maas, "Children in Long Term Foster Care," *Child Welfare* 48 (June 1969):321–33. David Fanshel, "Status Changes of Children in Foster Care: Final Results of the Columbia University Longitudinal Study," *Child Welfare* 55 (March 1976):143–71.

5. Jones et al., op. cit., p. 55.

6. Deborah Shapiro, *Agencies and Foster Children* (New York: Columbia University Press, 1976), p. 74.

7. Gruber, loc. cit.; Temporary State Commission on Child Welfare, loc. cit.; Rein et al., op. cit.

8. Baltimore County Department of Social Services, "Pilot Project: Experiences with a Specialized Caseload of Natural Parents" (Townsend, Md.: the Department, 1971), p. 6 (mimeographed); Emlen et al., op. cit., p. 30; Helen D. Stone, "An Orientation to Foster Care Theory and Values: An Introduction," in Stone, op. cit., p. 6.

9. Lela B. Costin, *Child Welfare: Policies and Practice* (New York: McGraw-Hill, 1972), p. 287; Marvin R. Burt and Louis H. Blair, *Options for Improving the Care of Neglected and Dependent Children* (Washington, D.C.: Urban Institute, 1971), p. 76.

10. Delmer J. Pascoe, *Review, Synthesis and Recommendations of Seven Foster Care Studies in California,* (Sacramento: Children's Research Institute of California, 1974), p. 22.

11. Edward T. Heck and Alan R. Gruber, *Treatment Alternatives Project* (Boston: Boston Children's Service Association, 1976), p. 196, agree. They use the term "effort-expenditure" to refer to the activity dimension of a case.

12. Shapiro, op. cit., p. 90.

13. Ibid.

14. Gilbert Y. Steiner, *The State of Welfare* (Washington, D.C.: Brookings Institution, 1971), p. 40.

15. State of California, Department of Social Welfare, *Children Waiting* (Sacramento: the Department, 1972); Deborah Shapiro, "Agency Investment in Foster Care: A Study," *Social Work* 17 (July 1972):20–28.

16. Eileen D. Gambrill and Kermit T. Wiltse, "Foster Care: Prescriptions for Change," *Public Welfare* 32 (Summer 1974):47.

17. Leon W. Chestang and Irmgard Heymann, "Reducing the Length of Foster Care," *Social Work* 18 (January 1973):88.

18. Cited in Anthony N. Maluccio, "Foster Family Care Revisited: Problems and Prospects," *Public Welfare* 31, no. 1 (Spring 1973):14.

19. Bernece K. Simon, "Social Casework Theory: An Overview," in Robert W. Roberts and Robert H. Nee, eds., *Theories of Social Casework* (Chicago: University of Chicago Press, 1970), p. 378.

20. Eileen D. Gambrill and Kermit T. Wiltse, "Foster Care: Plans and Actualities," *Public Welfare* 32 (Spring 1974):15.

21. Edward J. Mullen, "Casework Communication," *Social Casework* 49 (1968):546–51.

22. Jones et al., op. cit.

23. Theodore J. Stein, *A Content Analysis of Social Caseworker and Client Interaction in Foster Care* (D.S.W. Diss., unpublished, University of California, Berkeley, 1974), p. 74.

24. Sherman et al., op. cit., p. 45; Edmund A. Sherman, Michael H. Phillips, Barbara L. Haring, and Ann W. Shyne, *Service to Children in Their Own Homes: Its Nature and Outcome* (New York: Child Welfare League of America, 1973), p. 59.

25. Jones et al., op. cit., p. 68.

26. Sherman et al., *Service to Children in Their Own Homes,* p. 59.

27. Stein, op. cit., p. 286.

28. Ibid., ch. 4.

29. Jones et al., op. cit., p. 83.

30. Margaret K. Rosenheim, "Notes on Helping Juvenile Nuisances," in Margaret K. Rosenheim, ed., *Pursuing Justice for the Child* (Chicago: University of Chicago Press, 1976), p. 57; Kenniston et al., op. cit., p. 38; Shirley Jenkins and Elaine Norman, *Beyond Placement* (New York: Columbia University Press, 1975), p. 142.

31. Jenkins and Norman, loc. cit.

32. Emlen et al., op. cit., p. 3.

33. Ibid., p. 43.

34. Ronaele Whittington, Katarina Digman, and John M. Digman, "Judgment Analysis of One Social Worker's Decision to Help or not to Help," *Child Welfare* 53 (February 1974): 83.

35. Henry S. Maas and Richard E. Engler, *Children in Need of Parents* (New York: Columbia University Press, 1959); David Fanshel, "The Exit of Children from Foster Care: An Interim Research Report," *Child Welfare* 50 (February 1971):65–81; Stein and Gambrill, op. cit.

36. No relationship was found between six of the child and case outcome by either Fanshel, ibid., or H. B. M. Murphy, "Predicting Duration of Foster Care," *Child Welfare* 47 (February 1968):76–84; however, a significant relationship between sex and case planning was reported by Sherman et al., *Children Adrift in Foster Care*, p. 65. A relationship was found between ethnicity and outcome by Bernice Boehm, *Deterrents to the Adoption of Children in Foster Care* (New York: Child Welfare League of America, 1958), and Shirley Jenkins, "Duration of Foster Care: Some Relevant Antecedent Variables," *Child Welfare* 46 (October 1967):450–55, but not by Sherman et al., op. cit., p. 26, and Fanshel, ibid. A relationship was found between age and outcome by Jenkins, ibid.; a nonlinear relationship by Sherman et al., op. cit.; and no relationship by Fanshel, ibid., Murphy, op. cit., or Stein and Gambrill, op. cit.; Edmund A. Sherman, Renee Neumann, and Ann W. Shyne, *Children Adrift in Foster Care: A Study of Alternative Approaches* (New York: Child Welfare League of America, 1973), 1st case: p. 26, 2nd case: p. 24.

37. Jenkins, ibid.

38. David Fanshel and Henry S. Maas, "Factorial Dimensions of the Characteristics of Children in Placement and Their Families," *Child Development* 33 (March 1962):123–44; Fanshel, op. cit.; Jenkins, op. cit.; Alfred Kadushin, *Child Welfare Services* (2nd ed.; New York: MacMillan, 1974), p. 455.

39. Sherman et al., op. cit., p. 69; Maas, op. cit.

40. Jones et al., op. cit., p. 114.

41. Fanshel, "Status Changes of Children in Foster Care," p. 153.

42. Jenkins and Norman, op. cit., ch. 8.

43. Shapiro, *Agencies and Foster Children*, p. 91.

44. On turnover, see Temporary State Commission on Child Welfare, op. cit., p. 129; Jenkins and Norman, op. cit., p. 137.

On case records, see Bernice Q. Madison, "Changing Directions in Child Welfare Services," in Francine Sobey, ed., *Changing Roles in Social Work Practice* (Philadelphia: Temple University Press, 1977), p. 35; Joint Commission on Mental Health of Children, *The Mental Health of Children: Services, Research, and Manpower*, (New York: Harper and Row, 1973), p. 112.

45. Sherman et al., *Children Adrift in Foster Care*, p. 67.

46. David Fanshel, "Parental Failure and Consequences for Children: The Drug Abusing Mother Whose Children Are in Foster Care," *American Journal of Public Health* 65 (June 1975):604–62.

47. Jessica S. Pers, *Government as Parent: Administering Foster Care in California* (Berkeley: Institute of Governmental Studies, University of California, 1976), p. 87.

48. W. Eugene Claburn, Stephen Magura, and William Resnick, "Periodic Review of Foster Care: A Brief National Assessment," *Child Welfare* 55 (June 1976):395–405.

49. Ibid., p. 398.

50. Alfred Kadushin, *Supervision in Social Work* (New York: Columbia University Press, 1976), pp. 54–55.

51. Ibid., p. 59.

52. Shapiro, *Agencies and Foster Children*, p. 184.

53. David C. Bolin and Laurence Kivens, "Evaluation in a Community Mental Health Center, Huntsville, Alabama," *Evaluation* 2 (1974):26–35.

54. Eileen D. Gambrill and Theodore J. Stein, *A Training Manual for Social Work Supervisors* (to be published, summer 1978).

55. Madison, op. cit., p. 43; Pers, op. cit., p. 87; Office of Program Evaluation, *Placement in Foster Care: Issues and Concerns* (Oakland, Calif. the Office, 1977), p. 54; Gruber, op. cit., p. 27; Donald Brieland, Kenneth Watson, Philip Hovda, David Fanshel, and John J. Carey, *Differential Use of Manpower: A Team Model for Foster Care* (New York: Child Welfare League of America, 1968), p. 19.

56. John P. Steketee, "The CIP Story," *Juvenile Justice* 28 (May 1977):4.

57. Ibid., p. 5.

58. U.S. Congress, House of Representatives, *Foster Care, Adoption and Reform Act of 1977*, 95th Cong., 1st sess. (Washington, D.C.: U.S. Government Printing Office, 1977).

59. Arthur Young and Co., *Final Report: Alameda County Pilot Project on Human Services Planning* (Oakland, Calif.: Arthur Young and Co., 1976), p. V-8.

60. Pers, loc. cit.; U.S. Department of Health, Education and Welfare, Office of Human Development, *The Community Team: An Approach to Case Management and Prevention*, vol. 3, *Child Abuse and Neglect* D.H.E.W. publication no. (OHD) 75-30075 (Washington, D.C.: U.S. Government Printing Office, 1975), p. 117.

61. Edwina Leon, "Gatekeepers of the Profession" (Sacramento: California State University, 1977), ch. 4. (Mimeographed.)

62. Ibid.

63. Hobbs, op. cit., pp. 228–30.

64. Ibid., p. 228.

65. Leon, op. cit., p. 28.

66. Heck and Gruber, op. cit., p. 195; Emlen et al., op. cit., p. 35; Sherman et al., *Service to Children in Their Own Homes*, pp. 4–5; Shapiro *Agencies and Foster Children*, p. 61.

67. Madison, op. cit., p. 35; Joint Commission on the Mental Health of Children, op. cit., p. 97; Hobbs, op. cit., pp. 258–60; U.S. Department of Health, Education and Welfare, op. cit., p. 144.

68. National Conference of Lawyers and Social Workers, *Law and Social Work* (Washington, D.C.: National Association of Social Workers, 1973), p. 36.

69. Office of Program Evaluation, op. cit., p. 56; Madison loc. cit.; Marvin R. Burt and Ralph R. Balyeat, *A Comprehensive Emergency Services System for Neglected and Abused Children* (New York: Vantage Press, 1977), p. xviii.

70. See also Burt and Blair, op. cit., Burt and Balyeat, op. cit.

71. National Conference of Lawyers and Social Workers, op. cit., p. 38.

72. Emlen et al., op. cit., p. 43.

73. Cynthia Bell, "Legal Consultation for Child Welfare Workers," *Public Welfare* 33, no. 1 (Summer 1975):43.

74. Ibid., p. 38; Michael S. Wald, "State Intervention of Behalf of 'Neglected' Children: Standards for Removal of Children from Their Homes, Monitoring the Status of Children in Foster Care, and Termination of Parental Rights," *Stanford Law Review* 28 (April 1976):659.

75. Child Abuse and Neglect Project, Education Commission of the States, *Child Abuse and Neglect in the States: A Digest of Critical Elements of Reporting and Central Registries* (New York: The Commission, 1976); and *Trends in Child Abuse and Neglect Reporting Statues* (New York: the Commission, 1977).

76. Bell, op. cit., p. 36.

77. Eileen D. Gambrill and Kermit T. Wiltse, "Foster Care: Plans and Actualities," p. 14;

Sherman et al., *Service to Children in Their Own Homes*, p. 58; David Fanshel and John Grundy, *CWIS Report* (New York: Child Welfare Information Services, 1975), pp. 11, 25.

78. Joel Fischer, "Is Casework Effective: A Review," *Social Work* 18 (January 1973):5–20; Melvin B. Mogulof, *Special Revenue Sharing in Support of the Public Social Services* (Washington, D.C.: Urban Institute, 1973), p. 2.

79. Josephine S. Hirsch, Jacquelynne Gailey, and Eleanor Schmerl, "A Child Welfare Agency's Program of Service to Children in Their Own Homes," *Child Welfare* 55 (March 1976):193–204; Theodore J. Stein and Eileen D. Gambrill, "Behavioral Techniques in Foster Care," *Social Work* 21 (January 1976):34–39; Elizabeth T. McInnis and David Margolin II, "Individualizing Behavior Therapy for Children in Group Settings," *Child Welfare* 56 (July 1977):449–64; Diane B. Lillesand, "A Behavioral-Psychodynamic Approach to Day Treatment for Emotionally Disturbed Children," *Child Welfare* 56 (November 1977):613–20.

80. Gerald R. Patterson, Families (Champaign, Ill.: Research Press, 1971); Roland G. Tharp and Ralph J. Wetzel, *Behavior Modification in the Natural Environment* (New York: Academic Press, 1969); Donald L. Whaley and Richard W. Malott, *Elementary Principles of Behavior* (New York: Appleton-Century-Crofts, 1971); Robert E. Alberti and Michael L. Emmons, *Your Perfect Right* (San Luis Obispo, Calif.: Impact Press, 1970); Gerald R. Patterson, J. B. Reid, R. R. Jones, and R. E. Conger, *A Social Learning Approach to Family Intervention*, vol. 1 *Families with Aggressive Children* (Eugene, Ore.: Castalia, 1975); Albert Bandura, *Principles of Behavior Modification* (New York: Holt, Rinehart and Winston, 1969); Eileen D. Gambrill, Edwin J. Thomas, and Robert D. Carter, "Procedure for Sociobehavioral Practice in Open Settings," *Social Work* 16 (January 1971):51–62.

81. Theodore J. Stein and Eileen D. Gambrill, *Decision Making in Foster Care: A Training Manual* (Berkeley: University of California Extension Press, 1976).

82. Hobbs, op. cit., p. 178; Bandura, op. cit.

83. Pascoe, op. cit., p. 31.

84. See, for example, Bandura, op. cit.; National Commission on Productivity and Work Quality, *Productivity: Employee Incentives to Improve State and Local Government Productivity* (Washington, D.C.: the Commission, 1975); Public Services Administration; *A Guide: Protective Services for Abused and Neglected Children and Their Families* (New York: Community Research Applications, Inc., 1973), pp. 45–46; Robert H. Quilitch, "A Comparison of Three Staff-Management Procedures," *Journal of Applied Behavior Analysis* 8 (1975):59–66; Brian A. Iwata, Jon S. Bailey, Katrina J. Brown, Jerry J. Fosnee, and Michael Alpern, "A Performance-Based Lottery to Improve Residential Care and Training by Institutional Staff," *Journal of Applied Behavior Analysis* 9 (1976):417–31.

85. Heck and Gruber, op. cit., p. 27.

86. National Commission on Productivity and Work Quality, op. cit., p. 141.

87. Ibid., pp. 14–16.

88. Steketee, op. cit.

89. Gambrill and Stein, *A Training Manual for Social Work Supervisors*.

90. Burt and Blair, op. cit., p. 96; American Public Welfare Association, *Standards for Foster Family Service Systems* (Washington, D.C.: the Association, 1975), p. 23; Justine Wise Polier, "External and Internal Roadblocks to Effective Child Advocacy," *Child Welfare* 56 (October 1977):497–508; Burt and Balyeat, op. cit.

91. Heck and Gruber, op. cit., p. 247; Steketee, op. cit., p. 4.

92. Heck and Gruber, loc. cit.

93. Claburn et al., op. cit., p. 403; Research Center, Child Welfare League of America, *1975 Census of Requests for Child Welfare Services* (New York: the League, 1975), p. i.

94. State of California, Department of Health, *Data Matters* (Sacramento: the Department, Report Register no. 342-0395-502, September 30, 1974 [issued June 1975]).

95. Office of Program Evaluation, op. cit., p. 6.

96. Ibid.

97. Ibid., p. 48.

98. Madison, op. cit., pp. 32–34; Fanshel and Grundy, op. cit.; Steketee, op. cit.

99. U.S. Congress, House, op. cit., p. 17.

100. Ibid.

101. Len Trout, "Annual Report of the Project Evaluator" (Reno: Research and Educational Planning Center, University of Nevada, 1976), p. 12 (Mimeographed.)

102. Fanshel and Grundy, op. cit., p. 5.

103. Martha L. Jones, "Aggressive Adoption: A Program's Effect on a Child Welfare Agency," *Child Welfare* 56 (June 1977):403.

104. Arthur Young and Co., op. cit., p. V-7.

105. Hobbs, op. cit., p. 163.

106. See Heck and Gruber, op. cit.; Burt and Balyeat, op. cit.

107. Wald, op. cit., p. 681.

108. U.S. Congress, House, op. cit., p. 13.

109. Claburn et al., op. cit., p. 403.

110. Wald, op. cit., p. 682.

111. Hobbs, op. cit. op. 11.

112. Wald, op. cit., p. 684.

113. Ibid. p. 683.

114. Ibid., p. 684.

115. Steketee, op. cit.; Trout, op. cit.

116. Steketee, op. cit., p. 7.

117. See Trudy B. Festinger, "The New York Court Review of Children in Foster Care," *Child Welfare* 54 (April 1975); Trudy B. Festinger, "The Impact of the New York Court Review of Children in Foster Care: A Followup Report," *Child Welfare* 55 (October 1976):515–46.

118. Steketee, op. cit.

119. Ibid., p. 7.

120. Wald, op. cit., p. 681.

121. Ibid.

122. Claburn et al., op. cit., p. 401.

123. Juvenile Rights Project, *Children's Rights Report* (New York: American Civil Liberties Union, 1977), p. 1.

124. Ibid., p. 7.

125. Burt and Blair, op. cit., p. 27; Child Abuse and Neglect Project, Education Commission of the States, *Child Abuse and Neglect: Model Legislation for the States* (New York: the Commission, 1976), p. 52; U.S. Congress, House, op. cit., p. 18.

126. Charles E. Lister, "Privacy, Recordkeeping and Juvenile Justice," in Rosenheim, op. cit., ch. 10; Justine Wise Polier, "Myths and Realities in the Search for Juvenile Justice: A Statement by the Honorable Justine Wise Polier," *Harvard Education Review* 44 (February 1974):107–119.

127. Juvenile Rights Project, op. cit.

128. Comprehensive discussion of these issues can be found in Lister, op. cit.; Child Abuse and Neglect Project, *Child Abuse and Neglect: Model Legislation for the States*; Polier, ibid.

129. U.S. Department of Health, Education and Welfare, op. cit., pp. 117–18; Temporary State Commission on Child Welfare, op. cit., p. 124; Robert M. Mulford, Victor B. Wylegala, and Elwood F. Melson, *Caseworker and Judge in Neglect Cases* (New York: Child Welfare League of America, 1974); David Fanshel and Eugene B. Shinn, *Dollars and Sense in the Foster Care of Children* (New York: Child Welfare League of American, 1972), p. 30; Bell, op. cit., pp. 33–40; Children's Bureau, *Child Welfare in 25 States: An Overview* D.H.E.W. publication no. (OHD) 76-30090 (Washington, D.C.: U.S. Department of Health, Education and Welfare, 1976), p. xii.

130. Edward Foy, "The Decision Making Problem in Foster Care," *Child Welfare* 46 (November 1967):502; Bernice Boehm, "An Assessment of Family Adequacy in Protective Cases," *Child Welfare* 41 (January 1962):12; Michael H. Phillips, Ann W. Shyne, Edmund A.

Sherman, and Barbara L. Haring, *Factors Associated with Placement Decisions in' Child Welfare* (New York: Child Welfare League of America, 1971), p. 2; Simon, op. cit.; Bernece K. Simon, "Diversity and Unity in the Social Work Profession," *Social Work* 22 (September 1977):394–400.

131. Simon, "Diversity and Unity," p. 395.

132. Arlene Skolnick, *The Intimate' Environment: Exploring Marriage and the Family* (Boston: Little, Brown, 1973); Sheldon H. White, Mary C. Day, Phyllis K. Freeman, Stephen A. Hantman, and Katherine P. Messenger, *Federal Programs for Young Children: Review and Recommendations*, vol. 1, *Goals and Standards of Public Programs for Children* (Washington, D.C.: U.S. Department of Health, Education and Welfare, 1973).

133. Temporary State Commission on Child Welfare, op. cit., p. 77.

134. Arthur Emlen and staff, *Barriers to Planning for Children in Foster Care* (Portland, Ore.: Regional Research Institute for Human Services, 1976), ch. 4.

135. Temporary State Commission on Child Welfare, op. cit., p. 90.

136. Elwood F. Melson, "Interpreting, Testing and Proving Neglect," in Robert M. Mulford, Victor B. Wylegala, and Elwood F. Melson *Caseworker and Judge in Neglect Cases* (New York: Child Welfare League of America, 1970), pp. 20–31; Cynthia Bell and Wallace J. Mylniec, "Preparing for a Neglect Proceeding: A Guide for the Social Worker," *Public Welfare* 32 (Fall 1974):26–37; Bell, op. cit.; National Association of Attorneys General, *Legal Issues in Foster Care*, (Raleigh, N.C.: Committee on the Office of Attorney General, 1976); Temporary State Commission on Child Welfare, op. cit., p. 124.

137. Sanford N. Katz, Ruth-Arlene W. Howe, and Melba McGrath, "Child Neglect Laws in America," *Family Law Quarterly* 9 (Spring 1975):1–372.

138. Betty Reid Mandell, *Where Are the Children?* (Lexington, Mass.: D.C. Heath, 1973), p. 108; Paul Nejelski, "Diversion: Unleashing the Hound of Heaven?" in Rosenheim, op. cit., pp. 94–118; Sanford N. Katz, *When Parents Fail* (Boston: Beacon Press, 1971), p. 65; Hillary Rodham, "Children Under the Law," *Harvard Educational Review* 43 (1974):4.

139. Melson, op. cit.; Bell and Mylniec, op. cit.; Bell, op. cit.; National Association of Attorneys General, op. cit.; Temporary State Commission on Child Welfare, loc. cit.

140. Wald, op. cit., p. 681.

141. U.S. Congress, House, op. cit.; State of California, Department of Health, *Family Protection Act of 1976* (Sacramento: the Department, 1977), "Children's Social Services, Adoptions and Foster Care."

142. State of California, Department of Health, op. cit.; Norman A. Polansky, Carolyn Hally, and Nancy F. Polansky, *Profile of Neglect: A Survey of the State of Knowledge of Child Neglect* (Washington, D.C.: Social and Rehabilitation Service, U.S. Department of Health, Education and Welfare, 1973), p. 5; Burt and Balyeat, op. cit., p. xxix; Joseph Goldstein, Anna Freud, and Albert J. Solnit, *Beyond the Best Interests of the Child* (New York: Free Press, 1973).

143. Polansky et al., op. cit., p. 5; Mech, op. cit., p. 32.

144. Kenniston et al., op. cit., pp. 188–89.

145. Temporary State Commission on Child Welfare, op. cit., p. 98.

146. Katz, Howe, and McGrath, op. cit., p. 4; Michael Wald, "State Intervention on Behalf of Neglected Children: A Search for Realistic Standards," *Stanford Law Review* 27 (April 1975):1001.

147. Public Services Administration, op. cit., p. 25.

148. Gambrill and Stein, *A Training Manual for Social Work Supervisors.*

149. Scott Briar and Henry Miller, *Problems and Issues in Social Casework* (New York: Columbia University Press, 1971), p. 144.

150. L. Diane Bernard, "Education for Social Work," in *Encyclopedia of Social Work*, vol. 1 (Washington, D.C.: National Association of Social Workers, 1977).

151. Simon, "Social Casework Theory"; Simon, "Diversity and Unity . . ."; Madison, op. cit.

152. William J. Reid and Laura Epstein, *Task-Centered Casework* (New York: Columbia University Press, 1972); U.S. Department of Health, Education and Welfare, op. cit., p. 67; Kenniston et al., op. cit., p. 186; Leon G. Smith and Roger F. Jordan, *Results Oriented Recording in Public Social Service Agencies* (Salt Lake City: Division of Family Services, Utah Department of Social Services, 1977); Pike et al., op. cit.; Theodore J. Stein and Eileen D. Gambrill "Behavioral Techniques in Foster Care," *Social Work* 21 (January 1976):34–39.

153. U.S. Department of Health, Education and Welfare, op. cit.; Brieland et al., op. cit.; Madison, op. cit., p. 58.

154. Madison, op. cit., p. 31; Public Services Administration, op. cit., p. 121; Berkeley Planning Associates, *Planning and Implementing Child Abuse and Neglect Service Programs: The Experience of Eleven Demonstration Programs*, D.H.E.W. publication no. (OHD) 77–30093 (Washington, D.C.: National Center on Child Abuse and Neglect, Children's Bureau, 1977), p. 43.

155. Public Services Administration, op. cit., p. 121.

156. National Association of Social Workers, *National Association of Social Workers Newsletter*, "County Committees Gear up to Fight De-professionalism" 19 (December 1977):5; Harry Specht, "The Deprofessionalization of Social Work," *Social Work* 17 (March 1972):3–15.

6

BARRIERS TO THE USE OF SYSTEMATIC
CASE MANAGEMENT PROCEDURES

There is general agreement that the agency setting greatly influences social work practice. This can be seen dramatically in the variables that affect caseworkers' planning decisions compared with those that affect final case outcomes. For example, Arthur Emlen found that the placeability of a child, the condition of the parents, and the emotional bonds of a child to parents, siblings, and foster parents were major determinants in planning. These client variables were highly predictive of planning decisions, accounting for 89 percent of the variation in planning for children under 12, and for 61 percent for those over 12. However, Emlen found that the rational basis for decisions disappeared in a welter of constraints that actually determined practice. Consideration of the effects of institutional barriers erased most of the effects of client predictors: all but 17 percent of the variation for children ages 0–11, and 29 percent for those 12 and over.[1] Ann Shyne also found a discrepancy between ideal and actual planning decisions. The match between ideal and actual decisions varied from city to city, depending upon the availability of resources.[2] And Scott Briar noted that caseworker decisions were affected by practices in the employing agencies.[3]

The institutional barriers to which Emlen refers are multidimensional. They include caseworkers' attitudes, such as the belief that a child's age is a major determinant of planning options, or opposition to the state's exercise of its power to terminate parental rights. Emlen highlights the role of the "county climate" in affecting a worker's view of what is possible, with particular reference to workers' perceptions of the court as a barrier to planning. He also notes the failure of agencies to have decision making a procedural requirement, and the absence of routine case review.[4]

We have discussed problems in each of these areas and have made recommendations that might resolve some difficulties. Agencies must establish clearly stated policies and provide workers with written policy guidelines for implementation. Case monitoring and review are necessary to prevent the drift of children into unplanned long-term care. We also have discussed the importance of legal training and consultation for child welfare staff and of incentives to support goal-oriented behavior.

The results reported in this book indicate that a service delivery system can be designed that will help to assure more effective decision making for children in care. The results of the Oregon project reinforce our findings, for they demonstrate that aggressive planning and decision making achieve impressive results. As of October 31, 1976, of the 509 Oregon foster children identified on November 1, 1973, as not likely to return home, a successful plan had been implemented or was in progress for 90 percent.

Each local child welfare agency is part of a larger community system of children's services. Constraints emanating from this larger system limit the freedom of agencies to implement change. In the remainder of this chapter, we will examine a few of these barriers to implementing systematic case management procedures and will offer specific suggestions to reduce these barriers.

FISCAL CONSTRAINTS

The effects of fiscal policy upon agency autonomy are examined in this section. In providing funds for foster care services, the federal government cites as its objective that out-of-home placement be temporary and aimed at reuniting children and their families.[5] Toward this end, it contributes "75 percent for salaries of service workers, supervisors, and support staff, and 50 percent of the salaries of eligibility workers, administrative costs, overhead, and all other costs."[6] Unfortunately, federal policy specifying the conditions for receipt of these monies does not support its stated objective. The policy is that funds are available only if children are removed under court order (the judicial determinacy requirement). This requirement is counterproductive in important ways. First, it provides a disincentive to return dependent children to their families, since for each child returned, the state must absorb the loss of federal monies allocated for salaries and administrative costs. In addition, there is an incentive to make children dependents in order to receive this money.* Processing dependency petitions means an increase of paper work for child welfare workers, and stigmatization of parents who must be alleged as failing in some manner in order for the court to assume jurisdiction. Stigmatization makes problems appear more severe than they

---

*During the course of the project, the director was reminded by one member of county administration that our success in moving youngsters out of placement was costly to the county in terms of lost monies.

TABLE 6.1

Oregon Project Results, by Permanent Plan
(Status as of October 31, 1976)

Plan	Plan Implemented	Plan in Progress	Plan Not Successful	Total Number	Percent
Back to parent	131	5		136	27
Adoption	184	83		267	51
By foster parents	96	63		159	31
By new parents	88	20		108	21
Contractual foster care	37	3		40	8
Relatives	15	1		16	3
Other	—	—	50	50	10
Total	367	92	50	509	100%
	(72%)	(18%)	(10%)		

Source: Arthur Emlen, Janet Lahti, Glen Downs, Alex McKay, and Susan Downs, *Overcoming Barriers to Planning for Children in Foster Care* (Portland, Ore.: Regional Research Institute for Human Services, 1977), p. 5.

are, and may contribute to caseworkers' avoiding contact with natural parents.

There are two models of state-level administration of child welfare programs, state-administered and state-supervised, with program autonomy resting with local or county government in the state-supervised type. The state is required to insure that agencies comply with federal regulations for the receipt of federal monies. However, local influence is paramount when programs are administered by local or county government.[7] Even in states where programs are run directly by a state agency, the new community involvement provisions of Title XX of the Social Security Act shift a significant degree of decision-making autonomy to the local or county level.

In California, counties pay roughly 25 percent of the costs of welfare, the state contributes about 31 percent, and the federal government contributes roughly 45 percent of the total costs.[8] Since the 58 counties in California act autonomously in running their programs, a number of vested interest groups at that level vie for the limited monies available. The extent of this competition can be seen in the fact that there are 65 to 70 boards and commissions concerned with human services in Alameda County, plus "twenty-two advisory groups for social and health care services alone."[9] It is the task of the County Board of Supervisors to decide how to allocate these funds. With so many competing demands, this task is indeed formidable. Sharon Krefetz examines the influences on local board decision making, suggesting that the politics of this decision making are a function of whether board members are elected at large or by districts.[10] When elected at large, supervisors do not have direct responsibility to a single constituency, whereas board members elected from districts make decisions in accordance with the expressed or implied wishes of the clients who have elected them. In Alameda County supervisors are elected by district. Using the Krefetz model, a knowledge of constituent priorities should make prediction of supervisorial allocations to any given service program possible.

In accordance with the community involvement provisions of Title XX, community residents are asked to state their serviced needs as ranked priorities. Out of 16 possible service areas, Alameda county residents ranked out-of-home services as number 16.[11] (Employment, housing, legal assistance, and information and referral services were ranked as the four most needed services. Other services included day care, health care, homemaker service, home management, and family planning.) It is, therefore, not surprising that out of a human services budget for the county of approximately $500 million, county appropriations for maintenance of children in foster care accounted for only $3.5 million, or 7 percent.[12] The low priority given to foster care is reflected in a statewide cutback from 700 service workers in 1972 to 350 in 1976.[13]

The foregoing points to the fiscal constraints placed on local agencies and suggests that there are distinct limits to changes that agencies can make. We will consider now what might be accomplished within these boundaries.

AGENCY CONSTRAINTS

Within external fiscal constraints to change and internal limits to services that can be offered, the agency director remains "the pivotal figure in locally administered welfare programs."[14] There is much that the occupant of this position can do. Our prime interest is with internal management policies and the extent to which they support or discourage systematic case planning. For purposes of illustration, we will describe briefly some of the operational principles in the agency where this study was conducted, and consider their effects on service delivery. At the time of the study, the administration employed what was described as a "middle-management" model for determining staff assignments. The objective of this model was to allow all supervisory personnel to learn the operations of each part of the system, thereby gaining knowledge of the system as a whole. This was to be accomplished by rotating supervisors across service units (eligibility, foster home licensing, foster home carrying units, and so forth). Assignment to any one unit rarely exceeded one year. At the same time, line staff were being shifted interdepartmentally. The major shift was to move M.S.W. workers from foster care carrying units to adoption units, and to replace these workers with AFDC eligibility staff.

Understanding the operations of each part of the system may have its merits. However, these merits are dubious in light of the effects on service delivery. Consider the following examples. One staff person whose responsibility it was to oversee unit supervisors was placed in her position at the end of the first year of the project. She worked very closely with the project supervisor, offering full support for every facet of our work. Simultaneously, she was developing a framework to offer much-needed guidance to supervisors in methods for monitoring case movement in order to maximize worker opportunity to offer effective service. In keeping with the middle-management concept, she was transferred out of her position when she completed her framework (but before she had the opportunity to implement its tenets). Her framework was never implemented. It occupies shelf space along with other attempts at systematic change. The process of rotating supervisors and child welfare workers resulted, at best, in placing a supervisor in charge of a unit that had managed to maintain some experienced child welfare workers. While this resulted in role reversal (workers training the supervisor), it was superior to the not infrequent result of bringing together an inexperienced supervisor and an equally inexperienced staff. We believe that the lack of case movement in the follow-up year was attributable in part to this practice.

Administrators make management decisions for complex reasons. There are no simple answers as to why projects that demonstrate effective methods do not result in these procedures being made a regular part of agency practice, or why these procedures are not disseminated among other agencies. Perhaps the most famous example of a failure to continue or to diffuse a demonstrably effective program was the lodge system developed by George Fairweather and his colleagues. This system was shown to be much more effective than traditional hospitalization procedures in maintaining mental patients in their natural environment and in maintaining employment at a cost much lower than that of usual procedures provided in the hospital.[15] The lodge was composed of a group of patients that was formed within the hospital; upon discharge, members lived together in the community and functioned as an independent unit. The original lodge group ran a janitorial service. The host hospital did not continue the program, and even more sobering were the results of a later attempt to diffuse the innovation of the lodge system to other mental hospitals. Out of an original sample of 255 mental hospitals in the United States, 102 said that they were not interested in their staff even receiving brochures describing the lodge system. Of the remaining, only 117 permitted a workshop to be given concerning the lodge system, 23 permitted a two-month demonstration project in which a group (an integral aspect of the lodge program) was formed on the ward, and only 15 actually went on to form a lodge in the community.[16]

The effort to follow the Alameda Experimental Demonstration Project with an implementation phase was disappointing. The success of the project, shown in the significantly larger number of experimental than control children headed out of placement, was the stimulus to continue to a third year, in which project methods would be implemented within the county child welfare department. County child welfare staff were to receive training in the use of procedures developed and tested by the experimental project, and the project director was to offer consultation to assist them in using these methods with their clients. The results of this effort were to be evaluated through a simple research design using experimental and control groups of foster care workers and clients.[17]

The implementation was initially planned to span a 12-month period. This span actually was only five months. First, a long and demoralizing strike by employees during the summer of 1976 delayed the beginning of implementation. Time lost during this period produced a large backlog of agency work, and training of county staff could not take place until October 1976. The running time of the experiment was further reduced to allow final data to be collected and analyzed. This became necessary when it was determined that the grant could not be extended to allow for analysis and reporting during the summer of 1977. Hence, 7 of the 12 implementation months (58 percent) were lost.

There are several facets of this implementation phase that are worth noting in some detail. These facets highlight the importance of administrative support to maximize successful implementation efforts and to provide essential information on the problems encountered when the procedures developed in experimental projects are put into use as a regular part of agency routine.

In our opinion, a major problem was the failure of administration to involve line staff in deciding whether to implement a project, despite repeated requests by the project director that staff be included. Once the decision was made to do so, procedures were developed for implementation. Line worker input also was ignored in this phase, in spite of our repeated requests for their involvement. In all, there was a lapse of eight months from the time negotiations for implementation were first opened until administration included line workers in discussions. By this time procedures were fully developed and staff involvement was token at best. We can guess the demoralizing effect of this omission on those persons whose day-to-day work would be most affected. Under these conditions, we hardly can expect staff to embrace new procedures enthusiastically.

Once the implementation phase got under way, the administration made no attempt to see to it that staff followed the procedures outlined. Whether or not procedures that had been proved successful during the experimental phase were employed was left to individual staff discretion. Experimental workers were expected to use contracts with their families. Contracts were written for only 15 out of 88 families (17 percent) during this implementation phase. Workers were asked to record the same process data that had been compiled during the project. We believed this information would be useful in pinpointing the difficulties experienced in implementing these new procedures in agency routine. Such reports rarely were made. It was planned that cases selected for the implementation phase were to be only those in which decision was pending. In fact, no cases were excluded, specifically those in which decisions had already been made during the experimental project phase for 61 percent of the experimental families and 59 percent of those in control.

The project director's major role during implementation was to act as consultant on the use of case management methods that had been employed successfully by experimental project workers. Each time there was consultation with a line worker, the supervisor was expected to be present. It was planned that the project director's consultative role would decrease as supervisors became more familiar with the procedures, allowing them to assume responsibility for implementation. It was especially important they do so, because many of the supervisors were newly transferred to foster care units and had little knowledge of the intricacies of foster care decision making. In fact, out of approximately 200 hours of consulting time, supervisors were present for less than 12. We believe this datum to be a measure of agency administration's lack of support.

Returning to the question of why management decisions so often seem counter-productive to service delivery, Krefetz points to the importance of the background and training of the director of a public welfare agency and the effect this has on service delivery decisions.[18] She studied the welfare systems in two major cities, one where the agency director had been a social worker and another where the director came from a business and management background. She describes agency policy in the former city as "client-oriented" and the latter as "budget and rule" oriented. A client-oriented director will make decisions to utilize staff time in ways that are more beneficial to clients, whereas a business-oriented director assigns priority to paper work over services.

> . . . there is a high degree of corresponsence between the predispositions and orientations of the welfare agency heads and the behavior of the welfare systems in Baltimore and San Francisco. . . . there is a close fit between what each of the local agency heads believes ought to be done and what actually is done in the treatment of welfare client. . . . each [agency director] organizes his department in a way that reflects and promotes his values and priorities. . . . the director of Baltimore's welfare agency has placed primary emphasis upon concern for clients' needs and aggressive advocacy of their causes. . . . clients themselves have been brought into the policy making process of the department. Furthermore, by interacting frequently and sharing decision making with members of his staff . . . [he] is able to see to it that his views are widely known throughout the department and those charged with implementing them are, for the most part, in basic agreement. . . .

A very different situation exists in San Francisco. Its welfare agency head . . . with his background in business administration and accounting, has emphasized the need for his department's personnel to be concerned above all with strict adherence to the rules and with their responsibilities to keep spending down. . . . [the welfare director] concentrates on administrative matters rather than programatic or philosophical concerns . . . and involves few, if any, staff members, much less clients [in the decision-making process]. He has been criticized both within and without the department for failing to provide clear leadership on client-service matters and for contributing to poor staff morale.[19]

The business management orientation of the welfare department where the follow-up phase of the Alameda Project occurred is evident in several respects. The approach we described for staff assignment was not conducive to effective service delivery. The failure to involve staff in decision making that affected their daily work was demoralizing. Administrative priorities for staff time placed paper work at the top of the hierarchy, monitoring children already in placement next, and contact with natural parents last.[20] A projected plan to prepare a description of the social services available in the county and the clients eligible for these services was not completed until mandated by Title XX requirements for fiscal year 1975–76. Despite Title XX requirements that clients be involved in drafting service plans, "public input was not solicited."[21] The problems highlighted in our discussion of implications for administration—specifically the absence of clear policy statements to guide workers, of case monitoring and data collection systems, and of incentives and training programs to support worker commitment—can be understood in the light of the low priority assigned to service delivery.

It is necessary to recognize that many critical decisions affecting attainment of the objectives of foster home care are political in nature. By this we mean that variables unrelated to attaining the objectives of foster home care enter into decisions that affect the outcome of this service. It has been suggested, for example, that the number of votes a decision may cost a judge will influence his decision making at neglect and dependency hearings.[22] The competition among vested interest groups for funds allocated to social services is a central aspect of political decision making.* Revenue sharing illustrates this point. The principle behind revenue sharing was to take money that had been allocated to specific programs, such as AFDC foster care, and to combine these funds into a single block grant to the states. The state would then allocate funds to specific programs at their own discretion. No priorities or standards would be set by the federal government.[23] It is clear that "special interest groups with political strength will dictate how this money will be spent." Poor people, who constitute the bulk

---

*The public ranking of services was for the 1976–77 fiscal year.

of those using foster care services, are not noted for their political influence. The effects of the competing aspects of revenue sharing and the political basis for decision making are demonstrated in the following passage:

> In a three year period between the start of revenue sharing in 1972 and early 1975, municipalities spent 44% of their revenue sharing funds on public safety, 15% on public transportation, 13% on environmental protection, 15% on health, and a mere 1% on social services for the poor and aged. In many cases communities elected to drop services that were once provided with federal money as soon as revenue sharing with local control gave them the choice. A recent study of 37 cities reports that only seven used any revenue sharing funds to replace any terminating federal programs.[24]

No doubt the community involvement provisions of Title XX were included as a means of redressing the historical failure to involve clients in deciding how funds are best allocated. As noted in our example of the first county plan, there is no way to guarantee that this requirement will be honored.

The foregoing presents a picture of a system that is at "odds with itself." On the one hand, federal and state legislatures, the judiciary, and child welfare professionals espouse common goals for the provision of foster care services. Simultaneously, action taken by various parts of the system work against goal attainment. The judicial determinacy requirements was identified as one such impediment. Administrators may give priority to paper work because of the link between reporting and receipt of federal funds.[25] The federal government issues regulations, such as the community involvement provisions of Title XX, but fails to support them with guidelines for implementation or systems to monitor compliance. Federal regulations are meant to eliminate state-to-state inequalities in available services and eligibility requirements for use of these services. Because guidelines for implementation are not issued, the states are left to interpret regulations as they see fit, maintaining, rather than eliminating, the problems they are meant to address.[26]

Just as the federal government does not monitor compliance, so the states do not monitor compliance at the local level. In California there is only minimal contact between state and county officials. The characteristics of programs are not reviewed; instead, they are deduced from a cursory reading of case records. With regard to monitoring for compliance with federal and state regulations, reports to the state "routinely indicate that the county anticipates movement toward this goal." But the state uses no inducements nor sanctions to persuade or force counties to change their activities. Sanctions for noncompliance, such as withholding funds, have never been used, even when failure to comply is both overt and deliberate.[27] California collects data concerning children in out-of-home care from each county, and is supposed to compile and report this on a quarterly basis. In September 1977, when we requested copies of the most recent state reports, the most recent documents available at that time reported data compiled for June 1975. Despite a data collection system, no new reports were issued in almost two years.

The courts are expected to play an intermediary role between federal government and public welfare authorities. The judicial determinacy requirement was meant to act as a "safeguard . . . against arbitrary removal of children by public welfare agencies."[28] In addition, the courts were expected to monitor the progress of children who were removed, in order to insure that the objective of reunifying families was pursued. Their failure in this regard is evident in the spate of new legislation that we have discussed, all of which attempts to delineate steps to be followed to attain this objective.

Each part of the foster care system can point to the constraints under which it operates. As the foregoing discussion indicates, many of these are legitimate bases for complaints. Instead of a unified system operating to achieve common ends, we have a fragmented operation that functions in greater discord than harmony. Leadership must be established by delineating mechanisms for complying with regulations, systems to monitor compliance, and appropriate sanctions for noncompliance. The federal role in financing foster care is increasing, since the states are unable to carry the fiscal burden of these programs. While wanting to maintain their program autonomy, states call for greater federal involvement in the financing of these services.[29] It is likely that the federal government will increase its fiscal participation and establish additional regulations.[30] It seems that the responsibility for unifying the system must rest at the federal level.

GUIDELINES FOR INTRODUCING NEW PROGRAMS

There are steps that can be taken while awaiting change at higher levels of the system. Some are suggested by the results of the Oregon Permanent Planning Project. During the third year of this project, the Children's Services Division "moved vigorously to incorporate the permanent planning process."[31] This division now is in the process of implementing permanent planning statewide. Key members of the original demonstration staff were incorporated into a dissemination project, a systematic plan with Children's Bureau support for disseminating the decision-making methods tested in Oregon to 45 states over a four-year period that began in early 1977.[32]

Key elements in the evident success of the Oregon project in overcoming institutional barriers to permanent planning for children in foster care were leadership arising from within the system (that is, social workers who perceived the necessity for change and had the tools at hand to initiate a change process); an agency outside the welfare system, in this instance the Regional Research Institute for Human Services, where people were found who were responsive to an appeal to collaborating in a search for new directions, and a condition of timeliness, itself a product of many conditions in immediate state and national environments that are summed up in the statement that this project responded to an idea whose time had come— namely, the concern about children who drift in foster care.[33]

It will inform our discussion to consider some of the factors that Fairweather and his colleagues found in their attempt to diffuse the lodge system to other mental hospitals. They generated a number of principles, some of which are particularly relevant to the successful efforts of the Oregon project and to our own less successful effort to continue an innovation within a child welfare agency. It is not surprising that the first principle they extracted from their efforts is that of perseverance (by which they refer to hard work and tolerance for confusion):

> If there is a single general notion from our data and experiences that we would like to import to the reader, it is that effecting institutional innova- tion is a highly complex multivariate phenomenon that it takes a long time to achieve and that the payoff is often minimal when weighed against the effort expended.[34]

It is apparent, in light of this principle, that the time constraints (one year for the implementation phase) of the Alameda Project were minimal at best. Had the intended 12-month effort, rather than only 5, been available, the payoff might still have been "minimal when weighed against the effort expended." The evident success of the Oregon project in implementing change within the child welfare system, in light of this principle, is weighed against the fact it has had four years (as of the time of this writing) to have an impact upon the agency.

Although each of the principles elaborated by Fairweather are worth examination for their applicability to innovation within a child welfare agency, and it would be illuminating to consider each in juxtaposition with the experience of the Oregon Children's Service Division in implementing permanent planning strategies statewide, we will comment here on only one other. This eighth principle concerns the importance of a small social change group that spearheaded the change effort. It was a supervisor and a unit of social workers in one county office who saw the necessity for reorienting foster care and initiated the change process that gained momentum from additional ideas and adherents as it moved along. Project concepts and methods were systematically diffused (Fairweather's final principle) through workshops conducted in strategic areas of the state and through project staff, placed at the operating level in selected county offices, who modeled project values and demonstrated permanent planning methods.

We believe that the findings described by Fairweather and his col- leagues were implications for attempts to diffuse innovative programs within child welfare agencies. They offer grounds for both optimism and pessimism. Grounds for optimism relate to the finding that change can be implemented at various levels in an organization, and that degree of change is not related to a number of factors one cannot change, such as the community in which the agency exists, or that are difficult to alter, such as agency budgets. They also offer grounds for optimism in the continuation of innovations once new programs were implemented. That is, once a change actually occurred, it tended to stick. The findings from the diffusion study certainly are pessimistic in terms of the actual number of agencies that implemented the new program.

Viewing the results of our implementation phase in light of the Fairweather study, it is apparent why it was essentially a failure. No cohesive group of individuals was formed within the agency. Such a group was essential to the implementation of the community lodge program in the mental hospitals discussed ·above; and such a group was decisive in the success of the Oregon project in diffusing innovation throughout the state's foster care system. Dissemination among other state and local child welfare systems continues as of this writing, led by a nucleus group from the original Oregon project. It is too early to evaluate the results of this dissemination phase. There is evidence of a national ferment for change in foster care systems, stimulated not only by the Oregon project but also by many studies and reviews that are serving to pinpoint the issue of children drifting in foster care. Perhaps we can anticipate an improved climate for innovation at all levels of foster care administration.

In this chapter we identified some of the institutional barriers to the use of systematic case planning and case management procedures. These barriers are multideminsional, ranging from culturally mediated attitudes toward the exercise of state intervention in parent-child relationships, to failures in federal social policy implementation that leave state and local foster care agencies laboring under ambiguous mandates and with confused objectives. Local political and intra-agency constraints were illustrated by our experience with the county in which this experimental project was conducted, particularly by the disappointing results of our effort to implement methods of proved effectiveness within the regular foster care administration. Finally, we suggested some guides to diffusion of new methods and procedures among similar programs, and compared a successful and a less successful dissemination effort and identified the ingredients essential to success.

NOTES

1. Arthur C. Emlen and staff, *Barriers to Planning for Children in Foster Care*, (Portland, Ore.: Regional Research Institute for Human Services, 1976), pp. 8.3, 8.4.

2. Ann W. Shyne, *The Need for Foster Care* (New York: Child Welfare League of America, 1969).

3. Scott Briar, "Clinical Judgement in Foster Care Placement," *Child Welfare* 42 (1963): 161-69.

4. Emlen and staff, op. cit., pp. 8.4-8.9.

5. Winford Oliphant, *AFDC Foster Care: Problems and Recommendations* (New York: Child Welfare League of America, 1974), p. 3.

6. Jessica S. Pers, *Government as Parent: Administering Foster Care in California* (Berkeley, Institute of Governmental Studies, University of California, 1976), p. 83.

7. Ibid., ch. 2; Sharon P. Krefetz, *Welfare Policy Making and City Politics* (New York: Praeger, 1976), p. 12.

8. Krefetz, op. cit., p. 92.

9. Arthur Young and Co., *Final Report: Alameda County Project on Human Services Planning* (Oakland, Calif.: Arthur Young and Co., 1976), p. I–1.

10. Krefetz, op. cit., pp. 71–73.

11. California Department of Social Welfare, *Proposed Plan for the Delivery of Welfare Social Services* (Sacramento: the Department, 1976), p. 2.

12. Office of Program Evaluation, *Placement in Foster Care: Issues and Concerns* (Oakland, Calif.: the Office, 1977), p. 3.

13. Arthur Young & Co., op. cit., p. V–6.

14. Krefetz, op. cit., p. 95.

15. George W. Fairweather, David H. Sanders, David L. Cressler, and Hugo Maynard, *Community Life for the Mentally Ill: An Alternative to Institutional Care* (Chicago: Aldine, 1969).

16. George W. Fairweather, David H. Sanders, Louis G. Tornatzky, and Robert N. Harris, Jr., *Creating Change in Mental Health Organizations* (New York: Pergamon, 1974), pp. 162–65.

17. Theodore J. Stein, "Final Report of the Alameda Project Implementation" (Oakland, Calif., 1977) (unpublished).

18. Krefetz, op. cit., p. 132.

19. Ibid., pp. 136–37.

20. Office of Program Evaluation, op. cit., p. 54.

21. Arthur Young & Co., op. cit., p. V–2.

22. Norman A. Polansky, Carolyn Hally, and Nancy F. Polansky, *Profile of Neglect: A Survey of the State of Knowledge of Child Neglect* (Washington, D.C.: Social and Rehabilitation Service, U.S. Department of Health, Education and Welfare, 1973), p. 8.

23. Marian Wright Edelman, "A Political-Legislative Overview of Federal Child Care Proposals," in Nathan B. Talbot, ed., *Raising Children in Modern America* (Boston: Little, Brown, 1974), p. 313.

24. Kenneth Kenniston and the Carnegie Council on Children, *All Our Children: The American Family Under Pressure* (New York: Harcourt Brace Jovanovich, 1977), p. 148.

25. Children's Bureau, *Child Welfare in 25 States: An Overview* D.H.E.W. publication no. (OHD) 76-30090 (Washington, D.C.: U.S. Department of Health, Education and Welfare, 1976), p. xiii.

26. Oliphant, op. cit., p. 24.

27. Pers, op. cit., pp. 51–52.

28. Oliphant, op. cit., p. 2.

29. Robert Harris, *Federal Assumption of Welfare and Medicaid Costs: Issues and Budgetary Impacts* (Washington, D.C.: Urban Institute, 1977), p. 1.

30. The MacNeil/Lehrer Report, *Welfare Reform* (New York: WNET/13, 1977); Harris, op. cit.; Robert Harris, *Welfare Reform and Social Insurance: Program Issues and Budget Impacts* (Washington, D.C.: Urban Institute, 1977).

31. Arthur Emlen, Janet Lahti, Glen Downs, Alex McKay, and Susan Downs, *Overcoming Barriers to Planning for Children in Foster Care* (Portland, Ore.: Regional Research Institute for Human Service, 1977), p. 6.

32. Regional Research Institute for Human Services, *Dissemination and Utilization of Permanent Planning Strategies for Children in Long-Term Foster Care*, technical proposal submitted to U.S. Department of Health, Education and Welfare, September 1, 1976, RFP No. HEW-105-76-1181 (published only as an RFP) (Portland, Ore.: the Institute, 1976).

33. Emlen et al., op. cit., p. 7.

34. Fairweather et al., *Creating Change in Mental Health Organizations*, p. 182.

PART II

7

ASSESSMENT AND CONTRACTING

The first part of this chapter will introduce the steps in the behavioral assessment procedures employed in the Alameda Project.

STEP 1: IDENTIFYING PARENTAL OBJECTIVES FOR A CHILD'S FUTURE

The purpose of this step is to identify parental objectives for the future of a child. The context in which the worker and client meet, whether it is before or after placement, defines the range of possible alternatives. If they meet before placement, the parent either has decided that he or she wishes to place a child out of the home, or may wish to investigate this as a possibility. Postplacement decisions include the parent's wish to have a child restored to his or her care, the parent's indecision as to what he or she wants for the child's future, or the parent's decision to place a child for adoption or to have a foster parent, relative, or friend become the child's legal guardian.

Parental objectives usually can be determined within one to three interviews, during which time the worker and client create a problem profile. By identifying problems, the worker assists the client in selecting the most appropriate alternative. To illustrate construction of such a profile, let us assume a preplacement situation in which the client states a wish to investigate the possibility of placing the child outside of the home. The worker would first obtain from the client a preliminary statement of the problems he or she sees as the reasons for this request. The worker would explain that in order to assess the current situation completely and reach an appropriate decision, the worker will have to see the client one or two more times, with at least one of these visits in the client's home and with the child present. This will permit the worker to gain a more complete picture of the client's problems. One possible outcome is that community resources would be located to aid in problem resolution and avoid removing a child from his or her home.

Should the client say he or she has already decided to place a child outside of the home, the same process would occur, with the objective of preventing placement when possible.

If the child already is in placement, the parent is asked whether he or she wants the child restored to his or her care. In the Alameda Project, 95 percent of the biological parents responded affirmatively to this question. Together with the client, the social worker then identified the problems it was necessary to resolve before the child could be returned. The assessment process described later is applicable to either the preplacement or the postplacement situation. Before turning to this assessment, we should consider briefly parents who are undecided about their child's future, or parents who have reached a decision to place children for adoption or to have a foster parent or relative assume legal guardianship. It is the worker's task to make certain that the parents understand the implications of each decision. The consequences for a natural parent of deciding either to place a child for adoption or to have a legal guardian appointed may vary, depending upon agency policy or upon the attitude of the adoptive parents or of the foster parents who obtain legal guardianship. There may be complete severance of contact between the natural parent and child if either the agency or the new parents insist upon it; or continued contact may be permitted in instances where the adoptive parent or legal guardian is known to the natural parents.

For the parent who is undecided, the worker begins by clarifying the alternatives (restoration, adoption, guardianship, long-term care) and the implications of each. The client is informed that he or she will be assisted in reaching an appropriate decision, and that this is best achieved by conducting an assessment to identify the problems that must be confronted and then providing the parent with a framework for selecting among alternatives.

STEP 2: CONSTRUCTING A PROBLEM PROFILE

This step provides an overview of problem areas.[1] Problems noted include those mentioned by the client, those from case records and court reports, and those noted by the caseworker. The focus is upon changes that are needed to maintain a child in its own home, to restore a child who is already in care, or to assist the parent who has not reached a decision. A completed profile will contain the following:

1. A list of problems, such as, financial, housing, behavioral, or emotional
2. The source of identification of each problem (client, verbal report, case record, and so forth)

3. Who is said to have the problem (the child, the parent, other)
4. An example of behavior that defines the problem; for instance, the worker may determine that a child who is said to be "unmanageable" refuses to return home from school at an appointed hour
5. The context(s) in which the problem is displayed: Is the youngster "unmanageable" only in the parents' home, or is this a problem at school and in the home of relatives as well?
6. The date on which the problem(s) is identified

The manner in which various sources of information contribute to creating a problem profile is discussed below.

The Use of Client Verbal Reports

The worker lists problems that are identified by the clients. These may be problems presented at intake or, if the child is already in care, issues that a client thinks will have to be resolved if the child is to return home. The information can be obtained by asking a series of questions that focus directly on the task at hand while remaining open-ended so as to allow the client a wide range of responses. The following are examples of questions that might be asked:

1. What are the problems that led to your request that James be placed outside of your home?
2. What would have to be different before he could return home?
3. How would someone recognize this difference?
4. Do you have any personal problems that you think must be resolved before he can return home?
5. How would things be different if these were resolved?
6. What would an observer see if these differences occurred?

Additional questions may be needed to clarify information, as illustrated below:

Client: Nothing works any more, everything at home is a mess.
Caseworker: Please tell me, as best you can, what you mean when you say that "nothing works."
Client: I can't discipline him any more, he never listens to anything that I say, and we always end up fighting.

While the client's response is still not specific, it does indicate a general problem area, that of discipline.

Let us assume, for example, that in addition to problems in disciplining the son, the client reports financial problems, housing inadequate to raise his son. The problems would be listed on the profile, as shown below:

FIGURE 7.1

Beginning Problem Profile

Problem No.	Label	Who Labels	Who Has the Problem	Date	Examples	Situation
1	discipline	father	father/son	10-1-74		
2	finances	father	father	"		
3	inadequate housing	father	father	"		

Source: Compiled by author.

The Use of Care Reports and Court Records

In considering the contribution that case reports and court records will make to a problem profile, the age and the specificity of information in such documents must be considered. If a child has been in care for a year, it is possible that issues noted at the time of placement are no longer problematic. A client who abused alcohol or drugs one year ago may no longer do so. Similarly, factors that contributed to a child's behavior problem, such as the neighborhood in which the family lived or peer relationships, may have been eliminated by a change in environment. The concern with concreteness of information is no different when considering written sources of information than when obtaining verbal reports from a client. The usefulness of such records will depend upon whether or not specific examples of behaviors and related situation that define problem areas are offered along with information relevant to establishing a treatment program.

If the case reports or court records are relatively recent, more precise information may be obtained in discussion with the client. Court investigators or other social workers may be able to clarify what is meant by a "filthy" home or by the often used but general term, "neglect." However, when records are both nonspecific and old, they may have no utility for identifying current problems. At most, they may point to potential problem areas. When adding information to the profile from either of these sources, the type of document, its date, and the data source (such as probation officer or social worker) are noted on the profile if this information is available.

Problems Identified by the Worker

Problems also may be identified by the worker. For example, day care arrangements may have to be made for a child who will be restored to a working parent; problems may be noted in the course of observing parent-child interaction during a home visit. Let's say that a child is in placement, the parent visits only once each month, and the parent seeks restoration. Increasing parent-child visits will be an important consideration. A first step in deciding upon a visiting schedule is collecting information concerning the quality of parent-child interaction through observation.

At least one of the first three interviews may occur outside of the office in order to obtain such data. Observational periods usually are an hour long. Various problems may be observed during this period. For example, interaction between the parent and child may be minimal, or the parent may make no affectionate overtures toward the child, such as picking it up or engaging in verbal exchange. The child may call upon another adult, perhaps the foster parent or the social worker, if it wants anything. This information suggests that the caseworker probably will have to involve both parent and child so as to increase their positive contact, and that until this occurs, the frequency of visits and their length should be kept to a minimum. This information is added to the profile, with the caseworker noted as the source of problem identification. On the other hand, observation may reveal very positive contact between parent and child, indicating that visiting can be increased rapidly. The information obtained at this time is primarily suggestive. Additional data on parent-child interaction are gathered later. This initial information is important for establishing a visiting schedule.

STEP 2A: BEGINNING PROBLEM DEFINITION AND SITUATIONAL EXAMPLES

Clients are likely to use abstractions from behavior.[2] Inattention may refer to looking around the room. Jealousy may be used to describe one boy hitting another. Some clients concentrate upon motives rather than upon behaviors.[3] A client may say, "I guess the problem is that he's just lazy," or "He just doesn't want to do it." Such statements are offered as explanations for problems. "Motive analysis" can lead one away from the identification of relevant behaviors. Because of the frequent use of traits and motives to explain behaviors, clients are not accustomed to identifying behaviors-in-situations. They usually do not realize that problem behaviors occur only in certain specific situations.

Examples of behaviors that relate to each problem and information describing the contexts in which these occur are obtained. They may be supplied verbally by the client, abstracted from case or court records, or identified through worker observation. For example, a child who cannot be disciplined may be one who "runs out of the house each time the parents have a disagreement." Obtaining examples of behaviors-in-situations[4] to which the client is referring when he or she says that he or she cannot "discipline" a child serves two functions. Since different clients may employ identical labels to refer to different behaviors, it is only by asking for examples that the caseworker can be sure that he or she and the client are discussing the same behaviors. This information also will provide a focus for gathering observational data in the client's environment. In order to collect such information, the caseworker must know which behaviors are to be focused upon and the context in which such observation should occur. In addition, defining problems at this stage of assessment may enable specification of objectives for certain areas and immediate work geared toward problem resolution. To illustrate this briefly, consider the issue of finances. Let's say that the father is unemployed, but that he has work skills. The objective of obtaining employment and a means of accomplishing this may be identified at this time.

Some examples of behaviors-in-situations are given below.

Client Label	Examples	Situational Context
Jason is unmanageable	He runs around the house	home
	He does not follow	
	instructions	
My husband is mean	He seldom speaks at	
	dinner	home

Each of these behaviors is countable, and information is provided as to the situation in which it occurs. Examples are given below of behaviors that need to be pinpointed.

Terms That Need to Be Specified	Countable Behaviors
He is insecure	He holds on to his mother whenever they are together
She doesn't like anybody	She refuses to speak to anyone
She gets angry and explodes	She yells and screams when not given what she wants
He is depressed	He won't come out of his room
His mother is too protective	She answers questions for him before he has a chance to say anything

A helpful question to ask when specifying behaviors is whether two or more people could easily agree as to the occurrence of a behavior. If the answer is no, as it might be for many of the terms listed in the left column, further pinpointing is necessary.

Let us turn to a more detailed consideration of the process of obtaining information describing the behavioral referents of a client's labels and the situations in which these occur. Information may be gained through questions posed in the interview, through client-gathered records, or through observations by the worker.

Attention can be directed toward behavior if questions focus upon behavior rather than inquiring about feelings and attitudes; for instance, "Can you give me an example of what he does?" When one example is gained, others can be requested until it seems that the set of behaviors to which the client refers when employing a given word have been identified. Information also can be gained by asking what the person complained about would do if he or she displayed a state opposite to that complained of. A parent could be asked, "What would he do if he was good?" Care must be exercised not to impose referents upon the client by making suggestions. Rather, the client is guided toward the identification by the questions asked or by offering examples of specific behaviors from other settings. Specification also must be carried out when emotional behavior, such as anxiety, is of concern. The referents of the term should be identified and the situations in which such reactions occur determined.

Information concerning surrounding conditions may be gained from questions such as the following: When does this usually take place? What is going on when this happens? Are there any times when this hardly ever occurs? Does this occur at certain times of the day more than others? What happens right afterward? It may be found that the behavior varies according to the presence or absence of certain environmental factors. A child may be enuretic only at home but never when visiting friends or relatives. Only when a mother is fatigued may the child start acting up, since in the past she has reinforced this behavior when tired and the child can recognize this state. The question "When did this start?" may offer useful information on a change in the client's environment that is related to the present complaint. A boy may have started to wet his bed after another child came to live in the home.

An example of a dialogue between client and worker is illustrated below:

Caseworker: You said that your son does not "listen to you," and that you cannot "discipline" him. Can you give me an example of a request that you made of him?

Client: I asked him to clean up his room and to help around the house, and he didn't do it.

Caseworker: What do you do when he refuses to listen?

Client: We end up yelling and arguing, then he either locks himself in his room or runs outside of the house.

Caseworker: Besides helping around the house, are there other types of requests that your son will not listen to?

Client: Just that he won't come home when I tell him to; he's always an hour or so late.

Caseworker: Are there requests that he does follow?

The information gained can be added to the profile, as shown below.

Figure 7.2

Problem Profile with Examples and Identified Situations

Problem No.	Label	Who Labels	Who Has the Problem	Date	Examples	Situation
1	discipline	father	father/son	10-1-74	son won't do chores	at home
					son won't come home at appointed hour	"
					result: father/son argument	"
					result: son locks self in room	"
					result: son leaves house	

Source: Compiled by author.

Other problem areas are then clarified, and the information added to the profile. For purposes of further illustration, let us consider the area of finances, and questions to ask to define "financial problems":

Caseworker: You say that you are having financial problems. What is your current source of income?
Client: I'm collecting unemployment and using some savings that I have in the bank.
Caseworker: Have you been actively looking for a new job?
Client: Off and on, not too much, I guess.
Caseworker: What kind of work have you done in the past?
Client: I've operated a printing press and done warehouse work.

From this exchange the worker has learned that the father does have work skills and that he has not sought employment. Through further discussion with the client, through reading case records and court reports, and through observations, additional problem areas are identified, and behavioral examples and situational contexts clarified. As a result, we have a complete profile (see figures 7.3 and 7.4).

We may now begin to form a hypothesis about factors that contribute to a problem. To consider this in detail, we will use the problems of finances and the father's unemployment mentioned above. Let us assume that throughout the interview, the father was hesitant in answering questions (delayed quite a while before responding) and the responses he did offer were in the form of incomplete sentences. Let us also assume that he did not look at the worker when responding, gazing instead at the ceiling and floor. One

FIGURE 7.3

Completed Problem Profile

Problem No.	Label	Who Labels	Who Has the Problem	Date	Examples	Situation
1	discipline	father	father/son	10-1-74	son won't do chores son won't come home at appointed hour result: father/son argument result: son locks self in room result: son leaves house	at home at home at home at home
2	finances	father	father	10-1-74	collecting unemployment unused work skills: printing press operator and warehouseman	
3	inadequate housing	father	father	10-1-74	has studio apartment wants two-bedroom apartment	
4	can't get along with relatives	father	father	10-1-74	disagree over father's child-rearing practices	during visits, in presence of child
5	like to visit more often	father	father	10-1-74	visits only bimonthly	visits occur in foster home or nearby park
6	child care	worker	father	10-1-74	after-school care arrangements needed during father's working hours	
7	child un- manageable	case record	father/son	11-73	none provided in record	
8	drug abuse	court	father	5-73	two arrests for possession of heroin one admission to hospital detoxifica- tion unit	"street arrest" hospital

Source: Compiled by author.

171

FIGURE 7.4

Completed Problem Profile

Problem No.	Label	Who Labels	Who Has the Problem	Date	Examples	Situation
1	child abuse	court	mother	2-6-74	welts on child's back burns on child's arms and legs	unknown
2	therapeutic counseling	court	mother	2-6-74	mother must participate in a counseling program approved by the child welfare worker	doesn't apply
3	needs help around house	mother	mother	4-7-74	assistance with household chores (dishes, cleaning)	at home
4	no social life	mother	mother	4-7-74	stays home every evening no contact with other adults at any time	
5	youngster won't obey	mother	mother/child	4-7-74	will not comply with requests for assistance with chores won't come in from play when called "talks back" to mother (mimics, argues)	at home
6	finances	mother	mother	4-7-74	lost AFDC grant when child was removed	at home and in public

Source: Compiled by author.

172

may hypothesize that he lacks interview skills, and that an interview situation is uncomfortable for him. This may help to explain why he has not actively sought employment. Bearing in mind that his discomfort may be related only to this particular interview situation, this information would be noted as something to be explored more fully at a later date.

We have found it helpful to note possible contributing conditions on a separate sheet for ready reference. Such hypotheses usually are only tentative at this stage of assessment; that is, further information usually is necessary to identify relevant factors.

Label (from profile)	Behavior	Worker's Hypotheses on Controlling Conditions	Data Source	Date
Finances	interview skills	Client hesitates when responding to questions	worker	10-1-74
		responds with incomplete statements	"	"
		does not look directly at worker	"	"

In fact, we would like to emphasize the importance of such tentativeness, because plans often are made at this point without obtaining needed additional information.

STEP 3: PROBLEM SELECTION

The objective of this step is to select from the profile the areas that most need immediate attention. Aside from problems that must be addressed as a function of court directive, the worker and client jointly select additional problem areas whose resolution may be necessary if, for example, a child is to be restored to a parent's home. The written profile presented to the client offers a basis for problem selection. Before selection can begin, there are several factors that should be explained to the client.

First, only problem areas that relate directly to the parent's objectives for the child's future can be focused upon at this time. If the parent wishes the child to be restored to the home, decisions must be made on which areas relate to this objective. For purposes of illustration, consider problem number 4 in Figure 7.3, that of difficulties with relatives. The relation of this issue to achieving restoration may depend on whether or not the father must rely on relatives for child care assistance. If child care facilities are not available in the community, and the father's finances preclude hiring outside help, relatives may have to be called upon for such assistance, in which case this area may have to be focused upon immediately. If, however, alternative care facilities exist, and interaction between the parent and relatives is minimal, this issue may be seen as not bearing on the immediate objective and therefore would not be the focus of current intervention. This does not mean that parents are left with unresolved problems. It does suggest that certain areas can be dealt with at a later time and possibly by other community resources.

It is explained to the client that certain problem areas, such as "discipline," as well as the information from past case records regarding the child's "unmanageability," will have to be assessed in the client's natural environment before their scope and nature can be determined. The client is informed that the conditions for observation will have to be arranged, and that should any problems emerge as an outcome of such observations, these will be shared with the client and that he or she will be assisted in altering such problems. It is stated that observation will take place during visiting periods. If a court dependency is involved, and if the court has established certain conditions for the return of a child, the worker must arrange for these to be met. Let us assume that the court has directed that cessation of drug use must be established as a contingency for return. While the client may insist that he or she no longer uses drugs, the worker must explain that this will have to be established, probably by having the parent submit to weekly urinalyses.

If any problem areas have been added to the profile by the worker, the client is told why these areas are seen as conditions for return. The issue of "child care" in Figure 7.3 is a case in point.

Once the above explanations have been made, both client and worker may focus on the profile and select the areas that will be addressed first. Considering the profile in Figure 7.3, it can be seen that eight problem areas are listed. Items number 1 (discipline), 5 (increased visiting), and 7 (child's unmanageability) can be grouped together. The central issue here is for an increased visiting shcedule to be established and parent-child interaction to be assessed. Of these three items, the only one that constitutes a current problem is the low frequency of visiting. Whether or not there are problems in the other domains will not be known until visits are increased and parent-child interaction is observed.

Let us assume that item number 4, regarding relationships with relatives, can be eliminated because the parent indicates that contact is minimal, and the worker's knowledge of available community resources suggests that child care is available and that the father will not have to rely upon relatives for assistance in this area. Four areas remain: finances, housing, arranging for child care, and establishing cessation of drug use. All are directly related to the objective of restoration. The issue of increased visiting would be added to this, leaving five problem areas from the total of eight on the profile.

STEP 4: INITIAL SPECIFICATION OF OBJECTIVES, INCLUDING IDENTIFICATION OF SUBGOALS AND CLIENT'S ASSETS

For each problem selected from the profile, the expected goals are described. A fully specified objective includes description of the behavior(s) expected of the client(s), including their frequency, duration, or intensity; the conditions under which this (these) behavior(s) should be displayed; and any approximations that may be necessary to achieve the final goal. Careful identification of outcomes enables the worker and client to understand fully the purpose of their continued contact, and this permits the worker to assess whether or not he or she has the requisite skills to bring about such changes. Assuming the presence of such skills, it provides a focus for the worker to develop programs that will bring about necessary changes. Some objectives can be identified at an early point, whereas others are identified only through further assessment efforts. A failure to identify specific objectives is one deficit in case management procedure that has been noted in the literature.[5]

How Objectives Are Specified

For each problem selected from the profile, changes are identified in relation to one of the following outcomes: the acquisition of new skills (learning new job-related behaviors); the increase in desirable behaviors (an increase in positive parent-child interactions); the decrease of undesirable behaviors (reduction of the negative statements exchanged by a parent and child); the elimination of undesirable behavior (drug use); the maintenance of desired behavior at a certain rate (positive interactions over time); or the variation of behavior (increasing the number of ways a person may initiate a job interview). Examples of specified objectives include signing up for food stamps within one week; securing full-time employment within one month; talking with daughter for ten minutes after school on each weekday about her school work; thanking son after he completes a chore; spending half an hour a day playing a game with a child; spending two hours per week at a skill center, participating in center activities.

Identifying behaviors to be increased is given particular attention because it often is easier and more comfortable to decrease undesirable behaviors by increasing others. The client may find it difficult to offer examples of behaviors that he or she would like to see increased since his or her attention has been focused upon those he or she would like to decrease. This is often found when, from the client's perspective, the problem is a significant other, such as a child or a spouse. So much unpleasant interaction may have taken place that the client has become a "negative scanner" of the other's behavior, noting only behaviors that he or she does not like. Helpful questions include What does he do that you like? What would you like him to do? Answers to the first question sometimes will be "nothing," perhaps because of a history of negative interaction and because the client may not recognize the importance of reinforcing approximations to desired behavior. Special help in identifying behaviors to be increased may have to be provided. A parent could be asked what an ideal child would be like, and general labels then specified in terms of discrete behaviors.

Any person, no matter how deviant his or her repertoire, evidences approximations to desirable behaviors. Some of these may be incompatible with undesirable behaviors, and simply increasing them will decrease the latter. Two behaviors may be physically incompatible in that they cannot be performed at the same time. A child cannot sit in his seat and run around the room at the same time. A child cannot be simultaneously compliant and noncompliant, or isolate himself from other children while at the same time approaching them. Thus, some types of competing behaviors are immediately identified when their undesirable counterparts are specified. In other instances, competing behaviors may not be so readily isolated. In these situations, behaviors must be identified that are functionally, but not physically, incompatible with the undesirable behaviors.[6] This implies a search for behaviors that are not correlated with the problem behavior. When a child is playing with other children, he or she may not cry. Playing with other children could be increased to decrease crying.

After desirable behaviors are identified, the conditions that interfere with or prohibit their display can be explored during later stages of assessment, as can the conditions that would facilitate their performance. Some examples of desirable counterparts of problem behaviors are offered below.

Problem Behavior	Desirable Alternative
Does not follow instructions	follows instructions
Uncommunicative	Talks with spouse for one hour each day after work
Will not complete homework	completes homework before due date
Yells at children	requests children to do chores in a reasonable tone of voice

The most common error made in attempting to identify objectives is a lack of precision as to exactly what is to be done. Another common error is stating objectives in terms of not doing something—for example, not being rude to service people or not getting upset. Ogden Lindsley has called this the "dead man's error," in that these are objectives that could be satisfied by a dead person.[7] It is helpful to state objectives in positive terms whenever possible. In the latter example, we would identify what the client should do more of, such as thanking clerks for their help.

Identifying Subgoals and Client Assets

Outcomes are most efficiently attained by making use of client assets. It is important to identify these. Let us refer back to the problem of finances (Figure 7.3, problem 2). Given that the father would like to pursue work he has done before, his experience as a printing press operator and warehouseman would be assets in seeking employment. Skills related to problem 3 (inadequate housing) may include ability to locate possible living places and facility in making arrangements to see them. Thus, initial subgoals are selected in accord with client assets. Subgoals should consist of the closest approximations to the desired outcome that are comfortable for the client and are achievable. Let us assume that one objective is for the client to attend a neighborhood social center two evenings per week and to participate in activities offered by the center, such as art or dance classes. Subgoals and related skills may be as shown below.

Available Assets	Subgoals
Mrs. R. has access to a phone and has required "telephone skills" (what questions to ask, what information to offer)	Mrs. R. will telephone the _____ social center no later than _____ and request that information regarding center acties be mailed to her
Same as above regarding telephone skills, Mrs. R. has greater interest in some activities than in others	Mrs. R. will select one activity of interest to her from the brochure, and telephone the center director no later than _____ to arrange an appointment to discuss her possible participation

Simply telling Mrs. R. to participate in center activities twice each week probably would result in program failure if she does not have required skills. For example, she may not know how to initiate conversations, or may feel very uncomfortable entering a room full of strangers.

Let us assume that a goal is to obtain full-time employment as a printing press operator within 30 days. Assets and subgoals are shown below.

Available Assets	Subgoals (to be completed within four working days from this date)
He knows where the employment office is, and can fill out required forms	register at the state unemployment office

| | Subgoals (to be completed within |
Available Assets	four working days from this date)
He can identify relevant agencies and complete required forms and interviews	register with two employment agencies in the city
He has access to a newspaper and knows where to look for printing press operator jobs	review the newspaper want ads daily, specifically looking for job advertisements for a printing press operator
He has adequate "telephone skills" and needed "interview skills," and can manage his behavior to meet commitments	for any jobs that are identified through any of the above channels, Mr. I. will make and keep appointments for interviews for the position of concern

Subgoals and available assets can be written down on weekly assignment sheets.[8] Progress achieved with initial steps provides information as to what the next subgoals (intermediate steps) should be. Weekly assignment sheets describing the client's current relevant repertoire and the subgoals selected for that week can be used to make concrete the agreements on goals, in order to keep attention upon use of client assets and to provide a record of weekly progress.[9] Obligations of the social worker also should be written on weekly work sheets. For the work sheet illustrated directly above, the obligations included the following two items: Each day during the next week, the worker will contact Mr. I. by telephone and discuss his progress in each of the above areas; should Mr. I. encounter difficulty in accomplishing any of the steps, the worker agrees to meet with him and assist him in resolving them.

As a last example, let us consider the area of increasing the father's visits with his son. The goal is to return Ronald J. to his father's home for a court-ordered 90-day trial visit and to complete assessment of parent-child interaction. To accomplish this, the father agrees to increase his visits with his son and to permit the worker to observe and assess parent-child interaction on at least one-third of these visits. Assessment information will be shared with the father, and programs will be developed to alter any identified problems in the area of parent-child interaction.

Available Assets	Subgoal for First Month
Father and son enjoy each other's company. The father has a means of transportation available	The father will visit with his son each Saturday of the month between the hours of 9 A.M. and 5 P.M. The father agrees to pick up his son at the foster home, and to return him to the foster home according to this

Available Assets	Subgoal for First Month
	timetable. If the father is unable to visit with his son on any of the scheduled days, he agrees to telephone the foster mother at least one day in advance. The worker will observe three visits for a period of time that will be prearranged with the parent according to his plans for the day.

	Subgoal for the First Three Weeks of Second Month
Accomplishing subgoal no. 1 without identification of serious problems in parent-child interaction that would threaten longer visits	During the first three weeks of the second month, the father and son will spend weekends together. The father will pick up his son at the foster home at 9 A.M. on Saturday, and return him to the foster home by 5 P.M. on Sunday.

	Subgoal for Last Week of Second Month
Subgoal no. 2 becomes available asset for subgoal no. 3	A one-week trial visit will begin on the fourth weekend of the month (date). The father will pick up his son at the foster home on Saturday morning at 9 A.M. (date) and return him the following Sunday (date) by 5 P.M.

Perhaps the most common reason for failure to meet subgoals is that the steps agreed upon are too big for the client and smaller approximations are needed. Subgoals that the client is very likely to attain always should be selected, and thus it always is better to err on the conservative side rather than go too fast. If subgoals are not attained, a discussion is held to try to determine what prevented their accomplishment. A first question to raise is whether the program was carried out as agreed upon. If not, the reasons for this are pursued. Perhaps instructions were not clear, or the client did not understand fully the relationship of subgoals or the procedure selected to achievement of outcomes. If either of the latter reasons is related to failure of the client to carry out agreed-upon assignments, procedures and rationales can be reviewed and the assignment pursued the next week. Such a review also will help to bring out previously unexpressed client objections to subgoals or procedures, and will prohibit premature abandonment of effective tasks.

The client can be encouraged gradually to assume more responsibility for identifying subgoals and for selecting programs to achieve them by filling out a weekly work sheet in which he or she first identifies how subgoals relate to final goals.[10] This serves as a check that subgoals are clearly related to contracted goals. The client can then be requested to write down agenda items for the next session, including items that may not necessarily relate to contracted goals but that he or she would like to discuss. More responsibility is gradually assumed for stating subgoals and for identifying programs and variables related to their attainment.

Impediments to Specification of Objectives

The identification of specific outcomes and subgoals sounds deceptively easy, and this misperception of its difficulty hinders its completion. This perception hinders devotion of attention to this task, which often is a difficult one requiring time and careful observation. Another impediment is the view that subgoals seem unworthy of attention and not really germane to the overall objective. One component by itself may not seem particularly valuable. Thus, another difficulty is the failure to see the many tasks that may be required to achieve a given goal, and the relationship of each to the overall goal. A foster care caseworker may, for example, tell a natural parent that he or she must move into a new apartment in order to get the child back. Not only may the worker fail to identify essential features of the required housing space; he or she also may fail to realize that many behaviors are required for accomplishment of this objective, and that perhaps the client does not know how to carry out some of these or lacks requisite self-management skills for their completion. Does he or she know where to look for vacancies? Does he or she know what to find out about each apartment? Does he or she feel comfortable talking to landlords? Can he or she manage behavior so as to complete each necessary step?

A lack of commitment to a "constructual approach" to change[11] in which client assets are carefully considered may hinder careful identification of subgoals. A lack of exposure to the value of specific identification of outcomes and subgoals for case management purposes also may impede efforts in this direction. If subgoals are clearly identified and the client encounters difficulty, the factors related to this can be readily identified.

Another factor that hinders clear identification of objectives is a lack of requisite skills for accomplishing this task. The caseworker must be able to recognize when an objective is specified and when it is not. A series of questions useful in scanning outcomes and subgoals will help: Are behaviors specified? Have initial subgoals been identified? Are situations identified? Are performance criteria identified (that is, will I know when an objective has been accomplished)? Is there any way the objective could be satisfied in an unsatisfactory way? If a vague goal, such as "helping with housecleaning more often," was accepted, this could include a wide range of behaviors—cleaning the windows once a month; vacuuming the living room once a week; vacuuming every day; wiping down the kitchen once a week; straightening up the house every day. None of these may refer to what a client would like to achieve.

Lack of commitment to a clear counselor-client contract also may discourage identification of outcomes and promote disinterest in evaluation of change efforts. Only if objectives are clearly stated can evaluation take place. This process takes time and effort. Unless there is some incentive for doing so, it is unlikely that it will be accomplished. Perhaps not until the benefits are seen will this be carried out in every case.

STEP 5: FORMULATION OF A TREATMENT CONTRACT

Contracts clarify agreements between two or more parties, such as a worker and client or two clients. Written contracts may identify a client's long-range objectives, such as having a child returned; identify the range of alternatives for a child's future when a parent is unsure of his or her objectives (such as restoration or adoption); or clarify any arrangement between two clients, such as the division of household responsibilities or child care. The following items are included in all contracts: the names of those who will sign the contract; the objective and the steps necessary to attain it (this includes identification of the requisite tasks of each party); the gains that each person will receive for completing contractual responsibilities; and agreed-upon time limits for accomplishing objectives. If there are costs for failure to carry out contractual responsibilities, they are specified.

By putting a client's objectives in writing and by delineating the responsibilities of each party to the contract in achieving them, each person is recognized as an integral part of the process of problem resolution. The client(s) can choose to participate or not to participate in an informed manner, since expectations are clearly defined. In addition, signing a contract may provide an increase in client commitment to participation in efforts to change.

At this stage of assessment, a written, signed contract may accomplish two objectives. First, it may be used to start the client toward resolution of certain problems. The objective of locating employment offers an illustration of an area in which the client may begin to work toward immediate resolution. The contract also arranges the conditions for further assessment in the client's natural environment. For example, an increased visiting schedule may be described in a contract that includes an agreement between worker and client whereby parent-child interaction can be observed in order to identify any problems that may exist in this area.

It is possible that only one contract will be formed between the worker and client. If, for example, the objective is to restore a child, the initial goals, such as locating employment or new housing, and increasing the frequency of parental visiting, are fulfilled and no additional problems are identified, the child could be restored at the close of the contract period. However, should additional problem areas be revealed, the contract may have to be amended to include them.

Contract Components

Let us first consider a simple agreement between two clients, as shown in Figure 7.5. The left-hand column lists the contract features mentioned above, and the right-hand column provides examples of the kind of information that would be included under each heading. To highlight the differences, we will contrast this contract with a more complex one between clients and caseworker.

Objectives

This contract has the single objective of dividing child care responsibilities. These are carefully defined, and approximations readily follow from the stated objective. Once "child care responsibilities" have been defined, the approximations consist of indicating which of the parents will assume what responsibilities on what given schedule. This can be contrasted with a contract where the goal is to restore a child to natural parents. Such an agreement may have multiple objectives to be accomplished in order to attain the goal. In addition, all conditions for restoration cannot be fully specified until observation in the client's natural environment occurs.

The objective of dividing child care responsibilities is selected solely by the clients, whereas goal selection for a restoration contract may include court-ordered directives (for example, regarding cessation of drug use) and the caseworker's goal (such as arranging for child care during the parent's working hours). The goals of a restoration contract may not, from a client's point of view, be as logically related to the objective as is the contract shown in Figure 7.5. A client may, for instance, strongly disagree with having to submit to a weekly urinalysis and with the specificity with which the worker wishes to arrange for child care. Here, the worker has the additional task of enabling the client to understand and agree with pursuit of certain objectives.

Approximations

The approximations required to accomplish division of child care responsibilities readily follow from the objective. The husband and wife state

FIGURE 7.5

Sample Contract Between Two Clients

Names: This contract is entered into by Jack and Alice Jones.

Objective: The objective is to divide responsibilities for child care for their daughter Mary on weekday evenings between the hours of 5 and 7:30 P.M. Child care is defined as feeding, bathing, and putting Mary to bed. To accomplish this, each parent agrees to do the following:

Approxima-   *Jack agrees to:*
tions: Beginning on Monday (date) and continuing on alternate week nights, Jack will be responsible for child care as defined above. On the second week of this contract, beginning (date), Jack's responsibilities will begin on Tuesday evening and continue on alternate week nights.

Alice agrees to:
Provide care for their daughter Mary on the alternating week nights.

Reinforcers   Each parent agrees to permit the other to have one evening of free
and costs: time per week, to spend in any way he/she chooses. Should either parent fail to assume his/her child care responsibilities, he/she understands that this free time will not be available to him/her.

The evening selected by each parent may vary on a weekly basis; however, each party agrees to tell the other, by Sunday evening of each week, which night he/she intends to take off the following week. If either parent wishes to be free on an evening when he/she is responsible for child care, it is the prerogative of the parent who would have to assume child care responsibilities to grant or deny this request. If such a situation should occur, the timetable for child care will change so that no parent is responsible for providing care three nights in succession. For example, if Jack is responsible for care Monday, Wednesday, and Friday evenings, and agrees to assume care on Tuesday so that Alice can have that evening off, Alice agrees to resume her responsibilities on Wednesday, following which the pattern of alternating nights will resume. Also in regard to the latter situation, the parent who receives the evening of his/her choice agrees that should a similar request be made by the other parent at a future date, this request will be granted, as long as it is made one week in advance. Both agree that they are free to negotiate free time if, for example, either wishes to accumulate time toward a longer period, such as an entire day on the weekend.

Time Period: This contract is in effect from _____ until _____

Signed:

_____

Jack Jones

_____

Source: Compiled by author.   Alice Jones

that they are having difficulty in allocating child care tasks. The worker must find out what the needs are and on what schedule they must be attended to; how much time each parent has to devote to child care; and what the parents consider to be a fair allocation of responsibility (that is, what each considers to be "fair"). He or she must then help the clients to negotiate an acceptable method of sharing responsibilities. It is not our intent to suggest that the above may not be difficult, particularly as regards the negotiating shared responsibilities. However, the situation is far less complex than one where the worker's task is to develop approximations for cessation of drug or alcohol use.

Reinforcers and Cost

Accomplishing the objective of a contract, whether it is dividing child care tasks or having a child restored to parental care, should be viewed positively by clients. However, since it may be several months between the time a contract is written and the time objectives are reached, additional incentives may be required to encourage clients to engage in necessary tasks. Reinforcers that can be offered for approximations may have to be identified.

Often, as in Figure 7.5, the major objective points directly to more immediate reinforcers. One parent may wish a more equal division of child care tasks in order to have more free time. "More free time" can be used as a reinforcer for child care; that is, for x hours of child care, each parent may have y amount of free time. This may not be the case for a parent who may lose free time by increasing child care duties; and here other reinforcers must be offered. The cost is readily determined in this example; failure to complete child care tasks results in a loss of free time.

In a restoration contract, the objective does not necessarily point to immediate reinforcers. If visiting with a child is reinforcing to a client, such visits may be made contingent upon parental compliance with a court directive to submit to urinalyses. However, additional efforts often will have to be devoted to locating reinforcers during the initial stages of intervention.

Time Limits

Several considerations relate to establishing time limits for a contract. The sole determinant may be the wishes of a client, as in Figure 7.5. For example, both parties may agree to write the contract for a 30-day trial period, following which they may have an option (that can be written into the contract) to renegotiate its conditions upon the basis of their experience with those in the initial document. Until clients demonstrate skills in writing contracts, renegotiation should occur with the worker present in order to assure viability.

In a contract that deals with restoration, or with maintaining a child in its own home, other considerations are involved in defining contract length. If treatment programs are involved, such as for drug, alcohol, or child abuse, suggestions from the empirical literature, as well as from the worker's own experience concerning the length of time it may take to remedy a given problem, should be considered in determining time. Additional determinants include the number of problems and the temporal sequence in which they must be resolved. If a client is using alcohol to excess, is unemployed, and must locate new housing, the excess drinking must be reduced prior to locating and maintaining employment. Both employment and increased sobriety may be requisites for locating new housing.

The involvement of the court and/or social service agencies also must be considered in setting time limits in restoration contracts. Only those problems should be addressed that are necessary to assure that a child who is restored will not return to care, or that a child who is left in the home of parents will be able to remain there. It has been our experience in the Alameda Project that clients sometimes cite long-range goals, such as participating in a one-year job-training program or entering a two-year community college program, as conditions they deem necessary to having the child restored. The worker may assist a client in identifying methods of achieving such goals—for example, by locating day care resources or developing appropriate study programs and study schedules. However, it is not realistic to delay restoration until such goals are accomplished.

Restoration Contracts

Restoration contracts generally are written in two parts.[12] Information contained in the first part includes the client's objective (restoration of a child on a permanent or trial basis); the worker's agreement to support the parent's objective by making appropriate recommendations to the court, given that problems are altered, and developing intervention programs to assist the parents in removing identified problems; a statement of the potential consequences of nonparticipation by the parent(s) (that the objective of having the child returned cannot be recommended to the court and that alternative planning must occur); the desired outcomes, focusing specifically on the identified problems to be altered prior to the return of a child or children; and the time limits within which goals are to be accomplished.

The second section of the contract contains the steps to achieve each goal. These may be specific treatment programs for resolving identified problems, as in the area of parent-child interaction, or schedules to accomplish increased visiting or locating employment. In addition, the tasks of the client and others in the client's environment who may be involved in treatment programs are described, as are the resources that will be brought

FIGURE 7.6

Restoration Agreement

　　This contract is entered into between _____ social worker for the Alameda
Project of Children's Home Society, _____, child welfare worker, Alameda
County Human Resources Agency, and _____ father of _____ and _____,
at present dependent children of the Alameda County Juvenile Court.

　　In keeping with the wish of the father of _____ and _____ to have his sons
returned to his home on a 90-day trial basis, both _____ and _____ agree to
recommend such a trial return to the Alameda County Juvenile Court, contingent
upon attainment of the three goals listed below. It is understood by the father that
failure to comply with these goals will result in a statement to the Alameda County
Juvenile Court that, in the opinion of both social workers, such a return is not
feasible at the present time. The general goals of the program are as follows:

1. The father is to visit his children on a regular schedule established by both social
   workers and the father (schedule attached)
2. The father agrees to be at his home, with his children, during a portion of each of
   these visits. The objective here is for the worker to observe and assess parent-child
   interaction (see attached plan for details)
3. The father agrees to establish a plan for substitute care for his children on any
   occasion on which he is absent from the home, other than those times when the
   children are attending public school (see attached plan for details)

This contract will be in effect for one month from January 27, 1975, to February 28,
1975.

Signed:

_____   _____
Father   Social Worker, Alameda Project

_____   _____
Date   Child Welfare Worker, Alameda
                                     County Human Resources Agency

Source: Compiled by author.

to bear in addressing the problem. The role of the caseworker in achieving
goals also is included.

　　An example of a restoration contract between two social workers and
the biological father of two children in foster home care is shown in Figure
7.6. The first paragraph of the contract contains the names and agency
affiliations of both social workers, of the dependent children, and of the
natural father. The father's objective of having his children returned to his
care, the worker's agreement to recommend such a return to the court, and a
statement of the consequences for a lack of parental participation are
contained in the second paragraph.

Three goals are stated that have to be accomplished prior to restoration. Except for a low frequency of visiting by the father, there were no identified problems at the time the contract was written. The first goal focuses upon increasing the visits, while the second is concerned with worker observation and assessment of parent-child interaction during these visits. The third goal is concerned with the need to provide child care when the father is not at home. The final paragraph contains the time limits of the contract. Attachments to this contract contain the visiting schedule and the plan for worker observation and assessment. Finally, the plan for substitute care of the children is described. Figure 7.7 presents the specific plans related to each goal. These are attached to the contract and shared with the client as they are formed.

An example of worker-client contract to cover an eight week trial visit is presented in Figure 7.8.

STEP 6: GATHERING BASELINE DATA ON IDENTIFIED PROBLEMS

An estimate of the frequency, duration, or magnitude of a behavior prior to intervention allows evaluation of the effects of intervention. The information required to make this estimate can be gathered by the client, the caseworker, or a trained aide. A method is selected that will provide accurate information and will be fairly easy to carry out. Information concerning surrounding conditions often is collected at the same time. Thus a parent may note that he or she yells and screams at the children when fatigued or under stress. A baseline also allows for more accurate assessment of the severity of a problem. Such information may reveal that the client either overestimated or underestimated its frequency.

With some behaviors, the client's estimate of the frequency of a behavior can be accepted. This is particularly true with low-frequency behaviors, or when it is important to start intervention immediately, or when baseline information may be readily available, such as frequency of arrests or attendance at a drug program. Forms for gathering baseline data and baseline information from specific cases are presented in chapter 8.

STEP 7: SPECIFYING ADDITIONAL OBJECTIVES

One of the purposes of a contract is to arrange conditions for collection of needed assessment information—for example, through observation of parent-child interaction. Problem areas may be identified through such observation; and if they are, additional goals directed toward their resolution are specified as conditions of a child's restoration.

FIGURE 7.7

Contract Attachments: Plans for Goal Attainment

Four-Week Visiting Schedule (Attachment 1)

Mr. _____ will visit with his children in his home as per the schedule below. The father agrees to pick up his children at the foster home, and to return them to the foster home at the hours specified. If, for any reason, a visit must be canceled, Mr. _____ agrees to notify the foster parents and one of the social workers at least 24 hours in advance. If the father anticipates being late either in picking up or in returning the children, he agrees to telephone the foster home as soon as possible.

Week One: Saturday, January _____ 1975, from 9 A.M. to 5 P.M.

Weeks Two and Three: Saturday and Sunday, February _____ and _____, and Saturday and Sunday, February _____ and _____, from 9 A.M. on Saturday until 5 P.M. on Sunday.

Week Four: If all of the conditions of the contract have been met, the trial visit will begin with this fourth weekend. Mr. _____ will pick up the children on Friday, February _____, at 5:30 P.M. The worker agrees to have requested an ex parte order from the _____ juvenile court permitting the children to remain in their father's home for 90 days.

Worker Observation and Assessment (Attachment 2)

The worker will visit at Mr. _____'s home during each of the visiting periods specified above. The exact time for these observation periods will vary; however, the worker agrees to telephone the father on the Friday preceding each weekend between the hours of 7 and 9 P.M. as to the time for these visits.

The objective of these observation periods is to assess parent-child interaction and to identify strengths and weaknesses in child care. Should any problems be identified, they will be shared with the father and, where appropriate, programs will be developed to resolve such problems.

It is understood that if any problems are identified that are severe enough to threaten the stability of the 90-day trial visit, and if they cannot be resolved prior to the established time for that visit, this contract may have to be extended beyond the current 30 days. If the latter situation should occur, the reasons for extending the contract period will be explained to the father, and specific time limits of this extension will be established.

Substitute Care (Attachment 3)

Two separate plans must be established for substitute care. The first is a daily plan, with care provided between the hours of 3:30 and 5:30 P.M. These hours cover the period between the end of the school day and the time the father returns from work. The second plan is concerned with providing care when the father is absent for social, recreational, or other personal reasons.

Plan One: Daily After-School Care: Mr. _____ has identified two day care facilities within walking distance of the children's school. These are _____, located at _____, and _____, located at _____. Mr. _____ is to telephone both of these centers no later than Tuesday, February _____, to find out if there is space available for both of the children. If there is space available, he is to make

188

(Figure 7.7 *Continued*)

appointments for a personal interview with the person responsible for admissions. These appointments should be arranged as soon as possible, but not later than Tuesday, February _____.

The following information is to be obtained from each school: (a) whether or not the school is licensed by the county to provide child care; (b) the cost of having both children attend five days a week; (c) the activities in which the children would be engaged during the hours at the center (for example, types of recreational and/or educational activities provided); (d) whether or not the children could remain at the center after 5:30 P.M. if, for example, the father should be late returning from work. If staying beyond 5:30 is possible, the maximum length of additional stay should be determined; (e) the days on which the center is closed (national holidays and/or any other days); (f) what provisions the center makes if a child becomes ill and the parent cannot be located.

The above information should be available in writing (either from a school brochure or in the form of notes taken by the father during the interviews), to serve as a basis for discussions with the social worker regarding the father's choice of day care facility. Within two days after the last of these interviews, the father is to select which program he would like to have his children enter. His selection, and reasons for it, will be discussed with the worker during the second observation period, which will occur during the second weekend in February.

If space is available in either facility but is limited, necessitating a decision before the above appointment, the father agrees to call the worker during regular business hours, at which time the contingencies for making an earlier decision will be discussed.

Plan Two: Substitute Care for Recreational or Social Activities: There are two alternatives for substitute care during such periods. The first is to continue employing the services of Mrs. _____, who has provided such care for the children in the foster home. The second alternative is to identify two or three other individuals who might provide child care services if Mrs. _____ is not available.

Both Mr. _____ and the social workers agree that their first choice is to continue employing the services of Mrs. _____. This is the case because she has provided such services for over two years and has demonstrated excellent skills in caring for the children, and because she is willing to offer her services at the father's home, if he is away during the evening, or at her own home if he is away overnight.

To identify individuals who might provide alternative child care services, the father is to telephone the "baby-sitting service" at _____ Junior College no later than February _____, and to find out (a) whether the school provides the names of individuals offering such services, or if the school must be contacted each time a baby-sitter is required; (b) if names and telephone numbers of individuals are provided, he is to request three such names and numbers; (c) if the school must be contacted each time, he is to find out the hours they are open and the amount of advance notice that is required; (d) the fee; (e) whether overnight services are available, and if so, what the conditions are (for instance, must the children be brought to the home of the sitter, or will the sitter come to the father's home); (f) the tasks that a sitter will perform (such as preparing meals, putting the children to bed); (7) if fees and specific services offered are not established by the school, the three identified individuals are to be called, and the above information obtained from them.

Source: Compiled by author.

189

FIGURE 7.8

Sample Contract Between Client and Worker Regarding Trial Visit

Names and
Objective: This contract is entered into by Mr. C., social worker for _____
County Department of Social Services, and Ms. D., mother of J.D.,
at the present time a dependent child of the _____ Juvenile Court.
The objective of this contract is to have J.D. reside in his mother's
home for a two-week period, beginning on _____ through
_____.

Time Limits: This contract is in effect for eight weeks, beginning _____ and
ending _____. During this period the mother agrees to visit
with her son, and the worker agrees to observe a sample of these visits
as per the following schedule:

Approxima- Ms. D. agrees to visit with her son on the following schedule:
tions: 1. For the first four weeks, beginning _____, Ms. D. will
visit her son on Saturday from 9 A.M. to 5 P.M. Ms. D. will pick up
her son at the foster home, and return him to the foster home as per
the above timetable.
2. For the final four weeks, beginning _____, Ms. D. will
visit with her son from 9 A.M. on Saturday through 5 P.M. on
Sunday. Ms. D. will pick up her son at the foster home and return
him to the foster home as per the above timetable.

Mr. C. the caseworker, agrees to do the following:

1. To assist Ms. D. in developing a schedule of planned
activities for visiting periods
2. To take Ms. D. food shopping for the weekend visits and to
assist her in menu planning
3. To observe the mother and child for a minimum of __ hours
during these visits, the objectives of these observations being to
identify both strengths and weaknesses in parent-child interaction.
Should any problems be identified, they will be shared with the client,
and the worker agrees to develop programs to resolve any problems
that are identified
4. If no problems are identified, or if identified problems are
either resolved or, in the worker's estimation, close enough to
resolution so as to not threaten the stability of the trial visit, Mr. C.
agrees to obtain an ex parte order from the _____ Juvenile Court
permitting J.D. to reside in his mother's home for the two-week
period of time.

Cost: It is understood by Ms. D. that should she fail to maintain any of the
above visits, or fail to participate in resolution of any identified
problems, that the planned two-week visit cannot take place.

Signatures: _____
             Ms. D.
             _____
Source: Compiled by author.   Mr. C.

The plan presented in Figure 7.7 allows for this in what we have called open-ended contingencies. These are areas in which additional objectives may have to be specified. For example, if drug use is a problem, the original contract may call for weekly "clean" urinalyses to establish that drugs no longer are used. If it is found that the client is using drugs, a program to eliminate drug use may have to be included in the contracts. The process of specifying additional objectives is the same as the process of specifying initial objectives. The important point to note here is that the contract should include this as a possibility.

STEP 8: AMENDING CONTRACTS

Various situations may require a contract to be amended. Additional objectives may be identified, or changes may occur in an already specified objective. For example, a client who has stated an objective of gaining employment prior to having a child restored may decide instead to apply for an AFDC grant, and the worker may agree that this is an acceptable and possible substitute. Time limits may have to be changed. They may be reduced if observation indicates parent-child interaction is satisfactory and visiting can be accelerated more rapidly than originally planned. On the other hand, time limits may be extended. A parent may complete four of five contract objectives and request an extension to complete the fifth. Setting of additional objectives or changes in existing ones also may necessitate an increase in the original time limits.

When amendments are made, it is not necessary to rewrite the entire contract. A footnote may be added to the original document stating which of the objectives has been changed, and an attachment describing the change and related plans in detail may be included. The footnote is initialed by all concerned parties, and some notation is employed (such as an asterisk) to indicate which of the original objectives is being amended. Let's say that two of the weekend visits specified in Figure 7.7 had to be canceled because the children were ill and that, as a result, the time period is to be extended by two weeks to include two additional visiting periods. An additional visiting schedule would be prepared (see Figure 7.9) and an asterisk would be placed beside goal 1, in Figure 7.6, as well as beside the final sentence, in which time limits are specified; and the following footnote would be added:

The visiting schedule is amended and the time period of the contract extended to include two additional visiting periods (see amendment 1, attached). This is necessary since, due to illness of the children, two of the previously scheduled visits had to be canceled. All of the conditions for observation and assessment, noted in objective 2 and specified in attachment 2, will pertain during these two added visits. This contract is extended until March 14, 1975.

Initialed by:

_____ (Father)   _____ (Social Worker, Alameda Project)

                               _____ (Child Welfare Worker;
                               Alameda County)

The amended schedule (Figure 7.9) is shown below.

FIGURE 7.9

Amendment to Contract: Additional Two-Week Visiting Schedule

This amended visiting schedule covers a two-week period from February 28 through March 14, 1975. The two visits scheduled below replace visits 3 and 4, detailed in attachment 1 of the original contract. The conditions set forth in paragraph 1 of attachment 1, which dealt with picking up and returning the children to the foster home, and with notifying the foster parents and social worker in the event of a canceled visit, or the foster parents in the event of tardiness, remain in effect.

The new schedule is as follows:

Week Three: Saturday and Sunday, March _____ and _____, from 9 A.M. on Saturday until 5 P.M. on Sunday

Week Four: The 90-day trial visit will begin on this weekend if no problems in parent-child interaction that would threaten the stability of the visit are identified by the worker during the third visiting period. Mr. _____ will pick the children up on Friday, March _____, at 5:30 P.M. The worker agrees to have requested an ex parte order from the _____ Juvenile Court as stated in attachment 1.

Source: Compiled by author.

NOTES

1. Eileen D. Gambrill, Edwin J. Thomas, and Robert D. Carter, "Procedure for Sociobehavioral Practice in Open Settings," *Social Work* 16 (January 1971):51–62.
2. Robert G. Wahler and William H. Cormier, "The Ecological Interview: A First Step in Out-Patient Child Behavior Therapy," *Journal of Behavior Therapy and Experimental Psychiatry* 1 (1970):279–89.
3. David Watson and Roland Tharp, *Self-Directed Behavior: Self-Modification for Personal Adjustment* (Monterey, Calif.: Brooks/Cole, 1972).
4. Ibid.
5. Eileen D. Gambrill and Kermit T. Wiltse, "Foster Care: Plans and Actualities," *Public Welfare* 32 (Spring 1974):12–21.
6. Wahler and Cormier, op. cit.

7. Ogden R. Lindsley, "A Reliable Wrist Counter for Recording Behavior Rates," *Journal of Applied Behavior Analysis* 1 (1968):77–78.

8. Arthur Schwartz and Israel Goldiamond, *Social Casework: A Behavioral Approach* (New York: Columbia University Press, 1975), ch. 3.

9. Ibid.

10. Ibid.

11. Ibid.

12. Theodore J. Stein, Eileen D. Gambrill, and Kermit T. Wiltse, "Foster Care: The Use of Contracts," *Public Welfare* 32 (1974):20–25.

8

INTERVENTION

Three of the most frequent problem areas in making decisions for children in out-of-home care are (a) deficient verbal communication between parents and their children, or between two adults, (b) alcoholism, and (c) child abuse. Case examples related to these areas are presented below.

Problem verbal communication is manifested either by the content of communication (such as statements beginning with disapproving remarks) or by the method of delivering the information. The content of communication may be quite appropriate, but the method of delivery unpleasant. For example, a parent may "yell" at a child or speak sarcastically. Examples of verbal problem categories are presented in Figure 8.1. Content and delivery problems may require either building an appropriate verbal repertoire (if this is absent) or, if positive skills are present but infrequently displayed, focus on increasing their frequency and decreasing inappropriate verbal comments.

While clients may identify communication as a problem during assessment, not infrequently the problem is stated as "difficulties in disciplining a child" or an "unmanageable" child. Home observation of the way in which parents and children speak to each other may reveal that Johnny may not be doing his chores because his parents' communications are incomplete concerning their expectations, or are delivered in an unpleasant manner. Assessment and intervention procedures for establishing desirable communication patterns are described in the first two case examples below.

CASE 1. THE JONES FAMILY*

Mike Jones, age 14, ran away from home and was picked up by the police. He refused to return to his father's house, stating that he no longer

*All names used in this and the following cases have been changed to protect the identity of clients.

FIGURE 8.1

Problems in Verbal Communication

Verbal Behavior	Examples
Yelling or shouting	Statements are made in a loud voice.
Disapproval	Sentences begin with a negative comment, such as "Why don't you ever . . ." or "You never . . ."
Sarcasm	The tone of voice is of concern here. For example, a parent may say, "I'm glad you cleaned up your room," but the message may be heard and meant as "Well, it's about time you cleaned up your room."
Whining	Messages are delivered in a tone of voice that is nasal, "high-pitched," or "falsetto."
Incomplete	A request is made, but the expectations are not clearly described. For example, a parent may say, "I'd like you to take out the trash," but does not say when this is to occur.
Command negative	Immediate compliance is demanded. No opportunity is given the listener to state a position. A threat of negative consequences for noncompliance may be included ("You do this, or else . . .").
Ignoring	Statements or questions are not answered. Repeated requests culminating in yelling or shouting may result.
Little or no communication	Long periods of silence occur between two people—for example, during parent-child visits. Nonverbal behavior (such as shuffling around in a seat or "fidgeting") may suggest discomfort by either or both parties.

Source: Gerald L. Patterson, J. B. Reid, L. R. Jones, and R. E. Conger, *A Social Learning Approach to Family Intervention*, vol, 1, *Families with Aggressive Children* (Eugene, Ore.: Castalia, 1975).

wished to live there "because he and his father continually fought." He said that his father was unfair, never gave him credit for anything that he did, and that it was impossible to please him, so "why bother trying?" Mr. Jones agreed with his son's observations that they could not discuss issues without "getting into a hassle." He said that the boy "never did anything he was asked to do"; and, though stating that he did want his son at home, thought that with things as they were, perhaps a foster home was the best solution for the present.

It was suggested that the problems they identified could best be dealt with if the boy returned to his father's home. Although a 600(a) (dependency) petition had been filed, he was put under supervision with his father after three weeks in temporary placement.

Assessment and Beginning Intervention

Assessment took place over a two-week period and included one office and three home visits. During the home visits, the worker focused on observing and recording the verbal behavior of father and son. This focus was taken for two reasons. First, verbal communication was cited by both clients as the most important problem. All discussions resulted in arguments. The father stated that his son did not listen to him when he was talking, nor did he comply with any of his requests, such as doing chores or being home at specified times; and the son stated that his father "always yells and shouts" and would not listen to his side of the story. Second, during the initial office interview, the worker noted that father and son frequently interrupted each other, and the interrupter would speak increasingly loudly to be heard above the speaker. The father's statement that his son "never did anything" did not appear to be entirely accurate, since both agreed that the boy did do some things. The issue was that he did not do them as his father thought they should be done.

A program to address the problem of chore completion was initiated while arrangements were made for the worker to gather assessment information regarding the verbal interaction between Mike and his father. This case provides a good example of starting intervention in one problem area while continuing to gather needed assessment information on other areas.

Intervention Program No. 1: Household Responsibilities

The father was asked to cite two household responsibilities that he thought his son should fulfill and the frequency with which they should be done. Cleaning up the kitchen each evening after dinner and washing the car once each week were cited. The son agreed that these were fair requests. Next, to clarify the father's expectations for each chore, he was asked to describe, in writing, what the kitchen and the car should look like after they were cleaned up. Regarding the kitchen, the father wrote that the dishes would be washed and stacked, the counter top and table wiped clean, the trash emptied, and the floor swept. The car would be washed on the outside, vacuumed and dusted on the interior, and the ash trays and trash bag emptied. The son was shown the written descriptions, and he stated that he understood what his father wanted and thought this was fair.

To identify reinforcers for the son, the worker asked whether he received an allowance, and if so, how much. The father replied that he gave his son $5 each week. The worker suggested that this allowance be earned for completing chores, with a set sum of money for each chore, and that she would assist the father and son in working this out. The father agreed willingly, the son somewhat reluctantly.

Next, the worker suggested that on the basis of what the father and son had said about their problems with verbal communication, of her observations of interrupting and shouting behavior in the office, it would be best if no verbal communication occurred between them relative to the chore program. She stated that she would make out a check list that could be used to indicate chore completion, and suggested that any problem that arose be written down by either party. To encourage the father's participation in the program, the worker asked him to cite two things that he enjoyed doing in the evenings. He noted that the only thing he did at night was to watch television. The worker suggested that the father's first half-hour of television watching be contingent upon his not discussing chore completion with his son. A second list was designed to note the absence of conversation relative to chores. This was to be checked by the son a half-hour after chore completion. If the father discussed chores, there would be no check mark and the father would forfeit the first half-hour of television. The worker stated that she would like to put the agreements into a written contract that both father and son would sign, and that she would make up a list to be posted for chore completion. (See Figures 8.2 and 8.3.) The worker went over the areas to be covered in the contract. After reaching agreement with the clients, she stated that she would bring the written document on her next visit for the three of them to sign. She next went over the check lists with father and son to be sure that they were understood. The worker said that she would telephone the father and son to check on their progress on each of the next three days, and asked them to call her if either of them had any difficulties.

The worker stated that she would like to visit the house three times in the next week, once during the dinner hour, once in the early evening immediately after dinner, and on Saturday morning between 10 and 11:30. She explained that the purpose of these visits would be to observe Mr. Jones and Mike in their home and to try to clarify the problems cited as "verbal communication." It was emphasized that her main role would be to observe and record during these sessions, rather than to discuss problems, but that a brief part of each session would be devoted to checking the chore completion program and dealing with any difficulties either party had. A promise was made to share the results of observation and to plan program(s) to modify any problems that were identified.

Baseline Data Describing Verbal Interaction. The data presented in Table 8.1 were collected during 3 hours and 15 minutes of home observation. A

FIGURE 8.2

Check List for Daily and Weekly Chores, and Dialogue Regarding Them

Clean kitchen	M	Tu	W	Th	Fr	Sat	Sun
Wash and stack dishes							
Clean counter and tabletop							
Sweep floor							
Empty trash							
Clean car							
Wash exterior							
Vacuum and dust interior, empty ash trays							

Clean kitchen: To be completed within one hour after dinner. A check mark is to be placed next to each chore each evening after it is done by Mike. Between an hour and an hour and a half after dinner, Mr. Jones will verify the chores that have been completed and make the appropriate check marks.

Clean car: To be done once each week. Mike will check off task completion. Mr. Jones will verify task completion and the check marks.

No-Dialogue Check List

Mon.		Fri.	
Tues.		Sat.	
Wed.		Sun.	
Thurs.			

Mike will place a check mark by each day of the week on which no dialogue has occurred relative to task completion.

Source: Compiled by author.

coding form utilizing five of the verbal categories in Figure 8.1, plus four additional ones to record positive verbal exchanges, was employed. Using a stopwatch and beginning on the hour, the worker coded in five-minute intervals. The worker coded for each interval during which either of the clients was speaking and the category most descriptive of each verbal

FIGURE 8.3

Contract Between Clients Regarding Daily and Weekly Chores

This contract is entered into between Mike Jones and his father, Frank Jones.
Mike agrees to:

Each evening, within one hour following dinner, Mike will clean up the kitchen. This includes washing and stacking the dinner dishes, cleaning off the counter and tabletop, emptying the trash, and sweeping the kitchen floor.

Each time Mike completes one of these tasks, he will place a check mark next to the task completed under the appropriate day.

Mike further agrees to wash the car once each week. This includes washing the exterior, vacuuming and dusting the interior, and emptying the ash trays. Mike agrees to place a check mark next to each of these tasks when they are completed. Mike further agrees to place a check mark on the "no-dialogue" list each evening and following car washing if no verbal exchange takes place between father and son regarding chores.

Mr. Jones agrees to:

Refrain from all discussion of task completion. Should any task not be completed to Mr. J's satisfaction, he will write down which aspect of the task wasn't completed and how it should have been done.

To pay Mike a weekly allowance, not to exceed $5. This amount of allowance earned is contingent upon task completion and is payable on the schedule listed below.

Finally, Mr. J agrees to forgo his first nightly half-hour of television watching should he engage in any dialogue with Mike regarding task completion.

Allowance Schedule: Maximum $5

Each of the four tasks involved in cleaning the kitchen has a value of $.10, or a maximum daily value of $.40 and a maximum weekly value of $2.80.

Washing the exterior of the car is valued at $.75, vacuuming and dusting the interior and emptying the ash trays at an additional $.75. Maximum value for cleaning the car is $1.50.

Bonus: If all kitchen cleaning tasks are completed each night, there will be a weekly bonus of $.35. If car washing tasks are completed once each week, there will be an additional $.35 bonus. This bonus for each chore category is payable only if all of the tasks within that category are completed.

Cost: For each task not completed, Mike will forfeit the value of that task. For example, if on any given evening Mike fails to sweep the floor, he can earn only $.30 for that evening.

Signed: ＿＿＿＿＿＿＿＿ F. Jones

Source: Compiled by author.   ＿＿＿＿＿＿＿＿ M. Jones

TABLE 8.1

Baseline Data Describing Verbal Interaction Between Mike Jones and His Father

No communication (10 intervals) Type of Verbalization	Father Fre- quency	Percent[a]	Son Fre- quency	Percent
1. Disapproval	10	20		
2. Yelling or shouting	9	18	8	29
3. Command negative	11	23		
4. Ignoring			12	43
5. Incomplete instructions	9	18		
6. Approval[b]	2	4	3	11
7. Command positive[c]	3	6		
8. Attending[d]	2	4	3	11
9. Positive verbal exchange[e]	3	6	2	7
Total	49		28	

Notes: Total recording time = 3 hours, 15 mins.

Length of recoding intervals = 5 mins.

Total intervals = 39.

Total responses recorded = 77.

No commnnication during 10 intervals.

More than one response can be recorded in any single interval. Also, a single statement, such as a disapproving comment or negative command, may be made in a "yelling" tone of voice, and would be coded twice.

[a]Percentages are of the total number of verbalizations made by each person.

[b]Recording categories not listed in Table 8.1. Definitions, as follows: *Approval* statements such as "thank you," or "you did a good job." Nonverbal behavior should compliment statement, i.e. speaker smiles and looks at person spoken to.

[c]Command positive (present) begins with a positive phrase or clause, such as "Would you please" or "I would appreciate it if you would," and is for something in the present. For example, "Please pass the salt." In command positive (future), immediate compliance is not demanded, and the listener is permitted to state a position. For example, in response to a request to go to the store, the listener may say, "It will be difficult for me to do that because . . ." and another way of obtaining what is needed at the store is found.

[d]In attending the listener looks at the speaker and responds almost immediately after the speaker has finished talking.

[e]Positive verbal exchange is an exchange of information about any topic, such as the son's school or the father's work, where each party attends and responds to the other and no negative methods of communication are employed.

Source: Compiled by author.

statement. At the end of each interval, coding would stop; it resumed when either client began a new statement. A statement was defined as any complete utterance; it began as soon as one person started to talk and ended when that person stopped speaking. Complete sentences and questions, as well as utterances such as "uh-huh" were included.

Sharing Assessment Data. At the end of the two-week assessment period, the information in Table 8.1 was shared with the clients and examples of statements defining each category were offered. The worker pointed out the high frequency of disapproving statements relative to approving ones, the frequency with which the father demanded compliance with his requests, and the high number of incomplete instructions. The effects of this pattern in relation to negative feelings and anger was noted. Incomplete instructions, negative commands, disapproval, and a low frequency of positive verbal responses contributed to the boy's feeling that he "never did anything right," and facilitated his ignoring and noncompliant behavior, which, in turn, encouraged the father's yelling and shouting. The son also had learned to model his father's behaviors. It was explained that such patterns gradually become established over time, so that each person becomes a cue to the other for such communication. Issues or problems rarely are dealt with, since each party responds to the "attack rather than the problem." [1]

The worker stressed that, although they occurred infrequently, the data showed that the father did have a repertoire of approval statements and that the son did attend to him when his remarks were positive. Hence, one treatment objective was to increase the frequency of the father's approval responses and the son's attending behavior.

An additional objective was to teach the father and son how to discuss problem areas in a manner that would lead to resolutions, and how to negotiate areas of disagreement. Work on the former was initiated during the fourth interview, and negotiation training was started during the fifth interview. A second counselor-client contract was drawn up, the objective of which was to dismiss the court dependency upon successful completion of the programs (see Figure 8.4). The clients were congratulated for their success during the past week with the chore completion program.

Intervention

*Increasing the Father's Approval Responses and the
Son's Attending Behavior*

The father was instructed to make one of the following verbal responses to his son each evening after checking the chore completion list, given that

FIGURE 8.4

Contract Between Worker and Clients to Dismiss Court Dependency

This contract is entered into between _____, social worker for _____, and Mr. J. Jones, father of Michael Jones, age 14, at the present time a dependent of the _____ Juvenile Court system, and Michael Jones. In keeping with the wish of both father and son to have the court dependency dismissed, _____ agrees to recommend such a dismissal to the _____ County Juvenile Court contingent upon completion of a treatment program to modify behaviors specified below, which both parties agree are currently problems. It is understood that failure to comply with such a program will result in a statement to the _____ County Juvenile Court that in the opinion of the social worker, dismissing the court dependency is inappropriate at the current time. The general goals of the program are as follows:

1. To increase the frequency of positive verbal communications between father and son
2. To engage in a program of negotiation training, the objective of which is to learn new methods of discussing problem areas and resolving problems in a positive manner
3. The previous contract entered into between the father and son, focusing on chore behaviors, will remain in effect for the duration of the current contract.

The specific plans for the first two goals are attached.
This contract will be in effect for a period of three months (90 days), beginning _____ and ending _____.

signed: _____

      J. Jones   Social Worker

_____

      M. Jones

Source: Compiled by author.

some chores had been completed: "The kitchen looks really nice, M., thank you for cleaning up" or "I appreciate the way you cleaned up after dinner." The boy was to listen to his father's statement, and after he had finished, to say simply, "Thank you, Dad." There were to be no negative comments made by either party. The details of the program and the reinforcers and costs identified by the clients are shown in Figures 8.5 and 8.6.

Negotiation Training

The purpose of negotiation training is to offer the client skills in resolving conflicts. Whenever two people live together, some behaviors of each will be bothersome; and many people do not possess negotiation skills, that is, positive ways to reach resolutions.[2] Assessment revealed a lack of these skills in this family. Nagging, yelling, shouting, and demands for change resulted. Negotiation training that involved the following steps was initiated.

First, training the clients to pinpoint behaviors, that is, to describe clearly what they would like. Dissatisfactions written down by the father and son were used as a basis for teaching the clients how to be specific. One method of accomplishing this is a series of questions that the worker poses during training sessions—for example, what particular aspect of the cleaning up was done well? Or what aspect was not done to your satisfaction? If this does not result in specific responses, questions can be asked regarding each of the separate tasks involved in cleaning up. For example, was the floor

FIGURE 8.5

Plan for Goal 1: Increasing Father's Approval Response and Son's Attending Behavior

The objectives of this program are to increase the frequency with which Mr. Jones praises Michael's chore behavior and to increase Michael's attending behavior and positive verbal responses to his father. To accomplish this, the following are to occur:

1. Each evening, after Michael has completed his chores as described in contract no. 1 [Figure 8.3], Mr. J. will monitor the chore completion chart and verbally reinforce M. for chores completed by saying "Thank you for cleaning up after dinner" or "The kitchen looks nice and clean, M., thank you."
2. Mr. J will refrain from all disapproving comments and from commenting on any aspects of the chores that have not been completed. Any type of noncompletion will be written down by Mr. J., as specified in contract no. 1.
3. M. will attend to his father's verbal approval statements by looking at his father and not interrupting. When Mr. J. has finished speaking, M. will respond by saying "Thank you" or "I'm glad you're pleased."
4. Both parties agree to maintain the attached record of approval and attending responses. The method for recording and the reinforcers and costs are described on the attached chart.

The social worker agrees to do the following:

1. Telephone Mr. J. and Mike twice each week for the first three weeks and once each week following that for the duration of the contract. The objective of the calls is to monitor the above program and to discuss any difficulties
2. To meet with Mr. J. and Mike each Thursday evening between 7 and 8:30 P.M. Negotiation training will begin during these sessions. In addition, the worker will monitor the chore completion and verbal response records, as well as any disapproval notes written by either father or son.

Source: Compiled by author.

FIGURE 8.6

Verbal Approval and Attending Behavior Check List

Mon. Tues. Wed. Thurs. Fri. Sat. Sun.

Mr. J. approval response
Michael approval response
Michael attending behavior

Instructions: Each evening, following an exchange of positive verbal responses as outlined in the plan for goal 1 [Figure 8.5], Mr. J. and Mike are to place a check mark in the appropriate box. If either party verbalizes a disapproving response, or should Michael not attend to his father, the box is to be left blank for the person concerned.

Reinforcers and Cost:

for Michael: Michael has expressed a wish to have his Saturday night curfew extended by one hour, and Mr. J. has agreed to this. This hour will be earned at the rate of ten minutes each evening: five minutes each for approval and attending behavior if check marks appear in the appropriate box. Should Mike not earn the entire hour, he will be permitted whatever extra time he has accumulated.

for Mr. Jones: Mr. Jones has expressed a wish to save $10 each week, to be used in any way he chooses. This will be accumulated at the rate of $1.50 for each check mark that appears. Michael has agreed to save this money for his father. Mr. J will give him the money each evening, after the above has been completed.

Source: Compiled by author.

swept? And so forth. In addition, clarification of incomplete statements can be obtained by asking, When did you want that done? Or what will "x" look like when it is finished? Or how would someone know when that was completed? It is of the utmost importance that clients avoid such global statements as "You didn't do a good job of cleaning up after dinner." These do not give credit for task components that have been well done, and do not specify which task components have not been completed satisfactorily.

Second, training the clients how to paraphrase each other's statements to insure clarity. Each person may be asked at several points to paraphrase what has been said.[3] For example, if the father says, "You came home after curfew last night," the son might respond, "You're saying I came home after 10 P.M." This step also includes recognition of the correctness of the other person's position even if one disagrees with it. Failure to do this leads to defensive verbal responses, that is, responding to attacks rather than to problems.

Third, trading, in which differences are resolved. An example of this can be seen in the chore behavior program, where the worker guided the clients to arrive at an exchange in which the father offered a set sum of money for a certain amount of task completion. Supervised practice sessions in arranging exchanges are held, and additional practice sessions are scheduled at home. Clients are forewarned that the initial practice sessions probably will be difficult because of well-established practices of destructive verbal communications. Sessions should occur at a preestablished time in a specified location—for example, once a week, between the hours of 5 and 6, in the living room. In this way, clients can avoid fighting and arguing at unscheduled times. If the clients have a high frequency of "zapping" each other, it is helpful to make a rule that practice negotiation sessions must be terminated if more than ten zaps occur. Zapping is a way of one person's "putting the other down" by making a vague, nondescriptive statement, such as "You're sloppy."[4] Such statements sidetrack the conversation and stop effective problem solving.

Clients should be requested to tape-record some of these sessions, so that progress can be monitored by the worker and clients can be assisted in resolving any difficulties that arise during these practice sessions. If this is not possible, clients are asked to write down areas of difficulty if they occur. Each person should do this, so that both opinions will be expressed. Consequences can be established for nonadherence to the practice session schedule. If it is anticipated that clients will have a hard time completing the entire negotiation process, their behavior should be "shaped" by asking them to carry out only one or two steps of the process during practice sessions. Thus, as a first assignment, they could be requested simply to try to define what each of them wants. They would not try to negotiate a trade. Their success with this step can be checked during the next session, and the negotiation completed with the worker's help. As their skill increases, the worker's help gradually fades. Figure 8.7 presents the plan shared with the clients and the agreements involved.

Outcome

The chore completion chart (Figure 8.2) was maintained for the 14 weeks of intervention. The data recorded by the clients was graphed by the worker to show the percentage of chores completed each week (see Figure 8.8). Chore completion ranged between 90 and 100 percent for the entire program, compared with the pre-baseline client verbal report of zero. Of the 14 days during which no dialogue regarding chores was to occur, the father complied with the worker's suggestion on 11 (79 percent) (see Figure 8.9). This information supports the assumption that lack of chore completion was due to negative communication between father and son, rather than skill deficits on the boy's part.

Verbal interaction between father and son was observed at home for 3.5 hours following negotiation training, using the same observational form

FIGURE 8.7

Plan for Goal 2: Negotiation Training

The objective of this program is to teach both parties methods of discussing issues in which there are differences of opinion, so that these differences can be resolved in a manner satisfactory to both clients. To accomplish this, the worker agrees to meet with the father and son each Thursday evening between 7 and 8:30 P.M. The focus of these meetings will be as follows:

a. To teach each party how to state an issue of concern in a specific manner, so that the other person understands the focus of the concern
b. To facilitate step (a), the worker will teach father and son how to "paraphrase" what the other has said. Paraphrasing involves having the listener repeat, in his words, what he has heard the speaker say. The speaker responds by stating either agreement or disagreement with what has been said
c. Finally, the worker will assist father and son in learning how to "trade" to resolve differences of opinion. Trading involves identifying what each party is willing to give or contribute to problem resolution.

The father and son agree to do the following:

1. To be present at their home during these regularly scheduled meetings.
2. To practice the tasks learned in negotiation sessions. These practice sessions will occur on _____ in _____ and at no other time
3. In any practice area in which there is disagreement or difficulty, each party agrees to write down his view of the difficulty. This should include a statement of the aspect of negotiation training (being specific, paraphrasing, trading) that is difficult. Within the identified area of difficulty, each party should write down who was speaking, what was said, and his perception of the difficulty and how it could have been resolved.
4. The worker agrees to go over any issues that are listed and to assist father and son in methods of resolving them.

Source: Compiled by author.

employed during baselining (see Table 8.2 and Figure 8.10). There were dramatic decreases in negative communication and increases in positive categories following training. On the basis of this information, the dependency was dismissed, as per the contract agreement.

CASE 2: CYNTHIA AND MRS. K.

Cynthia K., age 12, had been in foster care for six years under a 600(a) petition. Although her mother lived within several blocks of the foster home, she visited only once a month. These visits rarely exceeded 30 minutes. When asked about her plans for her daughter's future, Mrs. K. stated that

FIGURE 8.8

Percent of Chores Completed: 14 Weeks

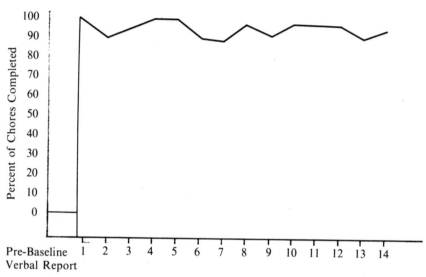

Pre-Baseline
Verbal Report

Source: Compiled by author.

she would like Cynthia to live with her, but expressed this with ambivalence. Cynthia said that she might like to live with her mother, but was not sure because she sometimes was uncomfortable with her. No problems other than deficits in visiting were identified by either client. The worker suggested that they not try to reach an immediate decision as to whether Cynthia would return to her mother's home. She stated that she would like the opportunity to observe Mrs. K. and Cynthia together during a set number of scheduled visits in order to identify any areas that might present problems. The worker emphasized that it was important to reach a decision about Cynthia's future as soon as possible, and that to facilitate this, she would like mother and daughter to visit together more frequently than was their current practice.

FIGURE 8.9

No Dialogue Relative to Chores: 2 Weeks

	Mon.	*Tues.*	*Wed.*	*Thurs.*	*Fri.*	*Sat.*	*Sun.*
Week 1	✓		✓		✓	✓	✓
Week 2	✓	✓	✓		✓	✓	✓

Note: Check mark indicates day with no dialogue.
Source: Compiled by author.

TABLE 8.2

Post-Negotiation Training Observational Data

Type of Verbalization	Father Fre-quency	Father Percent	Son Fre-quency	Son Percent
Disapproval	3	5		
Yelling or shouting	2	4		
Command negative				
Ignoring	1	2	2	5
Incomplete instructions	2	4	0	
Approval	12	22	9	23
Command positive	10	18		
Attending	11	20	12	30
Positive verbal exchange	14	25	17	43
Total	55		40	

Notes: Total recording time = 3 hrs., 30 mins.
Length of intervals = 5 mins.
Total intervals = 42.
Total responses recorded = 99.
No communication during three intervals.

Source: Compiled by author.

This information was exchanged during two 45-minute interviews. During these meetings, the worker noted that neither client looked at her when spoke and that their affects were minimal; for example, their facial expressions did not change when they went from periods of silence to periods of speaking. They rarely used facial expressions to complement their speech, such as raised eyebrows, smiles, or frowns. Their statements were very brief, rarely containing more than three or four words. Neither client requested any information from the worker, speaking only in response to her questions. The same pattern was observed in the few instances in which mother and daughter spoke to each other. If the verbal and nonverbal behaviors displayed in the worker's presence also occurred during visiting periods, the brevity and infrequency of visits was understandable. Further observation was felt to be needed before establishing a long-range visiting plan. The clients were informed that a regular plan for visits would be set up and that the options for Cynthia's future would be considered after completion of observation. The first observational period was set for three days hence at the mother's home, at 10 A.M.

FIGURE 8.10

Verbal Interaction Between Father and Son Before and After Intervention

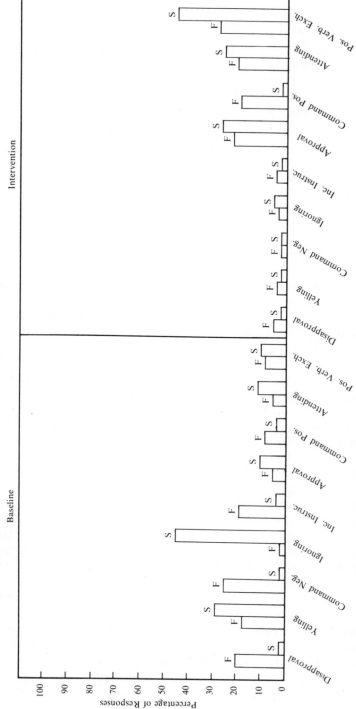

Source: Compiled by author.

Assessment

The major concern during assessment was with conversations between mother and daughter. A conversation was defined as either an attempt to engage the other in dialogue by asking a question or directing a statement to the other person, or an exchange of information in which each party spoke to the other. A conversation began with the first word spoken by either person and ended after a three-minute period of silence. Any dialogue occurring after the three minutes of silence was considered to be a new conversation. Using a stopwatch and coding form (see Figure 8.11), the worker first noted the observation period (first, second, and so on). Each time a person began to speak, she placed a check mark to indicate the person speaking and noted the duration of that person's verbalization. If the other responded, a check was placed in the appropriate column and the duration of the response recorded. In addition, each time a person began to speak, the worker would note whether she looked at the other person and whether the listener looked at the speaker. The absence of a check mark in these columns indicated that either party looked away—for example, at the floor or ceiling, or out the window. In addition, within the first 30 seconds after a person began to speak, she coded the person's "affective" response and the topic of conversation. The conversations were tape-recorded and used to provide examples of their conversational behavior for the clients.

The results of 90 minutes of observation are summarized in Table 8.3. These data show that between 68 and 83 percent of the time mother and daughter were together was spent in silence. When conversations did occur, they were quite brief, averaging 2.1 minutes. Conversational attending behavior was poor, with 60 to 70 percent of the codings indicating that mother or daughter looked away, rather than at, the other. There was an absence of affect 60 percent of the time for both parties. At the end of the final period of observation, a meeting was arranged for the next evening to discuss the assessment information with both clients.

The assessment information was discussed with the clients and portions of the tape-recorded material were played. The worker asked if their time together was usually spent in the way the data suggested, and they responded affirmatively. It was suggested that the brevity and infrequency of visits, as well as the mother's "ambivalence" and the daughter's "discomfort" relative to the issue of restoration, were due to a lack of more positive shared experiences. The worker recommended that during the next six weeks the three of them work together and focus upon trying to make visits more pleasurable. To accomplish this, they would work on increasing the verbal repertoire and nonverbal skills of both clients and on identifying mutually enjoyable outside activities in which mother and daughter could engage.

The worker informed the clients that she would like to draw up a written contract among the three of them. After explaining the general

Figure 8.11

Form for Coding Observations

Observation period:

Conversation no.	1		2		3		4		5		6		7		8		9		10		11		12
Speaker	M	D	M	D	M	D	M	D	M	D	M	D	M	D	M	D	M	D	M	D	M	D
Speaker looks at other																						
Listener looks at speaker																						
Duration (mins.)[a]																						
Initiator's verbalization																						
Responder's verbalization																						
Length of each conversation (mins.)																						
Total time per observation period																						
Conversation																						
Silence																						
Topic[b]																						
Affective responses[c]																						
Positive affect																						
Negative affect																						
No affect																						

[a] Time rounded off to nearest half or whole minute.

[b] Topic code: D's school = S; D's social activities = Sd; M's work = W; M's social activities = Sm; activity discussion (possible joint activities, such as going to a film or on a picnic) = A; misc. (weather) = M.

[c] Affect code: positive = P (smiling/laughing); negative = N (facial grimaces); no affect = N. (no show of interest or change of expression).

Source: Compiled by author.

TABLE 8.3

Summary Baseline Data: K. Family

Observation session	No. of Conversations Initiated Mo.	Dtr.	Total Conversations per Session	Total Mins. in Conv. Mo.	Dtr.	Mean Length of Conversations (mins.)	Total Time and Percent of Each Session in Convers. Time	%	Silence Time	%
1	1	2	3	2	4.5	2.2	6.5	22	23.5	78
2	3	2	5	5	4.5	1.9	9.5	32	20.5	68
3	1	1	2	3	2	2.5	5	17	25	83
Total	5	5	10	10	11	2.1	21	23	69	77

Conversational attending behavior

	Mo. Freq.	%	Dtr. Freq.	%
Speaker looks at other	2	20	1	10
Listener looks at speaker	2	20	2	20
Person looks at floor ceiling	6	60	7	70
Total conversations	10		10	

Affect data

	Mo. Freq.	%	Dtr. Freq.	%
Positive affect	4	40	2	20
Negative affect	0	0	2	20
No affect	6	60	6	60
Total conversations	10		10	

Topics Discussed

	Freq.	%
Dtr's school	3	30
Mo's work	2	20
Activities	1	10
Misc.	4	40
Total conversations	10	

Notes: Conversation is defined as either all of the dialogue exchanged between both clients, beginning with the first verbalization of either client, and ending after three minutes of silence, or an "attempt" to engage the other in conversation by making a statement or asking a question.

For affect data, percentage is of total affect responses coded.
No. of observations = 3.
Length of observation period = 30 mins.
Total observation time = 90 mins.

Source: Compiled by author.

purpose of contracts, she suggested one with the objectives of increasing psoitive experiences noted above, and, once they began to approximate this objective, to consider alternative decisions for the daughter's future (see Figure 8.12). It was considered imperative to increase positive verbal interaction between mother and daughter before planning for the child's future was discussed. Hence, intervention during the first three of the six weeks covered by the contract was concerned solely with verbal and nonverbal skills. Before concluding the meeting, the mother and daughter each were asked to identify one area of interest that they would like to discuss during the next session, to write it down, and to bring it to the meeting. This could be any subject at all, such as a favorite book or movie, a vacation or outing either would like to take, or some aspect of the daughter's schooling or mother's work. Next, to identify reinforcers that could be used, the clients were asked if there was any current joint activity they found pleasurable. Cynthia said that they "sometimes went to the movies together, and out to eat in a restaurant, and that she liked this." The mother agreed, and the worker stated that perhaps they could select one of these activities as

FIGURE 8.12

Contract Between Worker and Clients: K. Family

This contract is entered into between Sheila K., mother of Cynthia K., at the present time a dependent of the _____ County Juvenile Court, and _____, social worker for _____ County. The general objectives of this contract are listed below, and the plans for accomplishing these are attached:

1. To increase the verbal repertoire and appropriate nonverbal behaviors of both mother and daughter. The method for accomplishing this is attached as plan no. 1 [not included here]
2. To reach a decision regarding the future living arrangements of Cynthia K. Plan no. 2 lists the alternatives and the method to be employed in selecting among these [not included here].

This contract will be in effect for six weeks, beginning _____ and ending _____.

Signed:

_____   _____

Sheila K. (mother)   (Social Worker for _____ County)

_____

Cynthia K. (daughter)

Source: Compiled by author.

a reward for working toward objectives, given that money was available. They briefly discussed the cost of these activities, and ended the session with an agreement to meet at the same time the following week.

Intervention

Increasing Positive Verbal Communication

The assessment data revealed three deficits in verbal communication skills: the range of content areas discussed, accompanying affective responses, and the range of topics discussed within any one content area.[5] This assessment data is limited in two ways. First, it was gathered in one location (the mother's home); and while the clients stated that the exchanges observed were indicative of their usual communication, it is possible that if the observation periods had taken place during a specific activity, such as a picnic or movie, that provided a focus for the visits, the exchange might have been different. The second limitation was a lack of data regarding verbal and nonverbal skills of either client with other individuals. Therefore, it was not clear, and would not become clear until intervention began, whether the major issue was to teach new skills or to increase the frequency of skills already present but used infrequently. The worker could have engaged either client in conversation to gain additional data on verbal behavior or tried to observe either client with others. Another way to assess client skills would be to engage the client in role playing. The client could be asked who she enjoys talking to and can speak to with ease, and what content areas are discussed. A role-playing situation can then be carried out, with the worker assuming the role of the other person. The client may exhibit a more extensive repertoire in these situations.

Let us hypothesize that the clients have verval skills but do not share them with each other. Verbal behavior, like any other behavior, is maintained by its consequences. We may engage in dialogue with another because his or her nonverbal cues (such as looking at us when we speak, smiling, and laughing) indicate an interest in what we are saying. The nonverbal behavior of Mrs. K. and her daughter suggested a lack of interest in what was said; hence their verbal repertoires were not reinforced in each other's presence. When skills are present, the major emphasis during intervention is to "prompt" them so that they occur more frequently in selected situations, and to encourage significant others to reinforce each other's speech. Verbal behaviors often increase rapidly once they are reinforced (followed by attention or requests for further information, accurate paraphrasing, and so forth). If there are deficits in nonverbal reinforcing cues and in discussion skills, intervention would emphasize the acquisition of appropriate verbal and nonverbal skills.

One of the most rapid ways to establish new skills and to facilitate existing behaviors that occur infrequently is through observing models who engage in the behavior of concern.[6] The advantage of model presentation is that an entire chain of behavior can be demonstrated to the client and the client can then be requested to imitate it. Nonverbal behaviors, which are so important in social interaction, can be demonstrated as well; and the client's attention can be drawn to those that are especially vital. The effectiveness of model presentation in establishing new behaviors, in decreasing avoidance behaviors, and in facilitating behaviors is well documented.[7] Models are more effective if they are similar to the client in sex and age, if they are perceived to have a high status, if their reactions are followed by positive consequences, and if the client's attention is directed toward desired response elements.[8] For example, the client may be requested to notice the model's eye contact, the hand motions, and the orientation of posture toward the other person. The model may verbalize appropriate positive thoughts during the role playing if effective social skills are hampered by negative thoughts. Appropriate statements about himself or herself at first can be verbalized aloud by the client when imitating the model's behavior and then, via instruction, gradually moved to a cognitive level.

Prior to model presentation and rehearsal in the office,[9] the client may be instructed to watch people with effective behavior who are in similar roles, and to write down in a log the situation, what was done, and what happened. This increases exposure to a variety of effective models, offers examples to use during rehearsal, increases discrimination as to when to employ certain behaviors, and permits vicarious extinction of anxiety reactions through observation of positive reactions following effective behavior. The opportunity to see how negative reactions can be handled also may be provided. Client observations are carefully discussed, noting effective elements as well as other situations in which such behaviors may be usefully employed. These situations provide valuable material for rehearsal during office sessions in addition to the client's observations of his or her own behavior in the natural environment.

Following model presentation, the client is requested to practice (rehearse) the modeled behavior. Rehearsal (role playing) provides for learning new behaviors and their practice in a safe environment. Positive feedback is offered following each rehearsal. That is, positive aspects of the client's performance are carefully noted and praised. Focus is upon what the client did in a better way, noting even small improvements. Thus approximations to final behaviors are reinforced. Critical comments such as "You can do better" or "That wasn't too good" are avoided.[10] Such feedback helps the client to discriminate behavior that should be increased and decreased.

Instructions or signals are used to prompt (bring about) responses either prior to rehearsal or model presentation or during rehearsal.[11] Instructions can be given before the client rehearses a behavior that prompts him or her to engage in certain behaviors rather than others. Perhaps he or she did not look at the other person during the role playing, and is coached to look at the other person while speaking. Care must be taken to identify specific behaviors. Prompts should be faded out gradually as client skills increase.

Specific goals are established for each session. Perhaps only one or two nonverbal behaviors will be focused upon in any one session, or the client's initial repertoire may be such that he or she will be able to practice all needed verbal and nonverbal behaviors. Assessment of the client's behavior in relation to given situations will reveal the behaviors already possessed and training will build upon these. Thus goals are individually established for each client during each session. Reinforcement for improvement always is in relation to the client's past performance rather than in terms of comparisons with others.

Models are presented again as needed; and rehearsal, prompts, and feedback are continued until desired responses and comfort levels are demonstrated. It sometimes is necessary to establish hierarchies in terms of the degree of anxiety or anger that situations induce, in order to gradually establish new social skills. Rehearsal would start with situations inducing a small degree of anger or anxiety; and as these are mastered, higher-level scenes are introduced. Only after needed skill and comfort levels are attained are mutually agreed-upon assignments carried out by the client in the natural environment. As with any other assignment, a careful check is made at the next meeting to find out what happened. Client records or tape-recordings made at home aid in the discussion of assignments.

First Three Sessions: Modeling and Rehearsal

The worker and a female case aide first modeled verbal behaviors and related nonverbal cues. The clients were instructed to watch closely, because they would be asked to engage in the behaviors observed after their demonstration. The demonstrations were brief, never exceeding three minutes during the first session. After the clients engaged in the observed behaviors, the worker praised them for the approximations to the modeled skills and made suggestions in any area where there was room for improvement. Constructive feedback was employed: even small gains were generously praised and referents for this praise clearly noted. For example, the worker might say, "Your eye contact was much better that time; you looked at your daughter when you spoke, and you smiled at her."

The content areas for this session and for subsequent ones were issues identified by the clients or the shared activities designated as reinforcers (see Figure 8.13). Clients also were given practice in identifying specific topics related to a given content area. For 10 to 15 minutes of each session, using topics suggested by the clients, the worker presented ways in which topics in

FIGURE 8.13

Plan No. 1: Increasing Verbal Repertoire and Nonverbal Behaviors of Mother and Daughter

The objective of this plan, as stated above, will be accomplished in the following manner:

1. The worker and both clients will meet once each week for a period of six weeks. Each meeting will last a minimum of one hour and not more than one hour and a half. These meetings will occur on Wednesday evenings at the mother's home, beginning at 6:30 P.M. During these sessions, the following will take place:
   a. Focusing on areas of topical interest suggested by the clients, the worker and clients will operate in dyads, the worker alternately playing the role of mother and daughter, demonstrating different ways of discussing these areas and nonverbal behaviors that are appropriate to the dialogue
   b. The client whose role is being played by the worker will observe, and following the period of demonstration, will engage in those behaviors modeled by the worker.
2. On the basis of written instructions from the worker, both clients will be expected to rehearse these behaviors at specified sessions that are to occur between meetings with the worker.
   a. These sessions will occur once each week, at the mother's home, on Saturday mornings. They are to begin at 10 A.M. and are to continue for no longer than 45 minutes, but may terminate sooner at the request of either party should any difficulties arise.
   b. The clients agree to tape-record these rehearsal periods, using a recorder provided by the worker. The worker agrees to listen to these tapes and, on the basis of their content, to make suggestions to the clients in any areas in which there are difficulties.

Reinforcers and costs
   The clients identified two areas of activity that are mutually enjoyable, going to the movies and eating dinner in a restaurant. The cost of either of these activities is estimated as being between $5 and $6 per week. Mrs. K. said that she can afford to set aside $5 each week for an activity, and Cynthia has agreed to save $1 per week from the money that she earns baby-sitting. Following each meeting with the worker, and each rehearsal session between mother and daughter, each client will place half of the agreed-upon amount of money in an envelope that will be kept by Mrs. K.

If either client misses any of the meetings for any reason other than physical illness, the monetary value of that session will not be set aside and, hence, the total amount of weekly activity money will be reduced accordingly. Whatever amount of money has been set aside will be spent on an agreed-upon activity, and must be spent within the week it is saved.

Source: Compiled by author.

any one content area could be identified and used to further discussion. For example, "redecorating her house" was a content area the mother stated she would like to discuss during the first session. The worker suggested that one way to identify related topics was to write down all of the steps that would be involved in accomplishing this objective. The mother was asked what her house would look like after it was remodeled. She said, "The rooms would be painted and certain pieces of furniture replaced." From this, topics such as room color, who would do the painting, what furniture would be replaced, cost, and so forth were identified and written down. This information was used as discussion material during modeling and rehearsal.

At the end of each session, homework assignments were given to rehearse new discussion behaviors and to tape-record these sessions. The clients were loaned a cassette tape-recorder and blank tapes, and instructed to turn on the recorder during rehearsal periods. This material later was reviewed by the worker and used to point out gains that the clients were making, as well as to discuss any problem areas within a framework of constructive feedback.

During the second and third sessions, the worker and clients operated in dyads, with the worker in turn playing the role of mother and daughter. The client whose role the worker was taking was asked to observe, and later to engage in, the demonstrated behaviors. As the clients' skills increased, the length of the modeling sessions increased from three minutes in the first session to ten minutes in the third session; and there was a concomitant increase in alternative ways of discussing an issue and an increase in the variety of nonverbal cues and their frequency.

By the end of the third session, mother and daughter were engaging in uninterrupted conversations lasting between four and seven minutes, and displaying appropriate affective behaviors. Individual topic areas with content areas increased. During the next three weeks, the worker gradually decreased her participation and the clients assumed greater responsibility for initiating and maintaining conversations.

Cynthia's Future Living Arrangements

As stipulated in the contract, conversation regarding the daughter's future living arrangements took place during the last three sessions (see Figure 8.14). Both clients were much less equivocal in their expressed wish to live together. The mother raised concerns about finances, food, and medical issues; and the daughter's concerns related to how her foster parents might feel if she returned to her mother's home, and whether or not she would be able to continue seeing them. A budget was designed to estimate the actual additional costs that would be involved. The mother saw that her concerns regarding actual costs were somewhat exaggerated; and after the budget was

FIGURE 8.14

Plan No. 2: Decision Making for Cynthia K.'s Future Living Arrangements

The objective of this plan is to reach a decision regarding the future living arrangements of Cynthia K. There are two alternatives that have been discussed. Cynthia may be restored to the home of her mother, Sheila K., or Cynthia may remain in the foster home of Mr. and Mrs. L., where she has resided for the past six years. Mr. and Mrs. L. have expressed an interest in becoming Cynthia's legal guardians. Such an arrangement would involve Mrs. K.'s signing a consent form permitting Mr. and Mrs. L. to assume this role. The L.'s agreed that should Cynthia remain with them, Mrs. K. could continue to visit with Cynthia on an agreed-upon schedule that is acceptable to all parties.

A guardianship arrangement would accomplish two objectives: It would transfer the responsibility for primary decision making (for example, on medical and school-related issues) from the Department of Social Services to the L. family, and the current dependency action could be terminated.

To facilitate decision making, the following will occur. Beginning with the third of the six caseworker-client sessions covering the period of this contract [see Figure 8.15], a set amount of time will be used to discuss the implications of the two alternatives listed above. This discussion will include, but need not be limited to, the following areas:

Restoration:

1. The feeling of both clients regarding this possible outcome. Issues here may include Mrs. K.'s concerns about the responsibilities involved in assuming the role of full-time parent; the specific responsibilities that would be involved, and losses to the mother regarding her own free time
2. Cynthia's concerns about leaving the L. home; ways in which contact may be maintained between Cynthia and the L. family
3. Financial costs to Mrs. K. for assuming full-time care of Cynthia, and ways in which these might best be handled
4. Arrangements for Cynthia's care during those hours that Mrs. K. is employed

Guardianship:

1. The worker agrees to put in writing the full legal implications of such a decision
2. The worker further agrees to assist the mother and the L. family in making the necessary legal arrangements
3. The worker agrees to meet with Mrs. K., Cynthia, and Mr. and Mrs. L. to discuss any of these issues, should such a meeting be requested.

Source: Compiled by author.

completed, the worker assured her that she would be eligible for assistance from the food stamp program and for MediCal insurance for her daughter.

The mother stated that she would have no objections to Cynthia visiting the foster parents. Two meetings were arranged with the clients, worker, and foster parents. They assured Cynthia that they would be pleased to see her return to her mother and that they would continue to see her after such a return.

At the conclusion of these meetings, it was decided that Cynthia would return to her mother's home. However, the worker suggested that more extensive visits should occur first, since, at this point, visiting periods, including the rehearsal sessions and the weekly activity time earned, were still quite brief (see Figure 8.15). She suggested a 60-day contract, the objective of which would be restoration at the end of the first 30 days and dismissal of the court dependency at the end of 60 days (see Figure 8.16). To accomplish the first objective, they would increase the visiting periods on a prearranged schedule. The worker would continue to observe the mother-daughter interaction, and they would work together to resolve any problems that arose during this time. Both clients understood that should any problems be identified that could threaten restoration, it would have to be delayed until they were remedied. If restoration occurred at the end of the first 30 days, the worker would continue her visits with both clients for an additional 30 days, with the same objective of observing and aiding the clients in resolving any problems. The contingencies for recommended dismissal were the same as for restoration. Mother and daughter agreed, and a contract was drawn up by the worker and signed by all parties.

Outcome

The worker coded 15 minutes of the beginning, middle, or end of each of five tapes from the clients' rehearsal sessions, using a stopwatch and coding form. After identifying the portion of the tape to be coded, she began with the first verbalization made by either client and continued coding for 15 minutes. Material coded included who spoke first; the druation of the conversation; and, if more than two topics were discussed during any conversation, the first and second of these. The amount of "silent time" also was noted. The average length of conversations increased from the baseline time of 2.1 minutes to 8.6 minutes (see Table 8.4). In addition, the range of topics discussed increased to include redecorating the mother's house and the daughter's restoration to her mother's home, and more discussion focused upon outside activities earned as reinforcers.

Observational data gathered during the visiting periods (described in Figure 8.15) was compared with baseline data and client-recorded rehearsal sessions. The average length of conversations dramatically increased from

FIGURE 8.15

Extended Visiting Schedule and Worker Observations: K. Family

Period covered: Four Weeks

All visits are to occur in the mother's home, as per the following schedule:

First weekend: (dates)   Saturday afternoon at 5 P.M., to Sunday evening at 6 P.M.

Second and
third weekends: (dates)   Friday evening at 6 P.M. to Sunday evening at 6 P.M.

Fourth week: (dates)   Tuesday evening at 6 P.M. to Sunday at 6 P.M.

If, for any reason, the above schedule cannot be maintained, the clients agree to notify each other at least one day in advance, and to notify the worker as soon as possible thereafter.

The worker agrees to:

1. Visit at the mother's home during each of the above periods. The time and length of these visits will vary. The worker agrees to notify the mother one day in advance of each visit

2. During these visits, the worker will observe the interaction of mother and daughter, the objective of which will be to identify any problem areas. Should any be identified, the worker will discuss these issues, and methods of resolving them, with both clients

   a. In addition, the worker agrees to discuss any issues of concern to either party during these visits

   b. In addition to the home visits, the worker will telephone the mother's home during each of the visiting periods. Also, the mother or daughter may feel free to telephone the worker during regular business hours should either party deem this necessary

3. If no additional problem areas requiring extensive intervention are identified, the worker agrees to request an ex parte order from the juvenile court on _____. This will permit Cynthia to remain in her mother's home on a continuing basis beginning _____, the fourth week of this contract period

4. The worker will visit the mother's home during the last 30 days of this contract at least three times, on a prearranged schedule. The objectives of these visits will be the same as those noted under items 2 and 2(a) above. In addition, either client may telephone the worker during regular business hours, should this be deemed a necessity.

Source: Compiled by author.

2.1 minutes at baseline, to 8.6 minutes during intervention, to 10.7 minutes at post-intervention. The percentage of the mother's attending responses increased from 20 to 43 percent, and the percentage of Cynthia's attending responses from 10 to 20 to 29 to 43 percent, at post-intervention. The percentage of positive affective responses increased from 40 percent for the

FIGURE 8.16

Contract for Restoration and Dependency Dismissal: K. Family

This contract is entered into between _____, social worker for _____ County, and Mrs. Sheila K., mother of Cynthia K., at the present time a dependent of the _____ County Juvenile Court. In keeping with the wish of both mother and daughter to reside together, and to have the court dependency dismissed, the worker agrees to recommend the above to the court, contingent upon the following:

1. Extended visiting, as per the attached schedule [Figure 8.15] is to occur between mother and daughter. Some portion of each of these visits will be observed by the social worker
2. Should any problems be identified during these visits, the worker agrees to develop any necessary program(s) to resolve them
3. It is understood by both clients that should problems requiring modification arise, the period prior to restoration may have to be extended
4. If no problems have been identified at the end of the first 30 days, or if any identified problems have been resolved, a 30-day trial visit will begin on _____. The worker will continue to visit and observe during this 30-day period and, should any problems be identified, agrees to develop programs to resolve them.

If no problems have been identified, or identified problems been resolved, the worker agrees, at the end of this 30-day period, to recommend that the juvenile court dismiss the dependency of Cynthia K.

This contract will be in effect for 60 days, beginning _____ and ending _____.

Signed:

_____   _____
Sheila K. (mother)   (Social Worker for

_____   _____County)
Cynthia K. (daughter)

Source: Compiled by author.

mother and 20 percent for the daughter, to 71 and 57 percent, respectively (see Table 8.5).

No additional problem areas were identified during the 30-day period of extended visiting, and hence Cynthia remained in her mother's home as stipulated in the contract. The clients and foster parents arranged a visiting schedule once Cynthia returned to her mother's home. Biweekly personal and alternate-week telephone contact by the worker occurred during the 30-day restoration period, and the dependency was dismissed as specified in the contract.

TABLE 8.4

Coding of Tape-Recorded Material: K. Family

Tape No.	Conver-sation No.	Total Speaking Time (mins.) Mother	Daughter	Topic 1	2	Total Time and Percentage Conversation Time (mins.)	Silence Time (mins.)	%
1	1	3.5	2.5	S	A	6	40	9	60
2	2	5	3	W	A	8	53	7	47
3	3	6	4.5	H	S	10.5	70	4.5	30
4	4	3	6.5	R		9.5	63	5.5	37
5	5	5	4	A	R	9	60	6	40
Total		22.5	20.5			43		32	

Notes: Average length of conversation = 8.6 minutes.
Percent of time in conversation or silence is based on 15-minute coding period.
Topics are as follows: S = daughter's school; A = (joint) activity discussion; W = mother's work; H = redecorating mother's house (new topic); R = restoration of daughter to mother's home (new topic).
Number of tapes = 5.
Length of coding period = 15 mins.
Total coding time = 75 mins.
Source: Compiled by author.

CASE 3: THE W. FAMILY

Steven W., aged nine and a half years, was declared a dependent of the court on a 600(a) and (d) petition*; and criminal charges were filed against his father for abuse. Mrs. W. was not involved. No court action was taken in regard to the four other children at home: Joann, Richard, Mark, and Alice, ages eight, seven, five, and three and a half, respectively.

Assessment

The first visit with the family took place two days after S. was taken into emergency foster care. Both parents said that they wished to have their son returned. The father was not able to recall the specifics or sequence of events leading up to the abuse; corporal punishment had not been used extensively in the home, and was considered a last resort. Hence, the father's abusive behavior did not seem to be a typical response.

---

*600(a) alleges neglect; 600(d), abuse.

TABLE 8.5

Verbal Interaction Between Mrs. K. and Cynthia
Before and After Intervention

Outcome Comparative Data:

Observation Period	No. of Conversations Coded	Total Time in Conversation (mins.)	Average Length of Conversations (mins.)
Baseline	10	21	2.1
Intervention	5	43	8.6
Post-intervention	7	75	10.7

Attending Behavior

	Baseline				Post-Intervention			
	M		D		M		D	
	Freq.	%	Freq.	%	Freq.	%	Freq.	%
Speaker looks at other	2	20	1	10	3	43	2	29
Listener looks at speaker	2	20	2	20	3	43	3	43
Person looks away	6	60	7	70	1	14	2	29
Total conversations	10		10		7		7	

Affect Responses

	Baseline				Post-Intervention			
	M		D		M		D	
	Freq.	%	Freq.	%	Freq.	%	Freq.	%
Postive affect	4	40	2	20	5	71	4	57
Negative affect	0	0	2	20	0	0	0	0
No affect	6	60	6	60	2	29	3	43
Total conversations	10		10		7		7	

Note: Post-intervention observation time was held constant with baseline observation time. Hence, there were three observational periods, each lasting for 30 minutes, for a total of 90 minutes of observation.

Source: Compiled by author.

During the second interview, a problem profile was completed (see Figure 8.17). The worker and clients agreed to begin working on reducing the father's drinking, which was seen as the most important issue by both parents. According to Mrs. W., when Mr. W. drank in the evening, he "retreated" from the problems that were created by the children; this increased Mrs. W.'s responsibilities for dealing with the problems, and augmented her frustration. She stated that since she had no free time to herself, her "efficiency" at home was reduced; and she "resented the restriction upon her and the overall responsibility for running the house." Both drinking and frustration in relation to the children's lack of chore completion were considered to be factors in the abuse incident, and assessment efforts focused upon these areas. While fighting with her own mother was troublesome, Mrs. W. agreed that this did not occur often enough to give it priority over the first two problems; and the father felt that dealing with problems related to his work could wait until other issues were resolved. The worker agreed to assist Mr. W. in resolving the pending criminal charges.

The worker stated that he would like to arrange for both parents to visit their son for one hour on the following Saturday. The boy had been in care for nine days, and there had been no visits as yet. While Mr. W. said he was nervous about seeing his son, both he and his wife said they would like to do so. The worker agreed to speak to the son and foster parents, and to telephone the W.'s the next day with a plan for a first visit.

The parents were requested to gather baseline data on Mr. W.'s drinking behavior and the noncompliance of the children for seven days, and were given a recording form (see Figure 8.18) to facilitate this task.

The worker explained that this information would serve as a basis for establishing program goals. Prior to concluding the interview, he told the parents that he would like to draw up a written contract with them following collection of baseline information, and the use of contracts was explained. An appointment was arranged for the following week, and the worker informed the parents that he would call them in two days to check on the data-gathering process and that they should feel free to call him if difficulties arose.

Baseline Data

Mr. W. was consistent in keeping the records describing his drinking behavior. The information is summarized in Table 8.6.

Feelings of relaxation following drinking were noted for each day. The first two drinks each evening were said to be preceded by Mr. W.'s wish to quench his thirst and to relieve work-related tension. Later evening drinks were said to be preceded by "frustration and tension" caused by the children.

Although the parents recorded the total number of requests their children complied with, they did not record the total number they made; and thus the percentage of all requests that resulted in compliance was not known. They also were inconsistent in recording the time of day the request was made. They were more consistent in recording what the children did not do than what was done. The data presented below therefore must be viewed as suggestive.

FIGURE 8.17

Problem Profile: W. Family

Problem No.	Label	Who Labels	Who Has the Problem	Date	Examples	Situation
1	drinking	father	father	5-15	consumes "excessive" amounts of alcohol on a daily basis past history of drinking	at home on work breaks
2	frustration	mother/father	mother/father	5-15	mother assumes all child care and household responsibilities mother has no free time; children will not do chores or follow any instructions (such as to go to bed, to clean up rooms) father becomes angry at children's not complying with requests	all at home

3	criminal charges	father	father	5-15	father charged with 273(d) Penal Code (PC) for abuse	
4	fights with wife's mother	mother	mother	5-15	can't refuse mother's requests	telephone
5	work	father	father	5-15	doesn't like work schedule (hours vary randomly); would like more consistent schedule would like to transfer to a store nearer home	

Source: Compiled by author.

FIGURE 8.18

Recording Form for Baseline Information on Drinking Behavior and Children's Compliance Behavior: W. Family

Day: _____ Date: _____

Drinking Behavior

Drink No.	Type of Drink	Situation	Time	Thoughts		Feelings		Comments
				Before	After	Before	After	

Instructions: Each time you have an alcoholic drink, please note the following information in the appropriate column: whether it is the first, second, third (or other) drink of the day; the type of drink (beer, wine, highball, other); where you are (situation); the time of day; and what you thought and felt both before and after the drink was consumed. Please use the far right-hand column to indicate any comments.

Children's Compliance Behavior

Day: _____ Date: _____

Request Made	Who Makes It	Which Child Involved	Time	Child's Response	Response of Person Making Request

Instructions: One of these forms should be kept by each parent. Each time a request is made of one of the children, indicate in the appropriate column what the child was asked to do and by whom, as well as which child was asked, what time it was, what the child's response was, and what your reaction was.

Source: Compiled by author.

228

TABLE 8.6

Drinking Behavior: Mr. W. Over Seven-Day Period

Total drinks consumed		46
Average number per day		6 4/7ths
Type of beverage consumed		
Beer		27
Wine		16 glasses
Screwdriver		3
Context	at home	41 drinks (89%)
	work breaks	5 drinks (11%)
Time of day	midday	5 drinks (11%)
	evening	41 drinks (89%)

Source: Compiled by author.

Contract-Related Issues

County and project workers spoke to Steven in order to ascertain his feelings about returning to the home of his parents; he stated that he would like this, and would like to visit with his parents. The visit was observed and went well, except for a very brief hesitancy on the part of the father and son to look at and talk to each other. The parents and youngster discussed the other children at home and the boy's feelings about the foster home, and all parties expressed their wish to be together as soon as possible.

TABLE 8.7

W. Children's Compliance Behavior over Seven Days

Child	No. of Compliant Responses per Day
Alice	3.5
Mark	2
Richard	4
Joann	3.5

Notes: If parents considered a task incomplete, they recorded it as half done.

Chores least likely to be completed were picking up clothes in bedroom or around the house, making their own beds, getting dressed in the morning without assistance and/or arguing, feeding the dog, and setting the table for dinner.

Source: Compiled by author.

Intervention

On the basis of the above information and the baseline data, the worker suggested that a contract be drawn up with the objective of restoring Steven to his parents' home, contingent upon reducing the father's drinking and increasing the mother's free time and the children's performance of chores. Since Mr. W. did not show any effects of drinking until after the third drink, it was decided that he could have two drinks per day. In addition, it was expected that regular visits with Steven would be maintained. The parents agreed with this suggestion. The parents stated that they could afford $5 per week to be distributed among the children for completing their chores. Both parents agreed that Mrs. W.'s free time would be her reinforcer for assisting Mr. W. in reducing his drinking. Mr. W. said that it would be easier to reduce his alcohol consumption if he had one hour to himself each day after returning from work, and that he also would like to discuss his job with his wife. Mrs. W. was agreeable to both of these suggestions. The worker offered to discuss Mr. W.'s work with him during their sessions if the father complied with the drinking program, and that he would formulate treatment programs and a contract within the next four days. He also noted that once progress was observed with the problems in the contract, they would address Mrs. W.'s problems with her mother. The contract is presented in Figure 8.19 and specific plans for each goal in Figures 8.20 through 8.23.

Mother's Fights with Her Mother

Mrs. W. stated that her mother telephoned her three or four times a week and made continual requests that she mediate problems that she was having with her son, Mrs. W.'s younger brother. These calls lasted 20 to 30 minutes. In addition, since Steven had become a dependent of the court, she stated that her mother harassed her about this, blaming her for it. She said that she did not wish to intervene in the problems between her brother and mother, but did not tell her mother this, and that she found the phone calls exhausting but had no way of dealing with them. She wished to stop such conversations altogether for a period of time.

The worker said that he might be able to help her develop assertive skills that she could employ when her mother telephoned, and that they would spend a part of each home visit in modeling and rehearsal. A first step was to obtain a sample of the phone dialogue between Mrs. W. and her mother, in order to identify what Mrs. W. should do differently. Mrs. W. was first asked to role-play her own mother, trying to use the same tone of voice and inflection that her mother used on the telephone and to discuss the two topics (requests to mediate with her brother and Steven's dependency) that her mother spoke about. Mrs. W. had difficulty assuming the role of her

FIGURE 8.19

Contract with W. Family

This contract is entered into between ⎯⎯⎯⎯⎯, social worker for the Alameda Project, ⎯⎯⎯⎯⎯, child welfare worker for Alameda County, and Louise and Stewart W., parents of Steven W., at the present time a dependent of the Alameda County Juvenile Court.

In keeping with the wish of both parents to have their son Steven returned to their home on a trial basis, both ⎯⎯⎯⎯⎯ and ⎯⎯⎯⎯⎯ agree to recommend such a trial visit to the juvenile court, contingent upon the participation of both parents in a program to accomplish the following objectives:

1. To increase the frequency with which the children in the home complete their household chores (see attached)
2. To decrease Mr. W.'s alcohol consumption to no more than two drinks per day (see attached)
3. To increase Mrs. W.'s free time from zero to two hours per week
4. To visit with their son Steven as per the attached schedule.

It is understood by both parents that failure to comply with this program will result in a statement to the juvenile court that, in the opinion of both workers, the trial visit is not feasible at the present time.

The contract is in effect for ninety (90) days, beginning ⎯⎯⎯⎯⎯ and ending ⎯⎯⎯⎯⎯.

Signed:

Stewart W. (father)	⎯⎯⎯⎯⎯, Alameda Project Worker
Louise W. (mother)	⎯⎯⎯⎯⎯, Alameda County Child Welfare Worker
Date: ⎯⎯⎯⎯⎯	

Source: Compiled by author.

mother; and following several attempts, Mr. W. offered to play his mother-in-law, and Mrs. W. assumed her own role. Mr. W. was asked to begin the conversation in whatever manner Mrs. W.'s mother would use, and Mrs. W. was to respond as she usually would. During the next 20 minutes, Mr. W. engaged in three nonstop monologues, averaging three and a half minutes in length. During this time Mrs. W.'s only responses consisted of "Mm-hmm," "Uh-huh," and an occasional "yes, yes." When Mr. W. spoke about Mrs. W.'s brother, his tone of voice was pleading, as were his statements: "Please help me with this" or "I can't cope with that, and need you to help me." When the conversation turned to Steven's dependency, the tone of voice and

FIGURE 8.20

Plan for Chore Completion: W. Family

This plan lists chores to be completed each day. The objective is to increase the frequency with which the children complete chores with minimal direction from the parents.

Chore (2 points each)	Sun.			Mon.			Tues.			Wed.			Thurs.			Fri.			Sat.		
	A	J	R	M	A	J	R	M	A	J	R	M	A	J	R	M	A	J	R	M	A	J	R	M
Pick up clothes																								
Make bed																								
Get dressed																								
Feed dog																								
Set dinner table																								
Total																								

Instructions:

1. A check mark will be placed under each child's initial by either parent when the chore is completed. The total number of points earned will be tallied on a daily basis. If a chore is not completed, the space under the child's name will be left blank. At no time is physical punishment to be employed.

2. For every ten (10) points the child earns, (s)he will receive a nickel from the parents. The child may determine the manner in which it is spent. Failure to complete a chore will result in the subtraction of one

3. Feeding the dog and setting the table occur once each day, in the evening. Beginning on day 1, Alice will feed the dog and Mark will set the table. On day 2, Richard will feed the dog and Joann will set the table. On day 3, Alice will set the table and Mark will feed the dog and on day 4, Richard will set the table and Joann will feed the dog. On day 5, each child will resume the responsibilities designated under day 1, and the pattern for dividing responsibilities on ensuing days will be to follow the pattern of days 2 through 4.

4. Each week, the social worker will check the chart and discuss

FIGURE 8.21

Plan to Reduce Mr. W.'s Alcohol Consumption

The goal of this modification program is to reduce the number of drinks that the father consumes each day from 6-4/7 drinks to 2. The father states that his drinking behavior serves two functions: (1) to quench his thirst, and (2) to assist him in relaxing. This program is designed to make the father's drinking of alcoholic beverages contingent upon his drinking of nonalcoholic beverages to quench his thirst and upon his engaging in other relaxing behaviors while he is at home.

Before the father may drink an alcoholic beverage, he must first

1. Quench his thirst by drinking a nonalcoholic beverage such as orange juice, Pepsi-Cola, or lemonade
2. Attempt to relax by watching television, reading, or taking a bath

If he meets those two conditions, he may drink an alcoholic beverage. The total number of drinks per day may not exceed two (2). For complying with this program, the father will receive the following reinforcers:

1. If the father complies with steps (1) and (2) of his modification program, his wife will allow him to discuss his job with her for one-half hour each evening
2. For each day that the father has two drinks or fewer, he will earn one hour of time alone

The mother agrees to the following:

1. She will have nonalcoholic beverages readily available in the refrigerator
2. She will not discuss her husband's job unless he has complied with steps (1) and (2) of his modification program
3. She will keep records of "time alone" that he has earned, and will negotiate with him as to when that time will be used

The social worker agrees to the following:

1. To monitor the modification program at his weekly interviews with the parents
2. To discuss any problem areas in the implementation of the program and, if necessary, to make alterations in the program
3. Not to allow the father to discuss his job unless he has complied with steps (1) and (2) of his modification program on the day of the interview

Source: Compiled by author.

comments became sarcastic and accusing: "It's your fault that this has happened," "How could you permit this to occur to a son of yours?" "If you did a better job with your children, this would not have occurred."

Mrs. W. said that the discussion represented her telephone calls with her mother. The worker suggested that a way to resolve this problem would be for Mrs. W. to practice using one of several alternative responses that he wrote down. He pointed out that the longer Mrs. W. allowed her mother to

FIGURE 8.22

Plan to Increase Mrs. W.'s Free Time

The desired outcome of this plan is to provide the mother with time alone, as a respite from child care responsibilities and as an opportunity for her to pursue activities of her own choosing. Time alone will be contingent upon her monitoring the father's drinking program.

The mother agrees to do the following:

1. Have nonalcoholic beverages readily in the refrigerator
2. Keep records of "time alone" that he has earned
3. Reinforce him by allowing him to discuss his job if he has complied with steps (1) and (2) of his drinking program

If the mother complies with this program, she will earn two (2) hours per week of time alone.

The father agrees to the following:

1. That he will negotiate with ＿＿＿＿＿ as to when she will use her two hours of time alone each week
2. That during her "time alone," he will be responsible for managing the home, including caring for the children and other household chores

The social worker will review this program at his weekly interviews with the parents and will attempt fo facilitate its implementation and maintenance.

Source: Compiled by author.

talk, the more difficult it would be for her to stop the conversation, and stressed the importance of terminating the conversation as soon as possible. Examples offered included the following:

> "I'm sorry mother, but I can't talk right now because:
>   a. I'm in the middle of preparing dinner
>   b. Stewart and I are getting dressed to go out
>   c. I'm watching a television program, and would like to see it through
>   d. I'm tired and would prefer not to talk now
>   e. We have company and I can't talk

These were considered as merely suggestive, and Mrs. W. was encouraged to add her own alternatives with which she was comfortable. Mr. W. agreed to play the role of Mrs. W.'s mother during rehearsal periods. During practice Mrs. W. was to hold the list of alternatives and to verbalize one of the responses as soon as possible after Mr. W. began speaking.

The worker timed Mr. W.'s speech to determine how long Mrs. W. would allow him to talk before stopping the conversation. On the first of two practice sessions, it was 2 minutes and 20 seconds before Mrs. W. said

FIGURE 8.23

Plan for Increased Visiting: Steven W.

Period covered: three months

First month: (dates)	Saturday afternoon from 1 P.M. until 5 P.M.
Second two weeks: (dates)	Saturday from 9:30 A.M. until 5:00 P.M.

During this first month, to facilitate worker observation of the interaction between Steven and his parents, visits should include only the parents and Steven. Mrs. L., who has performed baby-sitting services for the W. family in the past, will stay with the four children during these visiting periods.

Second month: (all visits to occur in the parents' home)

First two weeks: (dates)	Saturday from 9:30 A.M. until 5 P.M.
Second two weeks: (dates)	Saturday from 9:30 A.M. until Sunday 5 P.M.

Either or both of the parents will pick up Steven at the foster home and return him to the foster home.

Third month:

First two weeks: (dates)	Friday 5:30 P.M. until Sunday 5 P.M.
Second two weeks: (dates)	Wednesday 5:30 P.M. until Sunday 5 P.M.

Either or both of the parents will pick up Steven at the foster home and return him to the foster home.

If for any reason any of the above visits have to be canceled, either Mr. or Mrs. W. will notify the foster home as much in advance as possible and will telephone the social worker.

The worker agrees to do the following:

1. To observe at least half of the above visits. The exact time for these observations will vary, but the worker agrees to notify the parents one day in advance
2. The worker will observe parent-child interaction, with the objective of identifying any problems that may exist. Should any be identified, the worker will discuss them with the parents and will develop a program to resolve them.
3. If no problem areas requiring extensive intervention are identified, or if any identified have been resolved, the workers both agree to request an ex parte order from the juvenile court on _____. This will permit Steven to remain in his parents' home on a continuing basis beginning _____, the last visit of this contract period.
4. The worker will continue to visit at the parents' home for a minimum of ninety (90) days following the start of the 90-day trial visit. The objective of these visits are the same as those noted in the second provision of this section.

Source: Compiled by author.

anything; and she spoke in a halting, almost stuttering voice. She did, however, make a request to terminate the conversation; and the worker and Mr. W. congratulated her for this. On the second attempt, she was able to stop the conversation after 1 minute and 48 seconds. The parents were asked to practice this on three separate days, for 15 minutes each time, prior to their next session, keeping in mind the importance of Mrs. W.'s responding as soon as she could after Mr. W. began to talk. Mrs. W. was instructed not to engage in this verbal behavior with her own mother until successful practice experiences.

At the next meeting, the couple reported progress. Mr. W. had timed the period between the onset of his speech and Mrs. W.'s, and reported that it was now 49 seconds. The worker suggested that Mrs. W. try her new verbal skills with her mother once during the following week, and recommended that the parents continue to engage in their rehearsal sessions as before.

Three weeks from the time the program began, Mrs. W. reported that the number of phone calls from her mother decreased from three or four per week to two, and that the average length of these calls decreased from 20 to 30 minutes to between four and seven minutes. Mrs. W. was very pleased with her progress, and reported that her mother now seemed more respectful of her. As the weeks went by, Mrs. W. reported that she was able to talk with her mother about other topics and that these conversations were enjoyable.

Outcome

Excellent progress was made in three of the four contract areas. Mr. W.'s drinking was reduced from a baseline of six and four-sevenths drinks per day to three and a half drinks per day at the end of the 60 days, to zero drinks at the end of 90 days (see Figure 8.24). He was earning his one hour of free time and engaging in nightly discussions with Mrs. W. about his work. Mrs. W.'s free time had increased beyond the contract objective of two hours per week, to eight hours. Mr. W. assumed child care responsibilities during this time (see Figure 8.25). The parents had negotiated the latter increase on their own, and both were satisfied with the arrangement. All visits with Steven had been made according to schedule, and no problems were observed by the worker or reported by the parents. The parents again were not consistent in maintaining records on chore completion. Information they did collect showed that at the beginning of the program, the children were earning an average of four points per day, and that this increased by approximately two points per child per day. An additional behavior problem with one of the older children was noted by the parents at this time. They said Joann was "disruptive" at bedtime, and that this had occurred almost nightly over the past two weeks. She shared a bedroom with her

FIGURE 8.24

Average Number of Alcoholic Drinks Consumed per Day by Mr. W.

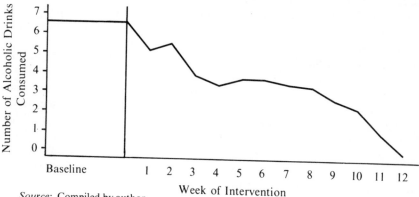

Source: Compiled by author.

younger sister, Alice; and her disruptive behavior (making a lot of noise and running in and out of the bedroom) prevented Alice from sleeping. When asked how they dealt with the problem, they said that they would take Joann in to watch television with them, allowing the younger child to fall asleep, and then "after about an hour, would put her back to bed." The possibility

FIGURE 8.25

Hours of Free Time per Week for Mrs. W.

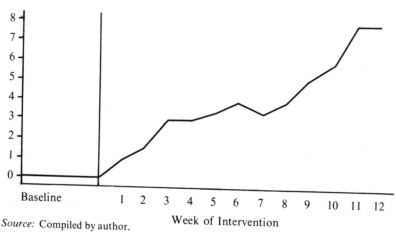

Source: Compiled by author.

of putting Joann to bed at a different hour was discussed. However, the parents wanted all the children to go to bed at the same time.

The worker suggested that the parents were reinforcing the disruptive behavior by permitting Joann to watch television with them, and presented a "time-out" procedure for eliminating this problem. This involves removing a child from a reinforcing environment to a nonreinforcing one, and is an effective method for eliminating problem behavior without the use of physical punishment.[12] The effectiveness of the procedure depends upon the method used to remove the child and the environment in which the child is placed. Removing the child should not itself be reinforcing. The child should be told in advance that each time he or she engages in certain behaviors, he or she will have to spend a certain amount of time in whatever area of the house is designated for "time out." When the misbehavior occurs, the child is reminded of the relationship between the undesirable behavior and the consequence of "time out," and told to go to the "time-out" place. If he or she does not go willingly, five minutes of time is added to the "time out" for each minute of refusal. The "time-out" area should not contain any items that might permit enjoyable activities—toys, books, or television. A downstairs bathroom was designated as a "time-out" space for Joann, and the parents were instructed to take her to this place and leave her there for two minutes as soon as the disruption began. At the end of that time she could return to her room. Should she engage in disruptive behavior a second time, the procedure described was to be followed again. Should it occur a third time, the length of time in the "time-out" space was to be increased. The procedure was to be fully described to Joann, including exactly what behavior would result in being placed in the "time-out" area.

The parents said that they used the "time-out" procedure on approximately four evenings during the first week, and that this eliminated the disruptive behavior. They explained the procedure to Joann and employed it on two occasions the first evening, on one occasion on the second and third evenings, and once toward the end of the week. During the following three weeks, they did not find it necessary to use "time out."

Two weeks before the end of the contract period, the father was transferred to a new store and placed on a new work schedule. He had not requested the transfer although, as indicated on the profile, he had desired it. Both he and Mrs. W. were very pleased.

Steven was returned to his parents' home as specified in the contract. The father was placed on one-year probation with a suspended 90-day sentence. For the first two months following restoration, the worker maintained biweekly personal contact and alternate-week telephone contact with the family. No problems were observed, nor were any reported by the parents. However, at the beginning of the third month following restoration, Mrs. W. reported that Steven was beginning to have tantrums and to fight with his younger siblings, although in his father's presence he was said to exhibit exemplary behavior. Mrs. W. usually was in some other part of the house, and would become aware of screaming and shouting. She said it seemed that the children would get into an argument over toys or what to watch on television; that Steven would bully the younger children; and that when he could not get his way, he would scream and shout.

When asked how she dealt with this problem, Mrs. W. said that she would separate Steven from the four younger children and talk with him about the problem, and that she was spending as much as half an hour to a full hour with Steven each afternoon following these scenes. This greatly distressed her, because it interfered with completion of her own chores. She said she knew she probably was supporting this behavior by spending so much time with Steven, but that her only concern was putting an end to the yelling and shouting and what she was doing was effective.

Shortly after Steven had been restored to his parents, the worker had suggested that they identify some activities, possibly at a neighborhood community center, that the children might engage in after school and on week-ends when Mr. W. was working, in order to relieve Mrs. W. of caring for all five children by herself. The worker broached this issue again as one method of resolving the current issue, and the parents agreed to contact the neighborhood center and obtain a list of appropriate activities for the children. The worker agreed to meet with the parents and the children in four days, to go over the list and discuss enrolling the children at the center. He suggested that should the problem occur in the meantime, Mrs. W. should not spend time talking with Steven but use the "time-out" procedure.

Two days later Mrs. W. telephoned the worker and told him that she and Mr. W. were convinced that Steven was hyperactive, and that they had decided to obtain medical consultation. The worker doubted that there was any organic basis for Steven's difficulties, but thought that if organicity could be ruled out, the parents might be more willing to engage in a program to eliminate these recent problems. Over the next several weeks, Steven underwent a general physical examination, glucose tolerance test, and EEG; psychiatric assessment; and psychological testing. None of the physical tests indicated any organic problems. The psychiatrist told the parents that he did not believe that psychotherapy was called for, and supported the case worker's recommendation regarding Steven and the younger children.

The parents then followed through with the suggestion that they identify appropriate programs at the community center. Steven subsequently joined the Cub Scouts and enrolled in an arts and crafts class that met twice each week at the center. The worker also suggested that since Steven was reinforced by time with his mother, she plan to set aside some time each week that she and Steven could spend together in a mutually pleasurable structured activity. Both stated that they had always enjoyed reading together and talking about what they read, but never had done this on a set schedule. Mrs. W. agreed to do this with Steven on afternoons that he was not at the community center, and that she would devote half an hour to an hour to this.

The worker remained with this case for 90 additional days of follow-up, reducing his contact to the biweekly personal and alternate-week telephone contact that had been arranged prior to the onset of the last problem. Steven was still reported to fight occasionally with his siblings, but not to an extent that was considered to be a problem. The court dependency was dismissed.

NOTES

1. Gerald L. Patterson, J. B. Reid, L. R. Jones, and R. E. Conger, *A Social Learning Approach to Family Intervention*, vol. 1, *Families with Aggressive Children* (Eugene, Ore.: Castalia, 1975).

2. Gerald L. Patterson and J. B. Reid, "Reciprocity and Coercion: Two Facets of Social Systems," in Charles Neuringer and John Michael, eds., *Behavior Modification in Clinical Psychology* (New York: Appleton-Century-Crofts, 1970), pp. 133–77.

3. Patterson, Reid, et al., op. cit.

4. Ibid.

5. Eileen D. Gambrill and Cheryl A. Richey, *It's up to You: Developing Assertive Social Skills* (Millbrae, Calif.: Les Femmes, 1976).

6. Albert Bandura, *Principles of Behavior Modification* (New York: Holt, Rinehart and Winston, 1969), ch. 3.

7. Ibid.

8. Ibid.

9. Marian MacDonald, "Teaching Assertion: A Paradigm for Therapeutic Intervention," *Psychotherapy, Theory and Research* 12 (1975): 60–67.

10. Robert P. Liberman, Larry W. King, William J. DeRisi, and Michael McCann, *Personal Effectiveness: Guiding People to Assert Themselves and Improve Their Social Skills* (Champaign, Ill.: Research Press, 1975).

11. Teodoro Ayllon and Nathan Azrin, *The Token Economy: A Motivational System for Therapy and Rehabilitation* (New York: Appleton-Century-Crofts, 1968).

12. Gerald R. Patterson, *Families: Applications of Social Learning Theory to Family Life* (Champaign, Ill. Research Press, 1971).

APPENDIXES

APPENDIX A:
Project Forms

CASE INFORMATION

1. Natural mother   Address:

2. Natural father   Address:

3. Marital status:

4. Financial status: (If employed, name and address of employer. Type of public assistance, if any.)
   a. Mother:
   b. Father:

5. Children in foster care:

Name	Age	Sex	Race	Reason Placed	Date Placed	Petition

6. Additional family, relationship, and address:

7. Who has custody?

8. Name, age, and sex of any nondependent children at home:

9. Foster parents: (if separate placements, list information by name of child)

Child's Name	Parent's Name	Address

10. Requested placement disposition (new intake):

11. Decision status (if any); list by child's name:

12. Plans (if any); list by child's name:

13. Evaluations (psychiatric, psychological, other):

14. Specific court directives:

15. Date of next hearing:

16. General notes:

CONTACTS WITH CHILDREN, NATURAL AND FOSTER PARENTS, AND COLLATERALS

Worker: _____

Month: _____

Case Name	Natural Parents IP or Phone, Purpose	Child IP or Phone, Purpose	Foster Parents IP or Phone, Purpose	Collaterals Who, Purpose

Note: IP = In-person.

Source: Compiled by author.

Project Form 3

QUARTERLY REPORT ON STATUS OF CHILDREN IN CARE

Case	Unchanged	To Be Dismissed	To Be Restored	Child Restored (now a/m)*	Undecided	Referred for Adoption	Referred for Guardian-ship	Long-Term Care	Closed for Misc. Reasons (such as change of jurisdiction)

*Dependency still open; objective is assessment of and maintenance of child at home.

Instructions: For each case, place a check mark in the column that describes the change(s) (if any) that occurred during the quarter.

Source: Compiled by author.

Project Form 4a

RESTORATION DECISIONS

Child's name:_____   Date: _____

Instructions:
    Each time a restoration decision is made for a child, indicate which of the reasons listed lies behind the decision, by placing a check mark to the left of the appropriate item. If more than one item pertains, check off as many as are appropriate; and, if at all possible, rank the reasons by placing a number 1 next to the most important, number 2 to the second most important, and so on.

_____ 1. The parent(s) has/have indicated that this is his/her express wish, and I should like to provide the opportunity to achieve this objective.

_____ 2. I have been working with this (these) parent(s) for some time, problems that were severe in the past are no longer so, and I believe that restoration is now a possibility.

_____ 3. I have been working with the child(ren) for some time, problems that were severe in the past are no longer so, and I believe that restoration is now a possibility.

_____ 4. The foster home placement is not a good one; and rather than move the child(ren) to a new home, I think that restoration could work out at this time.

_____ 5. A collateral resource (such as the Trauma Center, a psychiatrist) has indicated that major parental problems have been resolved and that restoration is appropriate at this time.

_____ 6. Same as 5, substituting children's resources and child for parent.

_____ 7. The parent has remarried, making restoration a possibility.

_____ 8. The child(ren) is (are) older now, and better able to cope with the home situation.

_____ 9. I think that this (these) child(ren) should not have been taken into placement, and that with immediate assistance, an early restoration can occur.

_____ 10. The parent(s) is (are) moving out of the community, restoration seems a possibility, and I should like to see this occur before the move takes place.

_____ 11. Placement occurred because of some temporary difficulty (such as parent was hospitalized for medical reasons), and early restoration appears likely.

_____ 12. The court has ordered that this (these) child(ren) be restored at this time.

_____ 13. Other (specify)

_____ 14. Indicate when you expect restoration to occur.

Source: Compiled by author.

Project Form 4b

ADOPTION DECISIONS

Child's name: _____   Date: _____

Instructions:
Each time an adoption decision is made for a child, indicate which of the reasons listed lies behind the decision, by placing a check mark to the left of the appropriate item. If more than one item pertains, check off as many as are appropriate; and, if at all possible, rank the reasons by placing a number 1 next to the most important, number 2 to the second most important, and so on.

_____ 1.   The parent(s) has (have) willingly relinquished the child(ren).

_____ 2.   The parent(s) have (have) abandoned the child(ren).

_____ 3.   Legal grounds exist for terminating parental rights on grounds other than abandonment. (Indicate which section of 232 is applicable here.)

_____ 4.   The relative with whom the child is placed wishes to pursue adoption, and the parent(s) is (are) agreeable.

_____ 5.   Same as 4, changing the word "relative" to "foster parent."

_____ 6.   A relative is privately pursuing this course of action.

_____ 7.   Same as 6, substituting "foster parent" for "relative."

_____ 8.   Other (specify) _____

Source: Compiled by author.

Project Form 4c

LONG-TERM CARE DECISIONS

Instructions:

Each time a long-term care decision is made for a child, indicate which of the reasons listed lies behind the decision, by placing a check mark to the left of the appropriate item. If more than one item pertains, check off as many as are appropriate and, if at all possible, rank the reasons by placing a number 1 next to the most important, number 2 to the second most important, and so on.

_____ 1. The child(ren) is (are) too old to be adopted.
_____ 2. There are no adoptive homes for (a) child(ren) of this race.
_____ 3. Physical handicap of the child precludes adoption.
_____ 4. There is (are) no adult(s) willing to assume the role of legal guardian.
_____ 5. The parent(s) is (are) not willing to relinquish, and legal grounds for termination do not exist.
_____ 6. The child(ren) is (are) with a relative who is not interested in either adopting or assuming guardianship. At the same time, I cannot remove this (these) child(ren) from the relative's home for placement in a preadoptive home.
_____ 7. The child's emotional/behavioral problems are such that long-term care seems most appropriate.
_____ 8. Parents' problems are so severe that restoration to their home does not appear to be a likely outcome, and this is the only alternative that I see for the near future.
_____ 9. The foster home is a good environment, the child has been there for quite some time, and I do not think that removal would be appropriate.
_____ 10. The parent(s) is (are) not willing to make himself/herself (themselves) available for treatment that would result in restoration.
_____ 11. Several siblings are in the same foster home, and I do not wish to separate them for adoption or guardianship elsewhere.
_____ 12. I am not sure what has to be done to bring about restoration.
_____ 13. Other (specify)

Source: Compiled by author.

248

Project Form 4d

GUARDIANSHIP DECISIONS

Child's name: _____ Date: _____

Instructions:

Each time a guardianship decision is made for a child, indicate which of the reasons listed lies behind the decision, by placing a check mark to the left of the appropriate item. If more than one item pertains, check off as many as are appropriate and, if at all possible, rank the reasons by placing a number 1 next to the most important, number 2 to the second most important, and so on.

_____ 1. The child(ren) is (are) with a relative who is willing to assume this role, but not the role of adoptive parent.

_____ 2. Same as 1, substituting "foster parent" for "relative."

_____ 3. The natural parent is willing to permit this alternative, but not adoption.

_____ 4. The child(ren) is (are) too old for adoption elsewhere, and this seems the most appropriate outcome.

_____ 5. While this (these) child(ren) is (are) probably adoptable, (s)he (they) has (have) been in this home too long to be removed to a preadoptive home; and that is the only alternative that the foster parents are willing to consider.

_____ 6. A relative is privately pursuing this course of action.

_____ 7. Same as 6, substituting "foster parent" for "relative."

_____ 8. Other (specify) _____

Source: Compiled by author.

249

Project Form 5

QUARTERLY REPORT ON PROBLEM AREAS OF NATURAL PARENTS

Case Name: _____   Frequency of parental visits to child(ren):

	Weekly	Monthly
Child 1	_____	_____
Child 2	_____	_____
Child 3	_____	_____
Child 4	_____	_____
Child 5	_____	_____

For each month in each quarter, indicate which of the following problem areas, if any, you are currently working on with natural parents. In the two right-hand columns, indicate, at the end of the quarter, whether the problem is currently resolved, or remains unresolved.

	Month 1	Month 2	Month 3	Resolved	Unresolved
1. Finances					
2. Employment					
3. Job training					
4. Housing					
5. Household furniture					
6. Housekeeping skills					
7. Clothing for children					
8. Food					
9. Nutrition					
10. Day care					
11. Medical care for parent(s)					
12. Medical care for child(ren)					
13. Visiting children					
14. Parent-child interaction					
15. Problems in keeping appointments with ancillary resources					
probation					
methadone maintenance					
alcohol program					
drug program					
other counseling service					

	Month 1	Month 2	Month 3	Resolved	Unresolved
16. Problems in relationships with significant others					
with relatives					
with spouse					
nonspouse adult					
misc. (landlord, employer)					
17. Legal/ criminal (abuse charges, other criminal charges)					
18. Parent's personal problems					
19. Decision making for child's future					
20. School-related problems					

If any of the following problem areas were originally alleged against your client(s), indicate whether or not there is current evidence for the existence of the problem.

	Never Evidenced by Client	Current Evidence
21. Drugs		
22. Alcohol		
23. Psychiatric problems		
24. Abuse		
25. Other		

Source: Compiled by author.

Project Form 6

CONTACTS WITH NATURAL PARENTS

Case name: _____

Date: _____

For each interview, check as many techniques as apply, then circle the predominant activity for the interview. Definitions are below.

Interviews Within a Single Month

	1	2	3	4	5	6	7	8
Exploration								
Structuring								
Support								
Directive techniques								
Reflective techniques								
Practical help								
Behavioral approach								

Definitions of Caseworker Activity Categories

Exploration: Worker seeks information about relevant present or past situation, attitudes, and behavior. Although this activity may encourage airing of emotion-laden subject matter, its primary purpose is to gain knowledge rather than to effect a change in the client's behavior or attitudes.

Structuring: Worker explains agency or court function, requirements, and expectations, so as to structure and clarify the nature of the agency-client and worker-client relationship. The primary purpose is to enhance the client's functioning in the role of client, rather than to affect his/her functioning in life situations.

Support: Worker expresses reassurance, understanding, encouragement, or sympathy with the client's feelings, situation, and efforts to cope with the situation.

Directive techniques: Worker attempts through advice, recommendations, or suggestions to prompt the client to engage in certain tasks, such as visits with a child. Such attempts by the worker can range from commands to implicit suggestions couched in the form of questions.

Reflective techniques: Worker raises questions or gives explanations to increase the client's understanding of his/her own behavior and attitudes, his/her situation, the consequences of his/her behavior, and the reactions of others to him/her.

Practical help: Worker arranges for or provides concrete services (such as homemaker service, transportation, money, goods, escort).

Behavioral approach: All dialogue that relates to a behavior approach belongs here. The way to determine whether something goes here, rather than in one of the other categories, is by the content of questions and statements. For example, if you are asking questions to gather information for a problem profile, or to identify reinforcers, even though questions fit the definition of "exploratory" verbalizations, they would be categorized here because the content relates to a behavioral approach to treatment. Similarly, if you are purposefully, verbally reinforcing a client for participating in a program—which could fit the definition of "support"—such reinforcement likewise would belong here.

Source: Compiled by author.

252

Project Form 7

CONSENT TO TAPE-RECORD INTERVIEWS IN THE
STUDY OF DECISION MAKING IN FOSTER CARE

I understand that _____, whose signature appears below, is part of a special project staff working with parents who have children placed in foster care under the supervision of the Alameda County Human Resources Agency. The purpose of the project is to study carefully how parents can be helped to plan for their children's future more effectively.

Tape-recording interviews between the project social worker and parents is one way of carefully studying how decisions are made to place children in foster care and continue to care for them away from their natural parents.

I give consent to tape-recording interviews between us, with the understanding that the following restrictions will apply very strictly to the use of these tapes:

1. When typed copies are made, all last names will be either left out or changed
2. As soon as a typed copy is made, the tape will be erased
3. The only persons who will see typed copies or listen to tapes are persons directly connected with the project staff
4. In any written or spoken reports about this project, no real names of parents, children, or social workers will ever be used.

I have been told that any questions I have about this project and what use will be made of the results or reports from it will be answered fully.

I freely consent to tape-recording of interviews and their use as described above. I understand that I may decide at any time that I do not wish to continue tape-recording, and that receiving social services in no way depends upon consenting to the tape-recording.

_____   _____
     Project Social Worker   Parent

Date: _____

Source: Compiled by author.

253

Project Form 8

ASSESSMENT OF HOME CONDITIONS

Name of parent(s): ―――――――――――――――――

Number of children and their ages: ――――――――――――――――――――

Household: (condition)

The following information is appropriate to any case where the parent(s) want(s) to have (a) child(ren) returned to parental care. Responding to these questions will enable you to identify household conditions that might have to be changed prior to making such a return. This portion of the assessment form could be used at different times (for example, as soon as a decision for return is made, one month later, two months later) to indicate the extent of improvement and areas that still require attention.

There probably are items that could be added to this list, and I should like you to do so when you come across areas of concern. However, I am concerned that in making additions, we bear in mind the difference between objectively dangerous conditions (that must be changed) and subjective judgments that reflect our own values (which should not be included).

1. Dangerous objects: (presence in home)
   broken glass ―――― broken toys (with sharp edges) ―――― knives ―――― scissors ――――
   (lying around) broken windows ―――― Does the parent keep potentially dangerous objects (knives, scissors) out of the reach of children? ――――
2. Odors: (these may indicate unsanitary/unhealthy conditions)
   garbage ―――― urine ―――― feces ―――― other (identify) ――――――――――――
3. Household equipment: (does household have)
   stove ―――― refrigerator ―――― beds for child(ren) ――――
   linen (for beds) ―――― cooking utensils ―――― dishes ――――
   flatware ―――― kitchen table ―――― chairs ――――

Medical care:
   It would seem most appropriate to gather this information just prior to returning (a) child(ren) to (a) parent(s).

1. Does client have Medi-Cal? yes ―――― no ―――― Private health insurance? yes ―――― no
   If no, is client eligible for Medi-Cal? yes ―――― no ――――
2. Is there a family doctor? yes ―――― no ――――
3. Is there a community clinic nearby? yes ―――― no ――――
4. How far from either (specify which) does the family live? ――――――――
5. Does the parent know the location of a community clinic? yes―――― no ――――
6. If the client has either Medi-Cal or private health insurance, is he or she knowledgeable regarding the circumstances under which it can and cannot be used? yes ――――
   no ――――
7. Do(es) the parent(s) know how to get to a clinic or physician by public transportation?
   yes ―――― no ―――― By automobile? yes ―――― no ――――
8. How frequently are children taken for checkups? ――――――――
9. Are there first aid supplies (bandages and so forth) in the house? yes ―――― no ――――
10. Does the child have any observable physical conditions that appear to require medical attention? (burns, open wounds or cuts, obvious infections)? yes ―――― no ――――
    If yes, specify ――――――――

254

Parent-child interaction:

Items 1 through 15 should be completed for all children who are in foster home placement. They are the only items you need complete if parent-child visiting is of brief duration (one to three hours) and occurs either in the foster home or in the physical environment around the foster home.

Items 16 through 26 focus on parent-child interaction that occurs either in the home of the parent(s) or in the physical environment around the parental home. These items are appropriate for children in care if they visit at their parents' home (regardless of the length of time involved) or for children who have been returned to their parents.

1. What is the schedule for parent-child visiting? If the schedule differs for each of several children, indicate the differences by child.

    a. If there are two parents, do they both visit? yes —— no ——
    b. If no, which parent does not?
    c. If both parents cannot visit at the same time, is there a separate schedule for each
        parent? yes —— no ——
2. How frequently do(es) the parent(s) actually visit the child? Does (s)he adhere to the schedule; yes —— no —— What is the duration of these visits?
3. Is there a plan to increase the frequency and length of visits?
4. If there is more than one child, are they in different foster homes? yes —— no ——
    a. If yes, in how many homes?
    b. Where is (are) the home(s) located geographically?
5. Are there any restrictions on the visits (for example, is the parent allowed to visit only in the foster home, or is visiting in the foster home precluded)? yes —— no —— If yes, state what these restrictions are and whether they refer to all of the children.
6. Using the following check list, describe as well as possible the response of the parent(s) to the child at the beginning of a visit:
    a. Smiles at child: yes —— no ——
    b. Verbally expresses pleasure at seeing child: yes —— no ——
    c. Physically embraces (hugs) child: yes —— no ——
    d. No discernible response: yes —— no ——
    e. Any other response (describe)
7. Using the following check list, describe the reaction of the child to the parent(s):
    a. Smiles at parent(s): yes —— no ——
    b. Verbally expresses pleasure at seeing parent: yes —— no ——
    c. Responds to parent physically (hugs parent back): yes —— no ——
    d. Child attempts to approach parent (holds out hand to be taken, tries to hug parent) and parent fails to respond: yes —— no ——
    e. Child accompanies parent willingly: yes —— no —— If no, what is the child's response (cries, runs away, other)?
    f. Any other response (describe).
8. Using the following check list, indicate how the parent and child spend their visits:
    Parent engages in playful activities with child (this item would be of concern with infants who cannot be engaged in more structured activities, and would consist of playful tossing around or attempts to amuse the child with various antics). yes —— no —— movies —— plays —— walks —— car rides —— museums —— reading to child —— discussion of shared interest (could include discussion of child in school or of child's activities) —— picnics —— nothing occurs (they sit and stare at each other) ——
    If the visits occur in the foster home, does the parent have access to playthings that are available in the home? yes —— no ——

9. If either the parent(s) or the child(ren) attempt to engage the other in any of the above activities, and it does not work out, why is this the case? For example, does one of the parties make suggestions, such as "Let's go to the movies, or the park," and the other respond negatively? Does one of the parties fail to respond to attempts at verbal interaction by not answering questions or by answering in such a way as to indicate non-interest in talking?

10. Does the parent look to you, or to the foster parent, to provide a structure for the visits? yes —— no ——

11. If the child misbehaves in any way, describe the parent's response (looks to you or the foster mother to discipline, ignores, responds by yelling at or hitting the child, or other). Is the parent's response different if the visit occurs in the foster home than if it occurs in a public space, such as a park or walking on the street? yes —— no ——

12. How does the parent respond to a child's request for "praise" (for example, if the child shows the parent work that [s]he has done at school, asks the parent[s] to watch some activity)?

   a. Listens to the child and provides a verbal response regarding the school paper, or activity, or other item. yes —— no ——

   b. Ignores the child's request. yes —— no ——

   c. Responds negatively (Go away, I'm too busy, Don't bother me with that now). yes —— no ——

   d. Other (describe)

13. Does the parent "bribe" the child (for example, "If you leave me alone now, I'll give you such and such later on")? yes —— no ——

14. Does the parent "set limits" for the child (for example, does the parent say "You may go as far as the corner, but you cannot cross the street," or "You can play outside for 'x' amount of time, but no more")? yes —— no ——

   a. If the answer is yes, are there any problems that follow the parent's rule-setting statement (for instance, does an argument begin between the parent and child as to the appropriateness of the limit set)? yes —— no ——

   b. If the answer to 14(a) is yes, describe the difficulty (for example, a five-minute fight begins regarding the appropriateness of the rule; the child says, "I won't do that," and runs out of the house).

15. When a parent(s) ask(s) or tell(s) a child to do something, are there clear contingencies for the request (for example, "If you go wash your hands, then we can go to the park," or "If you don't get your coat on, we will have to spend our visit indoors")? yes —— no ——

16. How much time each day do(es) the parent(s) and child(ren) spend together?

   ————————————

17. Is there an allotted period of time for the parent(s) and child(ren) to spend together? yes —— no —— If yes, how much time do they spend together? ——————.

18. Which of the following activities do the parent(s) and child(ren) engage in together? movies —— plays —— walks —— car rides —— museums —— reading to a child —— discussions of shared interests —— help with child's home-work —— hobbies (specify) ————— picnics —— cooking —— others (specify) —————

If either the parent(s) or the child(ren) attempt to engage the other in any of the above activities, and it does not work out, why is this the case? For example, does one of the parties make suggestions, such as "Let's go to the movies or the park," and the other respond negatively? Does one of the parties fail to respond to attempts at verbal interaction either by not answering questions, or by answering in such a way as to indicate non-interest in talking?

256

19. Using the above activity areas as a guide, what things would the parent like to do with the child? Why do they not engage in activities that they indicate as of interest (no money, no transportation, other)?
20. What equipment is available in the house for the child(ren) to play with?
books —— coloring books —— crayons —— pencils/pens —— toys ("age appropriate"? specify) ———————— bicycle —— other (specify) ——
21. Are there other children to play with? yes —— no ——
   a. If yes, how much time each day to they play together? ————
   b. Where do they play? – ————
   c. How frequently, when the child is playing outdoors, does the parent check on his or her whereabouts? ————
   d. Does the parent provide specific guidelines for the child relative to his or her going outdoors? For example, does the child know where he or she is to play? yes —— no ——

   1. Does the child know when (specific time) he or she is to come back indoors? yes —— no ——
   2. Is there an understanding that if the child wishes to "stray" from the specified area, he or she must inform the parent? yes —— no ——
22. If the child does not play with neighbor children, why is this the case? For example, does the mother/father consider the area unsafe for the child to be outdoors? Does the mother/father consider the neighborhood children "unsuitable" playmates?
23. Is the parent consistent in following through on promised activities with the child? yes —— no ——
   a. If no why is this the case? For example, does the parent promise to do things that are unrealistic (things that he or she cannot afford, or are plans made so far in advance that the parent forgets about them)?
   b. If the parent must "break plans" with the child, are the reasons for doing this explained to the child? yes —— no ——
   c. Does the parent "create" an alternative for the child when the plans have to be broken (does he or she create the possibility for the child engaging in the activity with someone else? Are the plans set for a future, specific date)? yes —— no ——
24. Is the home physically close to:
   parks —— playgrounds —— museums —— community recreational centers —— other (specify) ————
   a. Does the parent know the location of these facilities? yes —— no ——
   b. Does the parent know how to get to them by public transportation? yes —— no ——
   c. Does the parent know of their existence, and what activities are offered? yes —— no ——
25. In general, how does the child spend his/her time at home? ————
26. Does the child receive an allowance? yes —— no ——
   a. If yes, how much? ———— how frequently? ————
   b. If the child spends his or her allowance before the allowance period is over, what are the consequences (does the parent provide additional money, or must the child go without money until the next allowance is due)?

257

Child management

The items listed under this heading focus most specifically on situations where the child is at the parents' home for either a brief visit (such as a weekend or a one- or two-week trial, or for children who have been restored to their parents).

1. During an observation period which, if any, of the following positive physical interactions do you observe between parent(s) and child(ren)?
   a. Parent(s) and child(ren) hug or embrace each other. ———
   b. Parent(s) lift(s) child and engage(s) in playful activities. ———
   c. Parent(s) comfort(s) crying child (picks up and holds child or verbally tries to comfort child). ———
   d. Other (describe) ————

2. How does the parent respond to a child's request for praise (for example, if the child shows the parent work that (s)he has done at school, asks the parent[s] to watch some activity)?
   a. Listens to the child and provides a verbal response regarding the school paper or activity. yes —— no ——
   b. Ignores the child's request. yes —— no ——
   c. Responds negatively (Go away, I'm too busy, Don't bother me with that now). yes —— no ——
   d. Other (describe)

3. Which (or how many) of the following do(es) the parent(s) employ to control a child's behavior?
   a. Yells at child. ——
   b. Hits child. (where is the child hit? with what is child hit?) ———
   c. Sends child to room. —— (how long) ———
   d. Revokes a privilege. —— (what privilege? for how long?) ———
   e. Other (specify) ————

4. Describe the behavior of the child that evoked punishment (child drew pictures on living room wall with crayon; child screamed for one minute; and so on).

5. How long does the parent allow the misbehavior to go on before responding to it?
   ————

6. Does the parent ignore misbehavior? yes —— no ——

7. Is the parent consistent in following through on promised punishment? yes —— no ——

8. If the parent punishes the child, does he or she follow this with attention (for example, hitting a child, then cuddling him or her and saying "I love you")? yes —— no ——

9. Are promised punishments realistic (for instance, does the parent threaten something that cannot be followed through, such as "You cannot go out for six months")? yes —— no ——

9a. Does parent threaten the child with statements such as "I will leave you" or "I won't love you any more"? yes —— no ——

10. Do punishments for one child result in punishing of other children in the family? For example, if everyone is expecting to go on a picnic, and Johnny misbehaves, is the picnic canceled, so that everyone ends up being punished? yes —— no ——

11. Is the child told why he or she is being punished? yes —— no ——

12. If more than one of a family's children are involved in misbehavior, is punishment meted out uniformly? yes —— no ——

12a. If no, describe the inconsistency.

13. Is the child praised for a "job well done"? yes —— no ——

14. If verbal communication accompanies punishment, or if it is the form of punishment employed, are statements demeaning to the child (such as "You are so stupid, you never do anything right")? yes —— no —— If yes, describe the demeaning statement.
15. If the family has two parents, are all punishments meted out by one? —— Both? —— If one, which one? ————
16. If one parent punishes a child, does the child go to the other parent for comfort? yes —— no ——
    a. If yes, which parent? ————
    b. What is the response of the parent? (describe)
17. If two parents are present, and one is meting out punishment, what is the response of the nonpunishing parent? If (s)he disagrees, describe the disagreement statement and the response of the other parent and child.
18. If a child misbehaves, does the parent threaten that the child will be punished when the other parent returns from work? yes —— no —— If yes, what occurs when the parent returns home?
19. If there is a disagreement between parent and child about an infraction of rules, or the rules themselves, does the parent listen to the child's arguments? yes —— no ——
    a. If no, what is parental response to the child when the latter tries to explain his/her position?
    b. If yes, what is the outcome of the discussion (for instance, if the child's explanation is reasonable, does the parent acquiesce)?
20. Does the parent "bribe" the child (for example, "If you leave me alone now, I'll give you such and such later on")? yes —— no ——
21. Does the parent "set limits" for the child? For example, does the parent say "You may go as far as the street corner, but you cannot cross the street" or "You may play outside for 'x' amount of time, but no more"? yes —— no ——
    a. If the answer is yes, are there any problems that follow the parent's rule-setting statements (for instance, does an argument bein between the parent and child as to the appropriateness of the limit set)? yes —— no ——
    b. If the answer to 21(a) is yes, please describe the difficulty (for example, a five-minute fight begins regarding the appropriateness of the rule; the child says "I won't do that,"and runs out of the house).
22. When the parent(s) ask(s) or tell(s) a child to do something, are there clear contingencies for the request (for example, "If you go wash your hands, then we can go to the park," or "If you don't get your coat on, we will have to spend our visit indoors")? yes —— no ——

Household management (for child[ren] at home only):
1. Does each member of the household have a clear understanding of his or her responsibilities (such as chores)? yes —— no ——
    a. If yes, are chores carried through in accordance with plans? yes —— no ——
    b. If no, describe the consequence of not doing chores (the parent does the youngster's chore, the child is punished, other).
2. Does the family have any system for "negotiating" household tasks (such as discussing differences of opinion as to who is responsible for what)? yes —— no ——
    a. If yes, describe hos this is handled.
    b. If no, describe how disagreements are handled.

3. Is the division of labor "fair" (are chores equally distributed, or is one person responsible for most of them)? yes —— no —— If no, what person holds the greatest responsibility? ——

4. Are parental expectations too high? For example, is a four-year-old expected to baby-sit for younger children, or to run errands that require crossing streets that are unsafe? yes —— no —— If yes, describe the "too high" expectations.

5. If a request is made of a child, does the parent ask whether the child understands the request? yes —— no ——

Source: Compiled by author.

Project Form 9

STATEMENT OF PROBLEMS

Case:

No.:

Worker(s):

Problem No.	Label	Who Labels	Who Has Problem	Date Noted	Examples	Situational Context

Source: E. J. Thomas, R. D. Carter, and E. D. Gambrill, "Utilization and Appraisal of Socio-behavioral Techniques in Social Welfare," DHEW, SRS–CRD–425–CI–9.

Project Form 10

PROBLEM RESOURCE DATA

Case:

No:

Worker(s):

Date:

Potential Mediators	Reinforcers	Ancillary Resources	Method of Gathering Baseline Data and Who Will Gather

Source: Compiled by author.

Project Form 11

BEHAVIORAL SAMPLE (BASELINE) AND
ASSOCIATED CONDITIONS DATA

Case:

No:

Worker(s):

Gen. Prob. No.	Data Obtained	Data Source	Data Form	Data Location	Essential Results

Attach relevant baseline and behavior sample data, if available.

Source: E. J. Thomas, R. D. Carter, and E. D. Gambrill, "Utilization and Appraisal of Socio-behavioral Techniques in Social Welfare," DHEW, SRS-CRD-425-Cl-9.

Project Form 12

SUMMARY RESULTS OF BASELINE INFORMATION

Summarize results in most appropriate form, depending upon type of data.

Source: Compiled by author.

Project Form 13

CASE PLAN

Case:

No:

Worker(s):

Date:

Problem No.:

---

1. Objectives (overall): should include specification of what client will be doing, where, when, and with what frequency.
2. Specific steps to achieve these objectives: specify each intermediate step that is necessary to achieve the goal(s) stated in 1.
3. Specify other individuals in the client's environment who will participate in achieving the goal, and the role of these persons.
4. Reinforcers: Specify what reinforcers are to be employed, how they are to be provided, when, where, and by whom.
5. Specify your role in the plan: anticipated frequency of contact and any other tasks you've planned for yourself in assisting the client to implement the program.
6. What is the method for monitoring the implementation of the plan: what records are to be kept, by whom, and what is your plan for checking client record keeping?
7. Specify ancillary resources (such as other welfare agencies) that may be involved in this plan, and their role.

Source: Compiled by author.

Project Form 14

WORKER'S DEFINITIONS OF PROBLEMS

Case:

No:

Worker(s):

1. General problem (no.) selected to work on. _____ (from form 9).

2. Worker's behavioral analysis

Label (from form 9)	Behavior (from form 9)	Judgment of Controlling Conditions	Data Source	Date Obtained

Source: E. J. Thomas, R. D. Carter, and E. D. Gambrill, "Utilization and Appraisal of Socio-behavioral Techniques in Social Welfare," DHEW, SRC-CRD-425-CL-9.

Project Form 15

CASE MANAGEMENT RECORD

Case:

No:

Worker(s):

1. Overall intervention plan:

2. Departures from procedure or intervention plan

Date	Departure	What Departed From	Rationale	Apparent Consequences	Date Consequences Observed

Source: E. J. Thomas, R. D. Carter, and E. D. Gambrill, "Utilization and Appraisal of Socio-behavioral Techniques in Social Welfare," DHEW, SRS-CRD-425-Cl-9.

APPENDIX B:
California Civil Code Section 232

232. (a) An action may be brought for the purpose of having any person under the age of 18 years declared free from the custody and control of either or both of his parents when such person comes within any of the following descriptions:

(1) Who has been left without provision for his identification by his parent or parents or by others or has been left by both of his parents or his sole parent in the care and custody of another for a period of six months or by one parent in the care and custody of the other parent for a period of one year without any provision for his support, or without communication from such parent or parents, with the intent on the part of such parent or parents to abandon such person. Such failure to provide identification, failure to provide, or failure to communicate shall be presumptive evidence of the intent to abandon. Such person shall be deemed and called a person abandoned by the parent or parents abandoning him. If in the opinion of the court the evidence indicates that such parent or parents have made only token efforts to support or communicate with the child, the court may declare the child abandoned by such parent or parents. In those cases in which the child has been left without provision for his identification and the whereabouts of the parents are unknown, a petition may be filed after the 120th day following the discovery of the child and citation by publication may be commenced. The petition may not be heard until after the 180th day following the discovery of the child.

The fact that a child is in a foster care home, licensed under subdivision (a) of Section 16000 of the Welfare and Institutions Code, shall not prevent a licensed adoption agency which is planning adoption placement for the child, from instituting, under this subdivision, an action to declare such child free from the custody and control of his parents. When the requesting agency is a licensed county adoption agency, the county counsel, and if there is no county counsel, the district attorney, shall institute such action.

(2) Who has been cruelly treated or neglected by either or both of his parents, if such person has been a dependent child of the juvenile court, and such parent or parents deprived of his custody for the period of one year prior to the filing of a petition praying that he be declared free from the custody and control of such cruel or neglectful parent or parents.

(3) Whose parent or parents suffer a disability because of the habitual use of alcohol, or any of the controlled substances specified in Schedules I to V, inclusive, of Division 10 (commencing with Section 11000) of the Health and Safety Code, except when such controlled substances are used as part of a medically prescribed plan, or are morally depraved, if such person has been a dependent child of the juvenile court, and the parent or parents deprived of his custody because of such disability, or moral depravity, for the period of one year continuously immediately prior to the filing of the petition praying that he be declared free from the custody and control of such parent or parents. As used in this subdivision, "disability" means any physical or mental incapacity which

renders the parent or parents unable to adequately care for and control the child.

(4) Whose parent or parents are convicted of a felony, if the felony of which such parent or parents were convicted is of such nature as to prove the unfitness of such parent or parents to have the future custody and control of the child, or if any term of sentence of such parent or parents is of such length that the child will be deprived of a normal home for a period of years.

(5) Whose parent or parents have been declared by a court of competent jurisdiction wherever situated to be mentally deficient or mentally ill, if, in the state or county in which the parent or parents are hospitalized or resident, the State Director of Health, or his equivalent, if any, and the superintendent of the hospital of which, if any, such parent or parents are inmates or patients certify that such parent or parents so declared to be mentally deficient or mentally ill will not be capable of supporting or controlling the child in a proper manner.

(6) Whose parent or parents are, and will remain, incapable of supporting or controlling the child in a proper manner because of mental deficiency or mental illness, if there is testimony to this effect from two physicians and surgeons each of which must have been certified either by the American Board of Psychiatry and Neurology or under Section 6750 of the Welfare and Institutions Code. If, however, the parent or parents reside in another state or in a foreign country, the testimony herein may be supplied by two physicians and surgeons who are residents of such state or foreign country, if such physicians and surgeons have been certified by a medical organization or society of that state or foreign country to practice psychiatric or neurological medicine and if the court determines that the certification requirements of such organization or society are comparable to those of the American Board of Psychiatry and Neurology.

The parent or parents shall be cited to be present at the hearing, and if he or they have no attorney, the court shall appoint an attorney or attorneys to represent the parent or parents and fix the compensation to be paid by the county for such services, if he determines the parent or parents are not financially able to employ counsel.

(7) Who has been cared for in one or more foster homes under the supervision of the juvenile court, the county welfare department or other public or private licensed child-placing agency for two or more consecutive years, providing that the court finds clear and convincing evidence that return of the child to his parent or parents would be detrimental to the child and that the parent or parents have failed during such period, and are likely to fail in the future, to

(i) provide a home for said child;

(ii) provide care and control for the child;

(iii) maintain an adequate parental relationship with the child.

Physical custody of the child by the parent or parents for insubstantial periods of time during the required two-year period will not serve to interrupt the running of such period.

(b) A licensed adoption agency may institute under this section, an action to declare a child, as described in this section, free from the custody and control of his parents. When the requesting agency is a licensed county adoption agency, the county counsel, or if there is no county counsel, the district attorney, shall in a proper case institute such action.

269

AUTHOR INDEX

Alameda County, Office of Program Evaluation, 54
Alberti, R. E., 143
Alpern, M., 143
American Civil Liberties Union, 144
Assembly of Behavioral and Social Scientists, Advisory Committee on Child Development, 37
Atherton, C. R., 26, 27, 39
Ayllon, T., 240
Azrin, N., 240

Bailey, J. S., 143
Baltimore County, Department of Social Services, 36, 40, 140
Balyeat, R. R., 37, 125, 142
Bandura, A., 143, 240
Bell, C., 125, 142, 144, 145
Bernard, L. D., 145
Blair, L. H., 140
Boehm, B., 9, 20, 22, 34, 35, 41, 141, 144
Bolin, D. C., 142
Briar, S., 10, 12, 35, 145, 147, 158
Brieland, D., 11, 12, 14, 35, 142
Brown, K. J., 143
Bryce, M. W., 17, 37
Burt, M. R., 37, 125, 140, 142

California, Center for Health Statistics, 54, 143; Department of Health, 7, 38, 40; Department of Social Welfare, 41, 140, 159
Campbell, D. T., 40
Carey, J. J., 34, 142
Carnegie Council on Children, 139, 159
Carter, R. D., 143, 192, 261, 264, 265
Case, D., 39, 139
Chestang, L. W., 36, 101, 109, 140
Claburn, W. E., 100, 133, 141
Community Research Applications, Inc., 37
Conger, R. E., 143, 240
Connolly, P. R., 38
Connor, P., 41

Cormier, W. H., 192
Costin, L. B., 140
Cressler, D. L., 159

Day, M. C., 39, 145
De Risi, W. J., 240
Digman, J. M., 112, 141
Digman, K., 112, 141
Downs, G., 34, 39, 139, 158
Downs, S., 34, 39, 139, 158
Duster, T., 5, 7

Edelman, M. W., 159
Education Commission for the States, 142, 144
Ehlebt, R. C., 17, 37
Emlen, A. C., 13, 14, 18, 25, 34, 36, 39, 100, 112, 139, 145, 147, 158
Emmons, M. L., 143
Engler, R. E., 13, 23, 24, 27, 34, 35, 141
Epstein, L., 146
Ergo, R., 42

Fairweather, G. W., 151, 157, 159
Fanshel, D., 8, 13, 15, 18, 24, 27–28, 34, 36, 38, 39, 40, 41, 101, 113, 116, 130, 140, 141, 142, 143, 144
Fellner, I. W., 27, 39
Festinger, T. B., 7, 18, 27, 28, 29, 36, 134, 144
Fischer, J., 143
Fosnee, J. J., 143
Foy, E., 20, 144
Freeman, P. K., 39, 145
Freud, A., 39, 145

Gailey, J., 143
Gambrill, E. D., 13, 16, 18, 24, 27, 34, 35, 36, 38, 100, 101, 109, 126, 139, 140, 142, 143, 146, 192, 240, 261, 264, 265

Goffman, E., 22, 39
Golan, N., 11, 35
Goldiamond, I., 193
Goldstein, A. P., 39
Goldstein, J., 39, 145
Gross, B., 6
Gross, R., 6
Gruber, A. R., 6, 12, 13, 15, 18, 28, 34, 37,
   100, 108, 128, 129, 139, 140
Grundy, J. F., 13, 18, 24, 27–28, 36, 130, 143

Hally, C., 145, 159
Hantman, S. A., 38, 145
Hargrave, V., 41
Haring, B. L., 14, 34, 36, 140, 145
Harris, R., 159
Harris, R. N., Jr., 159
Hatry, H., 37
Heck, E. T., 15, 37, 100, 108, 128, 129, 140
Herstein, N., 16, 37
Heymann, I., 36, 101, 109, 140
Hirsch, J. S., 143
Hobbs, N., 37, 101, 123, 130, 133, 139
Hollis, F., 40, 66
Horejsi, J. E., 38
Hovda, P., 12, 34, 142

Iwata, B. A., 143

Jaffee, B., 41
Jenkins, S., 11, 15, 22, 35, 36, 100, 112, 114,
   141
Jeter, H. R., 13, 24, 27, 34
Jewish Child Care Association of New
   York, 40
Jones, M. A., 40, 106, 110–11, 113, 139
Jones, M. L., 26, 36, 130, 144
Jones, R. R., 143, 240
Jordan, R. F., 146

Kadushin, A., 10, 29, 34, 37, 41, 142
Kahn, A. J., 39
Katz, S. N., 7, 41, 101, 145
Kenniston, K., 139, 159
King, L. W., 240
Kivens, L., 142
Koshel, J., 100

Koss, M., 37
Krefetz, S. P., 149–50, 153–54, 159

Lahti, J., 34, 139, 149
Lemert, E. M., 39
Lemert, M., 101
Leon, E., 142
Lewis, M., 37
Liberman, R. P., 240
Lillesand, D. B., 143
Lindsley, O. R., 176, 193
Lister, C. E., 144

Maas, H. S., 13, 23, 24, 27, 34, 35, 39, 140,
   141
McAdams, P. J., 14, 36
McCann, M., 240
MacDonald, M., 240
McInnes, E. T., 143
McKay, A., 34, 139, 149
Madison, B. Q., 39, 141
Magura, S., 100, 141
Mahoney, K., 39
Mahoney, M. J., 39
Malott, R. W., 143
Maluccio, A. N., 140
Mandell, B. R., 145
Margolin, D., 143
Maynard, H., 159
Mech, E. V., 9, 10, 34, 100, 109, 139, 145
Melson, E. F., 144, 145
Messenger, K. P., 39, 145
Michael, J., 240
Michigan, Office of Children and Youth
   Services, 40
Millar, A., 37
Miller, H., 145
Minahan, A., 37
Mnookin, R. H., 6, 7, 36, 42, 101
Mogulof, M. B., 143
Morisey, P. G., 41
Mulford, R. M., 144
Mullen, E. J., 109–10, 111, 140
Murphy, H. B. M., 100, 141
Myniec, W. J., 145

National Association of Attorneys General,
   6, 34

National Association of Social Workers, 146
National Center for Child Advocacy, 159
National Commission of Productivity and Work Quality, 38
National Conference of Lawyers and Social Workers, 142
Nebraska, Department of Public Welfare, 36
Nee, R. H., 140
Nejelski, P., 145
Neuman, R., 13, 25, 26, 27, 35, 40, 106, 139
Neuringer, C., 240
New York State, Department of Social Services, 139
Norman, E., 15, 22, 36, 112, 114, 141
Nutt, T. E., 139

Oakland, California, Office of Program Evaluation, 159
Oliphant, W., 158

Palmer, S. E., 34
Pascoe, D. J., 19, 35, 101, 140, 143
Patterson, G. R., 143, 240
Pers, J. S., 6, 15, 17, 35, 37, 100, 141, 159
Peterson, M. V., 40
Phillips, M. H., 10, 12, 14, 20, 22, 34, 36, 140, 144
Pike, V., 39, 139, 145
Piliavin, I., 35
Pincus, A., 37
Polansky, N. A., 145, 159
Polansky, N. F., 145, 159
Polier, J. W., 38, 143, 144
Portland State University, Regional Research Institute for Human Services, 159

Quilitch, R. H., 143

Radinsky, E. K., 37
Reid, J. B., 143, 240
Reid, W. J., 146
Rein, M., 139
Resnick, W., 100, 141
Richey, C. A., 240
Roberts, R. W., 140

Rodham, H., 6, 7, 39, 145
Rosenheim, M. K., 112, 141, 144, 145

Sanders, D. H., 159
Sauber, M., 11, 35
Scheff, T. J., 39, 101
Schmerl, E., 143
Schmidt, D. M., 39
Schorr, A. S., 139
Schur, E. M., 39
Schwartz, A., 193
Selznick, P., 6
Shapiro, D., 14, 15, 36, 40, 101, 106, 108, 114, 118, 140
Shapiro, M., 39
Sherman, E. A., 10, 12, 13, 14, 15, 19, 20, 25, 27, 34, 35, 36, 110–11, 116, 139, 140, 144
Shinn, E. B., 10, 38, 144
Shireman, J., 41
Shyne, A. W., 10, 11–12, 13, 20, 25, 26, 27, 34, 35, 36, 40, 106, 139, 140, 144, 147, 158
Simon, B. K., 109, 136, 140, 145
Skolnick, A., 21, 39, 145
Smith, L. G., 146
Sobey, F., 141
Solnit, A. J., 39, 145
Solomon, C., 27, 39
Stanley, J. C., 40
Stein, T. J., 10–11, 27, 35, 38, 100, 101, 111, 126, 140, 143, 145, 146, 159, 193
Steiner, G. Y., 140
Steketee, J. P., 18, 27, 37, 145
Stone, H. D, 34, 36, 100, 149, 145
Szasz, T., 4, 7

Talbot, N. B., 159
Taylor, H., 39
Tharp, R. G., 143, 192
Thomas, E. J., 143, 192
Tornatzky, L. G., 159
Trout, L., 130, 144

United States, Bureau of the Census, 54; House of Representatives, 7; Department of Health, Education and Welfare, Office of Human Development, 37

Wahler, R. G., 192
Wald, M., 6, 7, 38, 133, 142, 145
Walker, R., 42
Walz, T., 38
Watson, D., 192
Watson, K., 12, 34, 142
Weaver, E. T., 20, 35
Weiss, H., 139
Wetzel, R. J., 143
Whaley, D. L., 143

White, S. H., 21, 39, 145
Whittington, R., 112, 141
Wiltse, K. T., 13, 16, 18, 24, 27, 34, 35, 36,
   100, 109, 139, 140, 143, 192
Wolins, M., 8, 10, 34, 35
Wylegala, V. B., 144

Young, A. and Company, 159

SUBJECT INDEX

abandonment, and adoption, 30–31; proof of, 60–61; and termination of parental rights, 62
abstractions, and behavioral descriptions, 167–68
abuse, and termination of parental rights, 60–61
accountability, 5
administrators, Alameda study's implications for, 122–28; and data collection, 131; management decisions of, 150–51; and project implementation, 151–65; training and background of, 153–54 (see also, supervisors)
adoption, 26–32; and contact frequency, 66; contracting and, 91; decision form for, 53, 245; decision making and, 11; in follow-up period, 95 97; as outcome, 55–56, 58–59, 63–64, 80; predictors of, 80, 83–87; record keeping and, 120–21; subsidized, 29–30, 32
affect (see, nonverbal behavior)
age factors, 44; in experimental and control groups, 49; as placement factor, 13, 27–28, 29; as predictor variable, 80–81, 83–86 (see also, demographic variables)
aides, 128, 134
Alameda County, Ca., caseload size in, 108; childcare statistics, 43–44; Department of Social Services, 47
Alameda Project, case descriptions, 47–50; case-sharing in, 25–26, 50–52, 73–78; caseload size in, 46; casework methods used, 109–11; data collection forms, 52–54, 241–65; discussion of, 58–100; follow-up, 93–96; implementation of, 151–53; implications of, 102–39; intervention histories, 194–240; limitations of, 93; objectives of, 43; outcomes of, 79–91; results by permanent plan, 149; selection of cases in, 44–46; setting of, 44; staff workers in, 46 (see also, case-sharing, caseload, control cases, county worker, experimental cases, intervention, outcomes, project worker)
alcohol abuse (see, drinking behavior)
analytic methods, 67–68, 110–11, 250

approval behavior, 201–02; check list, 203–04; goal plan example, 204
approximations toward goals (see, subgoals)
assessment, 51; in communications problem example, 207–13; forms, 53, 252–57; and intervention, 138–39; and outcome, 56; of parent-child interaction, 103–05; of program effectiveness, 54; and sharing of data, 198–201; 212–13; and stereotyping, 21–22; in verbal communications example, 194–99, 210–24
attending behavior, 201–02; check list, 203–04; goal plan example, 204
attention-seeking behaviors, intervention examples, 237–40

Baltimore, Md., welfare administration, 153
"banking" of cases, 98–99
baseline data, 187; gathering of, 53–54, 261–62; sample chart for client completion, 228; in verbal communications example, 198–201 (see also, data collection)
behavioral approach, 43, 67–67; 109–11, 126, 250; analysis form, 264 (see also, contracts, intervention, problem areas, reinforcements)
behaviors, approximations to, 96; pinpointing of, 167–70, 203; specifying changes in, 175–81; specifying deficiencies in, 167–70 (see also problem areas, verbal communication)
"budget and rule" oriented administration, 153–54

California, abandonment statutes in, 31; Annual Service Plan, 1975–1976, 24; child welfare legislation in, 18; Civil Code, section 232, 60–62; 267–68; data collection in, 129, 155–56; Department of Health, 19, 33, 38; guardianship policy of, 33; incentive programs in, 19–20, 29–30; Legislative Audit Committee, 28; restoration statistics, 24–25; Social Welfare

Board, 33; Welfare and Institutions Code, section 600, 47; welfare funding in, 149–50

case management, agency constraints in, 150–54; check list, 120; fiscal constraints in, 148–50; judicial constraints in, 283–284; and outcomes, 56; political constraints in, 154; recording form, 265 (*see also*, decision making, supervisors)

case planning, 51; indicators of, 106–08; major considerations of, 103; and outcome, 55; and service delivery, 12–14 (*see also*, decision making)

case review (*see*, review)

case-sharing, 25–26, 50–52, 79; contacts between workers, 73–76, 76–77; and decision making, 76; and personal advocacy, 77–78; practical aspects of, 78; supervisors' perceptions of, 76

caseload, 8, 19, 44; in Alameda project, 46; and length of time in care, 99; and service delivery, 15, 108–09

casework methods, 14–15; activity categories of, 66–68, 250; in Alameda project, 109–11

check list, of chore completion, 198, 232; of conversational skills, 210–13; of communications skills, 203–04

child care, 182–83; assessment forms, 256–57; sample contract for, 182–83; and science, 4–5; state intervention in, 3–5

Child Welfare League of America, 11, 30, 35

child welfare workers, Alameda project's implications for, 102–17; attitudes of and placement, 32; competency of, 109–12; decision making by, 8–22; profile of, 46; and program implementation, 152, 154; rotation of, 46; skills of, 14–15; training of, 17, 119, 123–28; turnover of, 18–19, 115, 118 (*see also*, county worker, project worker)

children, at risk of placement, 131–32; contacts with, 53; demographic profiles, 49–50; goals ascertained, 103; number entering by year, 45–46; reasons for placement, 47–48; tantrum behavior in, 238–40

Children's Bill of Rights, 4

Children's Bureau, 30–31

Children's Home Society, Oakland, Ca., 43

"choice points" (*see*, decision making)

chore completion, chart, 207, 232; check list, 198, 232; compliance table, 229; con-

tract for, 199, 202–06; intervention example, 196–97, 230 (*see also*, household responsibilities)

class, and stereotyping of clients, 21–22

client, assets of, 177–80; as informant, 54; rights of, 135, 136; sample data forms for, 228; verbal reports of, 165–66 (*see also*, children, foster parents, parents)

client-counselor contact, frequency of, 15, 53, 65–66, 73–78, 248–50; methods employed, 66–68; purpose of, 68–69

"client oriented" administration, 153

closing (*see*, outcomes)

collateral resources, contacts with, 53, 65–66, 71–72; and contracts, 185; coordination of, 123–25; and decision making, 11–12; identifying of, 53, 79; and multiple problem areas, 104, 105; and placement minimization, 132; and planning of cases, 16–17

communication (*see*, data collection, verbal communication)

communications skills, attending and approval, 201–02, 203–04; conversational, 207–24; reinforcing of, 194–207 (*see also*, conversational skills, verbal communication)

community resources (*see*, collateral resources)

computerized data storage, 125; and review, 132

confidentiality of information, 134–35

contact frequency, 15, 53; and outcome, 65–66, 109; with parents, 248–50; between workers sharing cases, 73–78 (*see also*, client-counselor contact)

continuity, as goal of foster care, 96–98

contracts, 51–52; amendment of, 191–92; for assessing parent-child interaction, 105; and case planning, 114–15; components of, 180, 182–85, 190; drafting of, 53, 263; forms of, 242; and outcomes, 56, 91; renegotiation of, 184; for restoration, 185–86; and review, 121; samples, 184, 186, 188–89, 192, 199, 202, 207, 213, 221, 222, 231, 232, 233, 235

contributing conditions, 170

control cases, adoption and guardianship of, 58–59; caseload size, 108; casework methods, 67–68; and collateral services, 71–72; contact frequency in, 65–66; and long-term placement, 106; outcomes of,

55-56, 63-64; predictor variables and outcomes of, 80-90; problem areas of, 69-71; purpose of contacts in, 68-69; restorations by year, 57; volunteered from intake, 45;
conversational skills, check list, 212; coding form, 211; intervention examples, 206-24 (*see also*, communications skills)
counselor-client contacts (*see*, client, contact frequency)
counties, and family services, 17
county worker, role of, 50-52, 72-78, 79, 112
courts, and adoption, 27; attitudes toward, 134, 136; and casework methods, 111; and childrearing, 3-5; closings ordered by, 56-57; and contracting, 116; directives for therapy from, 105; and guardianship, 33; reports and records of, 166; review of cases by, 18, 118, 120-21, 132-34, 137; workers' responsibility to, 76-77
cueing of appropriate behaviors, 128
curriculum recommendations (*see*, social work education, training of staff)

data collection, Alameda projects implications for, 128-35; computerized, 125, 132, 134; confidentiality and, 134-35; and court review, 132-34; critical areas of, 120-21; currency of, 166; and decision making, 10-11; on follow up, 95; forms for, 52-54, 241-65; legislation proposed for, 129; on parental abuse, 61; and periodic review, 132-34; process of, 130-31; and sharing, 124; and utilization, 131-32; (*see also*, baseline data; record keeping)
"dead man's error," 176
decision making, and case-sharing, 76; framework for, 20-26, 43-45, 102-06, 137; incentives for, 19; and long-term care, 98-99; and moralistic concerns, 4-5; overview of, 8-22; and personal advocacy, 77-78; and prediction, 112-16
decision status forms, 53, 243-47
demographic variables, as predictors, 80; of study participants, 49-51
directive techniques, 67, 110-11, 250
directors (*see*, administrators)
discipline problem, questioning examples, 169-70

dissemination guidelines, 156-58
drinking behavior, assessment example, 223-29; consumption chart, 237; plan for decreasing, 233

ethnic background, of participants, 50; as predictor, 80-81 (*see also*, demographic variables)
experimental cases, adoption and guardianship of, 58-59, 64; caseload size of, 108; casework methods used, 67-68; closing of, 55-56, 63-64; and collateral resources, 71-72; contact frequency in, 65-66; outcomes and predictor variables in, 80-91; problem areas of, 69-71; purposes of contact in, 68-69; restorations by year, 56; services to parents, 106; volunteered from intake, 45
exploration method, 66-67, 110-11, 250

family, autonomy of, 3-5; composition of, 51, 80-81; concepts and decision making, 9-10 (*see also*, parents)
federal government, funding by, 4, 13; role in social services, 154-56
fiscal policy, 148-50, 154-56
follow up, 52, 93-96
forms, 52-54, 241-63
foster care, entry into, 47-48; exit from, 24-33; goals of, 131; state involvement in, 3-5, 150; time spent in, 13, 14, 83-88, 107, 114 (*see also*, guardianship)
Foster Care Adoption and Reform Act of 1977, 97, 122-23
foster parents, contracts with, 53; as focus of service, 107; frequency of contacts with, 65-66; services to, 33, 50

goal plan, of approval and attending behavior, 203; in drinking problem, 233; in negotiation training example, 206 (*see also*, contracts)
goals, in contracting, 188-89; of foster care administration, 96-97; for interviews, 10-11; of parents, 51-52; setting of by administration, 122-23 (*see also*, objectives, subgoals)
guardianship, 32-33; and contact frequency,

66; decision form for, 53; in follow up period, 95–96; as outcome, 58–60, 63–64, 80; predictors of, 80, 83–87; service requirements of, 108

hard-to-place children, 19, 29–30
Hollis' typology of casework techniques, 25–26, 66–68, 109
household responsibilities, assessment form, 252, 256–57; increasing of, 194–208 (see also, chore completion)

identified problems (see, problem areas)
Illinois, restoration study, 26
implementation guidelines, 156–58
incentive systems, for caseworkers, 127–28; and decision making, 19–20
information (see, baseline data, data collection, record keeping)
information seeking technique (see, exploration method)
intensive services, and case sharing, 74 (see also, collateral resources)
intervention, in chore completion example, 196–97; in conversational skills example, 214–20; in drinking problem example, 230–37; goals of, 139; monitoring of, 53–54; mother's free-time example, 230–34, 237; and outcome, 56; and program development, 53; in verbal communications examples, 194–206, 207–24
interviews, and decision making, 10–11 (see also, contact frequency)

judges, decision making by, 10, 154 (see also, courts)
judicial determinacy requirement, 148, 155

labeling, of parents, 21–22; and problem definition, 168
law, and childrearing, 3–5; and social workers, 125–26 (see also, courts)
lodge system, 151, 157
long-term care, and contact frequency, 65–66; decision form for, 53, 246; in follow up period, 96; as outcome, 55–56,

63–64, 80; predictors of, 80–88; service requirements of, 108
Los Angeles County, 108

Massachusetts, abandonment statute, 31; Division of Family Services, 28; foster care study, 28–29
maternal factors, free time of, 230, 237; generational conflict, 230, 231–36; and placement, 9–10
medical care, assessment of, 252
mental health professions, 16 (see also, collateral, resources)
Michigan, restoration figures, 25
Model Act to Free Children for Permanent Placement, 30
Model Subsidized Adoption Act, 30
modeling, 215–17
monitoring, 17–18
morality, and problem identification, 4–5, 9
"motive analysis," 167
multidisciplinary teams, 139 (see also, case-sharing; collateral resources)

Nashville, Tenn., 125
Nebraska, adoption figures, 27; restoration figures, 24–25
neglect, defining, 115–16
negotiation training, 202–05; post training data, 208 (see also, verbal communication)
New York City, adoption in, 27, 28, 29, 113–14; case review in, 18; data collection in, 130; incentive system in, 19; restoration in, 24–25, 26, 113
New York State Charities Aid Association, 28
"no fault" foster care, 22
nonverbal behavior, comparison chart sample, 224; goal plan sample, 217 (see also, conversational skills)
"normalizing" view, 117

objectives, approximations to, 176–80; contracting for, 182–83; identifying of, 163–64; misperception of, 180–81; specifying of, 175–76, 187–91 (see also, goals, subgoals)

Oregon, adoption study, 31; Children's Services Division, 156, 157; Permanent Planning Project, 156–59; restoration figures, 25
outcomes, categories of, 55–56; changes in, 58–60; miscellaneous, 57–58; predictors of, 79–91; unplanned, 55–56

paraphrasing, 204
parent-child interactions, assessment and scheduling of, 166–67; assessment form for, 253–55; attending approval, 201–02, 203, 204; chore completion and communication example, 194–208; conversational skills example, 206–22; negotiation training, 201–05; visiting, 235 (see also, communications skills, contact frequency, verbal communication)
parents, caseworkers' views of, 21–22, 107–08, 112; contacts with, 53, 68–69, 107, 248–50; frequency of contacts with, 28–29, 65–66; implementing goals of, 103, 163–64; involvement of, 106, 214–15; restoration to, 14–15; rights of, and state, 3–5; service delivery to, 13–14, 25–26, 43, 44, 50; termination of rights, 30–32, 59–62
paternal factors, and placement, 9–10
"pathological view," 112, 137–38
personal advocacy, 77–78 (see also, case-sharing)
placement, factors relating to, 8–11; and "family adequacy," 9–10; parental objectives identified, 163–164; reasons for, 47–49, 82–83; type of, as predictor, 81–83, 113
planning (see, case management, decision making, goal plan, objectives)
politics, and welfare services, 149, 154–55
practical help techniques, 67, 110–11, 250
predictor variables, contracts as, 91; and decision making, 112–16; defining of, 114–16; demographic, 80–83; problem areas as, 88–90; reasons for placement as, 82–83; time in care as, 83–88
President's Commission on Population Growth, 29
problem areas, assessment of, 103–05; baseline data on, 187; and contracting, 114–15; contributing conditions to, 170–73; court identified, 166; defining of, 167–72; number of, and outcomes, 69,

88–89, 105–06; parent identified, 165–66, 173; as predictor variable, 80–81; ranking of, 132; resolution of, 89–90, 105, 114–15, specification of, 53, 173–74, 248–50, 259, 264; unresolved, 112; worker identified, 166–67, 173 (see also, intervention)
problem profile, 163; construction of, 4–5, 164–67; sample, 226–27
project worker, and case-sharing, 73–78, 79; as service coordinator, 105; tasks of, 50–52, 103 (see also, county worker)
psychological issues, 20–21
public welfare agencies, decision making in, 19–20; monitoring by, 17–18; policies of, 17

questioning procedures, for goal selection, 175–76; for problem profile, 165, 168–70

race, of project participants, 50; as predictor variable, 80–81 (see also, demographic variables)
record keeping, 18, 31; and contracting, 115; frequency of, 130; and review, 119–21 (see also, data collection)
reflective techniques, 67–68, 110–11, 250
Regional Research Institute for Human Services, 156
rehearsal, 215–18
reinforcers, and contracting, 184; identifying of, 53, 260, 263
relatives, placement with, 80
report and review hearings, 52 (see also, review)
restoration, 24–26; and contact frequency, 65–66; contracting and, 90–91, 185–86; decision form for, 53, 244; in follow up period, 96–97; as outcome, 55–57, 63, 80; predictors of, 80, 83, 89–90; and time in care, 23, 107, 114; by year in project, 56
revenue sharing, 154–55
review, by courts, 118, 132–36, 238; and data collection, 132–34; supervisory, 117–21
Rhode Island, 18, 27
Riverside County, Ca., 108
role playing, 215–18

San Francisco, Ca., 108, 154
service delivery, case planning and, 12–14;
   and caseload 108–09; and coordination,
   123–25; guidelines for, 102–06; impediments to, 14–17; and worker attitudes,
   112; and worker competence, 109–12
sex, of experimental and control groups,
   49–50; as predictor variable, 81 (*see also*,
   demographic variables)
Social Security Act, 1962 Amendments, 24;
   Title XX, 149, 154, 155
social work education, Alameda study's
   implications for, 135–39 (*see also*, training of staff)
specification, impediments to, 180–81; of
   objectives, 163–64, 174–76; of problems,
   167–72 (*see also*, problem areas)
state, and child rearing, 3–5 (*see also*,
   courts)
states, and child welfare, 149–154, 154
stereotyping (*see*, labeling)
structuring techniques, 67, 110–11, 250
subgoals, 175, 177–80
supervisor, Alameda study's implications
   for, 117–21; and case sharing, 74–76; and
   contracting, 115; as innovators, 157; participation of, 153; and problem resolution, 107; as resource persons, 105; review
   by, 132; rotation of, 150–51
support technique, 67–68, 250

tantrum behavior, 238–40
tape recording, coding sample, 223; in
   communications problems, 205; consent
   form, 53, 251; use of, 54

time factors, and adoptions, 27–29; in contracts, 184–85; and placement statistics, 8;
   and restoration, 23; time in care, 83–88,
   107, 114 (*see also*, long-term care)
time out procedure, 238
Title XX, Social Security Act, 149, 154, 155
tracking, 17–18, 119–20, 125
trading, as communications skill, 204–05
training of staff, 123–24; legal procedures,
   125–26; in service coordination, 123–25;
   in service provision, 126–27 (*see also*,
   social work education)
trial visit, sample consent for, 190

United States, Department of Health, Education and Welfare, 134; funding of social
   services in, 4, 12; role in social services,
   154–56

verbal behavior, of case workers, 110–11
verbal communication; as problem area,
   194–206, 210–23 (*see also*, communications skills; conversational skills)
verbal reports, of client, 165–67
visiting (*see*, parent-child interactions)
voluntary placement, 18
volunteer workers, 134 (*see also*, aides)

Worker Effort Expenditure, 15

zapping, 205

ABOUT THE AUTHORS

THEODORE J. STEIN is assistant professor of Social Welfare, School of Social Work, California State University, Sacramento. He has contributed to various social work journals and co-authored, with Eileen Gambrill, *Decision-Making in Foster Care: A Training Manual*. Dr. Stein holds the MSW and PhD degrees from the University of California, Berkeley.

EILEEN D. GAMBRILL is associate professor, School of Social Welfare, University of California, Berkeley. She is author of *Behavior Modification: Handbook of Assessment, Intervention, and Evaluation, and* co-author of *It's Up to You: Developing Assertive Social Skills*. Dr. Gambrill has contributed to many professional journals and holds a doctorate in Social Work and Psychology from the University of Michigan.

KERMIT T. WILTSE has been affiliated with the School of Social Welfare, University of California, Berkeley, since 1950. He co-authored *Group Methods in the Public Welfare Program* and *The Field of Social Work*, and has contributed to many journals and several book collections. He holds a DSW from the School of Social Work, University of Pittsburg.

RELATED TITLES

published by
Praeger Special Studies

*THE AGED IN THE COMMUNITY: Managing Senility and Deviance
Dwight Frankfather

CHILDREN'S TELEVISION: An Analysis of Programming and Advertising
F. Earl Barcus, with Rachel Wolkin

COORDINATING SOCIAL SERVICES: An Analysis of Community, Organizational, and Staff Characteristics
Neil Gilbert and Harry Specht

*THE CYCLE OF VIOLENCE: Assertive, Aggressive, and Abusive Family Interaction
Suzanne K. Steinmetz

HOUSING AND SOCIAL SERVICES FOR THE ELDERLY: Social Policy Trends
Elizabeth D. Huttman

SPECIAL EDUCATION: A Sociological Study of California Programs
Carl Milofsky

YOUTH CRIME AND JUVENILE JUSTICE: International Perspectives
edited by Paul C. Friday
and V. Lorne Stewart

---

*Available in paperback.